BUSINESS 121
LAB MANUAL
and Readings

Twenty-Seventh Edition

School of Business & Economics
Wilfrid Laurier University

2012

Captus Press

Handwritten annotations:

- hard copy (dropbox)
- turnitin (course io learning space)
- electronic copy dropbox on mls

Informal

To ~
Frn ~
memo
Problem
Recom
D.C.
- given
- own (yurs
date/time person

make up one.
1 given
required 2 alternatives

explaing why chosen
alternative (recmedation)
and satisfying D.C.

#only pick one recmedation

- each paragraph
descripe why
gets D.C.

- no describing
alternates
didn't choose

High Info
Headings

dont explain
(unting CEO
thinking already
understand)

few paragraphs

Business 121 Lab Manual and Readings
Twenty-Seventh Edition

© 2012 by Captus Press Inc.

ISBN-13 978-1-55322-257-6

CAPTUS PRESS INC.
Units 14 & 15
1600 Steeles Avenue West
Concord, Ontario
Canada L4K 4M2

Phone: (416) 736-5537
Fax: (416) 736-5793
Email: info@captus.com
Website: www.captus.com

Canada ▮▮▮ We acknowledge the financial support of the Government of Canada through the Canada Book Fund for our publishing activities.

0 9 8 7 6 5 4 3 2 1
Printed and bound in Canada

Therefore NWC would appear to be too high, with such a high acid test and quick receivables turnover, they could lower the NWC and invest the money to earn a higher return.

(b) *Leverage* $= \$195{,}000 \div 186{,}645 = \; > 1:1$

Compared to the rule of thumb this firm is highly levered

Interest Coverage Ratio $= \$91{,}750 \div 4500 = 20x$

According to the rule of thumb of $> 3x$, this indicates that the firm is quite capable of carrying a high degree of leverage, the risk is quite low, therefore investors should not be concerned about the long-term viability of the company, and the firm could in fact increase the leverage to increase return.

(c) *GPM* $= \$206{,}900 \div 719{,}100 = 28.8\%$

Compared with the industry average of 30%, this would appear within the norm

NPM $= \$69{,}800 \div 719{,}100 = 9.7\%$

Compared with the industry average of 15%, this would appear low — perhaps due to high operating expenses, and/or other expenses

ROI $= \$69{,}800 \div 186{,}645 = 37.4\%$

Compared with the industry average of 25% it would appear that this company is meeting its obligations to shareholders by maximizing their individual returns (even though the NPM is low).

Solutions — C-V-P

1. The Wicks Corporation

   (a) Assume the following: From the information given, if the company produces anything at all its fixed costs will be $340,000.

   Knowing that the S.P./unit = $25.00 and knowing that the Variable Costs/unit are $8.00 ($800,000/100,000), the following applies:

   $$B.\ E.\ P.\ =\ \frac{Fixed\ Costs}{Unit\ Contribution\ Margin}$$

   $$=\ \frac{\$340,000}{\$17.00}$$

   $$=\ 20,000\ units\ (Sales\ of\ \$500,000)$$

   (b) We know that if the factory is completely shut down (idle), its operating losses (fixed costs) would equal $200,000.

   It is necessary for us to determine the number of units we would have to sell to incur a loss of $200,000, keeping in mind that each unit produced will cost $8.00 in variable costs, that fixed expenses are $340,000, and that each unit sold will bring in revenue of $25.00.

   A simple relationship can be set up:

Let X	=	the number of units which must be sold to incur a loss of $200,000.
Sales	=	Variable Costs + Fixed Costs + Desired Profit
$25X	=	$8X + $340,000 + (−$200,000)
$17X	=	$140,000
X	=	8,235 units

In other words, if 8,235 units were produced, the company would incur a loss approximately equal to that if the company did not produce and sell any units at all. Therefore, if the company felt it could sell at least that number of units or more, then it would pay to continue operating (*i.e.* minimizing their losses). If it could not sell at least 8,235 units it would be cheaper to stop producing completely and bear the loss of your fixed costs (*i.e.* $200,000).

2.   (a) Using the information given:

$$\text{B. E. P.} = \frac{\text{Fixed Costs}}{\text{Unit Contribution Margin}}$$

$$= \frac{\$225,000}{\$1.50}$$

$$= 150,000 \text{ in units (or } \$600,000 \text{ in sales)}$$

(b) If sales are increased by 10,000 units, the company will realize an additional profit of:

$$10,000 @ \$4.00 = \$40,000$$

$$\text{V. C. } (\$2.50 @ 10,000) = \underline{\$25,000}$$

$$\$15,000$$

(c) At 170,000 units, in order to break even, the company must charge a unit price of:

Let X	=	the unit selling price
Sales	=	Variable Costs + Fixed Costs
170,000X	=	(170,000 × $2.50/unit) + $225,000
170,000X	=	$425,000 + $225,000
170,000X	=	$650,000
X	=	$3.82

The unit price charged would have to be $3.82 to break even at 170,000 units.

3.   (a) Let X be the selling price:

X	=	FC + VC + P
9,000X	=	$24,000 + (9,000 × $3.00) + $30,000
9,000X	=	$81,000
X	=	$9.00
Contribution margin per unit	=	$9.00 – $3.00 or $6.00 per unit.
Contribution margin in total	=	$6.00 × 9,000 or $54,000.

(b) Let X be the number of units to be sold:

$7.00X	=	$84,000 + $3.00X + $76,000
$4.00X	=	$160,000
X	=	40,000 units

or

$$\frac{\text{Fixed Cost + Profit}}{\text{Contribution Margin per unit}} = \frac{(\$24,000 + \$10,000 + \$50,000) + \$76,000}{\$4.00}$$

$$= \frac{\$160,000}{\$4.00}$$

$$= 40,000 \text{ units}$$

SOLUTIONS

4. (a) Let d = the number of doughnuts.

Semi-Automatic	Automatic
$.05d = $.02d + $3,000$	$.05d = $.015d + $5,000$
$.03d = $3,000$	$.035d = $5,000$
$d = 100,000$	$d = 142,857$

(b) **Total Annual Costs of 300,000 Units**

	Present Supplier		Semi-Automatic		Automatic	
Purchase costs	@$.05	$15,000				
Variable costs of production			@$.02	$6,000	@.015	$4,500
Fixed Costs				3,000		5,000
Total Annual Costs		$15,000		$9,000		$9,500

The choice should be the semi-automatic machine, as it will produce the doughnuts at the lowest cost, and therefore produce the greatest profit.

(c) **Total Annual Costs of 600,000 Units**

	Present Supplier		Semi-Automatic		Automatic	
Purchase costs	@$.05	$30,000				
Variable costs of production			@$.02	$12,000	@$.015	$9,000
Fixed Costs				3,000		5,000
Total Annual Costs		$30,000		$15,000		$14,000

The choice should be the automatic machine.

(d) The volume level would be that which produces the same total costs for each machine.

Let X	=	volume level
$3,000 + $.02X$	=	$5,000 + $.015X$
$.005X$	=	$2,000$
X	=	400,000 doughnuts

5. Currently selling 150 units for $750 each with variable costs of $500, therefore $250 unit contribution margin.

    (a) $800 price – $500 variable cost = $ 300 unit contribution margin
                                          ×   135 (90% of 150 units)
                                          = $40,500 total contribution

    vs. current total contribution $250/unit × 150 units = $37,500
    therefore, $3,000 greater contribution for $3,000 increase in fixed costs
    Makes no difference quantitatively, must consider qualitative factors — how will customers respond to higher price long term?, what marketing message are you trying to project — is this consistent?, etc.

    (b) 80 units × $250 unit contribution = $20,000 vs. fixed costs $25,000
        therefore, not covering fixed costs — any contribution is helpful
              $750 – $600 variable   = $ 150 contribution margin
                                     ×   30 units
                                     = $ 4,500

    Yes, still not covering fixed costs, but not as great a loss.

    (c) $750 – $350 variable cost   = $ 400 unit contribution margin
                                          ×   150 units
                                          = $60,000 total contribution

    vs. current $250 unit contribution margin × 150 units = $37,500
    therefore, $22,500 greater contribution for $15,000 increase in fixed costs
    Yes, $7,500 increase in bottom line.

    (d) $725 price – $350 variable   = $ 375 unit contribution margin
                                          ×   165 (110% of 150 units)
                                          = $61,875 total contribution

    vs. $60,000 (from part c)
    Yes, $1,875 increase in bottom line.

SOLUTIONS

6. (a)

Variable Costs	Fixed Costs
$ 42,000	$ 90,000
63,000	40,000
75,000	80,000
$180,000	$210,000

Contribution margin:

$$= \frac{\$210,000 \text{ fixed costs}}{1 - \left(\frac{\$180,000 \text{ variable costs}}{\$600,000 \text{ sales}} \right)}$$

$$= \frac{\$210,000}{1 - 0.3}$$

$$= \frac{\$210,000}{0.7}$$

$$= \$300,000$$

Break-even units at $50 price

$$= \$300,000 \div \$50$$

$$= 6,000 \text{ units}$$

(b) If there are already 5 major competitors in the market, the likelihood of achieving break-even let alone exceeding it is slim, so the company should not pursue this new product, or at least re-examine the cost structure to see if costs can be decreased to bring down the break-even point.

7. Existing Contribution margin = $700 price − $300 variable cost = $400/unit

Total contribution = $400/unit × 200 units = $80,000

Proposed Contribution margin = $650 price × $300 = $350/unit

Total proposed contribution = $350/unit × 250 units (25% increase) = $87,500

Additional contribution = $87,500 × 80,000 = $7,500
vs. additional fixed costs = $9,000
= loss of $1,500

On a purely quantitative basis, you should not drop your price and increase your advertising.

On a qualitative basis however, you must examine that much of the competition has dropped its price, and depending how sensitive your market is to price and whether the consumer will see your product as being worth the higher price, you may not have any option but to lower your price. You would therefore need to focus on lowering variable or fixed costs.

Table of Contents

Acknowledgements

Over the past year, the first year business courses (BU111 and BU121) have been extensively reviewed and revised. We believe these changes will lead to more successful students and graduates, with the skills required to compete in today's business world.

I'd like to thank Jim McCutcheon, who set up the courses in their original form (many years ago) and was the greatest colleague anyone could hope for, for listening and providing sound advice throughout the revision process. And I'd also like to thank the Teaching Assistants who tested out some of the new ideas for this course, and provided invaluable feedback that allowed me to make adjustments that hopefully will create a win–win for everyone involved. I couldn't have done this without them.

I hope you enjoy the course. But most importantly — I hope you learn new things and new skills that will make you more successful in school and in your careers.

Laura Allan
Co-ordinator, BU121

Note to the Students

This Lab Manual is designed to be used by you to prepare for and learn from the lab component of the Business 121 course in the School of Business and Economics at Wilfrid Laurier University.

To enhance the large lecture hall learning that takes place in a course of this size, you will meet in small groups/labs once a week with your Business 121 Teaching Assistant. In these smaller groups you will immerse yourself in the material in a way that cannot be done in the lecture hall alone.

This lab experience is unique to Wilfrid Laurier. Use it to your advantage. Follow the instructions carefully as to what you need to have prepared for each lab. Participate in the lab to the fullest extent possible. This is essential to gain the maximum advantage from the lab experience. Accumulate all the knowledge you can from your Teaching Assistant. These students are among our best and brightest, and most importantly they want to help you learn, and share their experiences with you.

You will also be assigned a participation mark from your Teaching Assistant, which will be used by the teaching professors in assigning final grades. Participation will form part of your grade in most of the business courses that you take at Laurier, sometimes a rather large part. It is essential that you start practising and getting comfortable with participating NOW. On the next page you will find a copy of the guidelines we give to the TAs to assist in assigning participation marks. Examine this closely so that you know what is expected of you.

After the participation rubric you will find *Codes of Conduct* for business students, Teaching Assistants, and Professors. This is a professional school, designed to prepare you for careers in the professional world. As such, you are expected to adhere to codes of conduct in school as would be expected of you in your careers. You can also expect that we, as educators, will adhere to professional codes of conduct as well. These have therefore been provided for your reference.

You will also find a *Statement of Academic Integrity* that you are expected to <u>fill out and bring to your first lab</u>. This is a requirement of the course. Your TA will continue to ask for it until you bring it to lab, and penalties could be applied if you have not provided a signed statement within the timeline specified by your TA.

The Lab Manual is arranged by week, so that you know exactly what you need to prepare each week for labs, as well as what you are expected to have prepared (from the Lab Manual) for class. Further preparation for class is required from the text, as indicated on the course outline/syllabus. This course outline will give you a step-by-step approach to tackling the requirements of the course. <u>All dates on the outline should be immediately placed on a calendar that you look at daily</u>.

Readings, discussions, cases, problems, and experiential exercises will be used to elaborate on the material covered in the text and in classes. They will help you to apply the concepts presented as well as introduce new concepts, and allow you to become involved in situations so that you can learn from your own observations and experiences.

PARTICIPATION
Expectations and Marking Guidelines

	4 exceeded expectations	3 met expectations	2 below expectations	1–0 failed to meet expectations	GRADE
PREPARATION	• always prepared — completes required exercises, readings and cases	• usually prepared	• sometimes prepared	• seldom prepared	
CONSISTENCY OF PARTICIPATION	• always participates — answers questions, offers insights, assists other students • does not dominate or attempt to dominate discussions	• usually participates • sometimes attempts to dominate discussions	• sometimes participates • OR participates at a level that makes it difficult for others to participate	• seldom participates	
QUALITY OF PARTICIPATION	• always participates in a quality manner — good answers to questions, useful or insightful comments, stimulates discussion — shines!	• usually offers quality participation — above average	• sometimes offers quality participation, but usually average	• seldom of a quality nature — below average and/or sometimes disruptive	

Note: Participation marks will be calculated /12 and then computed to a mark /10. You are allowed to miss 2 labs without penalty to your overall grade, however you will not receive participation marks for those missed labs. Beware of the fact that simply being in attendance at the lab does not constitute participation. Instead, quality participation involves exhibiting "Level 4" behaviour (see above) throughout the term. Failing grades for participation will be handed out to students who do not participate and/or hinder the effectiveness of the lab for other students.

Code of Conduct for *Business Students*
Core Ethical Values and Principles

As an Honours Bachelor of Business Administration student in the School of Business and Economics at Wilfrid Laurier University, you are preparing to embark upon a professional career in management. Ethical standards of behaviour are extremely important in today's business world. In the School of Business and Economics, we expect our students to exhibit the same levels of professionalism and ethical standards of behaviour that will be expected of you in both co-op placements and your chosen career after graduation. These expectations are as follows ...

Respect: A business student treats others with *respect*.

- Treat others (students, staff and faculty) in the same manner as you would want to be treated
- Do not demean other students (through put-downs or ridicule, etc.) in or out of the classroom
- Avoid derogatory comments regarding other students or instructors (TAs or professors)
- Respect differing points of view
- Do your fair share of group work — work should be equally distributed between all group members
- Respect that other students are here to learn — do not disrupt the class
- Turn off cell phones and shut down extraneous computer programs when in class
- Respect university property and those who use it — take your trash with you or deposit it in the nearest trash receptacle when you leave the classroom

Professionalism: A business student acts in a *professional* manner.

- Behave as you would in a business setting with your colleagues and/or superiors
- Don't read or play computer games, answer e-mails, etc., while in class — be there in mind as well as body
- Don't sleep in class
- Don't be late for class and don't leave early, unless cleared with your professor ahead of time
- Once class begins, do not leave and re-enter the classroom unless absolutely necessary
- Do not talk in class when others are talking
- Remember when you are off campus that your behaviour reflects on the S.B.E. — you are ambassadors to the school, and as such these same principles apply off-campus as well
- Do not use either the Internet, e-mail, or discussion forums to display or send inappropriate material or messages — those that others may find offensive (as outlined under *Principles in the Use of Information Technology* in the Regulations section of the University Undergraduate Calendar)

CODE OF CONDUCT FOR BUSINESS STUDENTS

Integrity: A business student behaves with *integrity*.

- Avoid any acts which would result in gaining an unfair advantage over other students (as outlined under *Academic Privileges and Responsibilities — Academic and Research Misconduct* in the Regulations section of the University Undergraduate Calendar):
    - Do not plagiarize — do not use the unacknowledged work of others as your own (in whole or part, in written or oral form, on assignments or tests, etc.) — all work of others must be acknowledged as such. This includes material taken from the Internet
    - Do not collaborate on an assignment when you have been asked for individual work
    - Do not cheat — do not use, give, sell, receive (or attempt to do so), any unauthorized information before or during a test or when doing an assignment — do not copy or allow someone else to copy, and don't smuggle notes into a test
    - Do not purchase or otherwise obtain assignments for submission as your own
    - Do not submit the same piece of work or any portion of it for more than one course without the permission of both professors — this includes work previously submitted elsewhere
    - Do not impersonate someone, or arrange to have someone impersonate you in a test
    - Do not falsify or otherwise misrepresent academic records or supporting documents, or documents used when requesting an extension or exception to course requirements — either through your professor, or through the formal petition process

- Seek assistance before you feel the pressure to breach your integrity
- Report any cases of academic misconduct that you become aware of to your professor (all reports will be kept strictly confidential)

Code of Conduct for *Teaching Assistants*
Core Ethical Values and Principles

As a teaching assistant in the School of Business & Economics at WLU you play a valuable and integral role in shaping the ethical direction of first year students in the program. You are ambassadors and role models. As such, the following principles must be adhered to...

Respect: A Business 111/121 TA treats others with *respect*.

- Treat others (students, staff, and faculty) in the same manner as you would want to be treated
- Do not demean students (through put-downs or ridicule, etc.) in or out of the classroom
- Avoid derogatory comments regarding other instructors (TAs or professors) and students
- Respect differing points of view
- Respect students' privacy by maintaining confidentiality (grades, personal information, student number, etc.)

Trustworthiness: A Business 111/121 TA acts in a *trustworthy* manner.

- Be honest with students (admit when you don't know the answer and endeavour to find it)
- Keep any promises made to students (office hours, etc.)
- Acknowledge academic references if materials originated from these sources — and do share your ideas with other TAs
- Use the TA office for TA business only — do not use for group meetings or snacks, and pick up after yourself
- Never leave the TA office unattended!
- Do not use photocopier and other SBE assets for personal use

Fairness: A Business 111/121 TA treats students *fairly*.

- Avoid favouritism which could be created or perceived through close personal relationships with students
- Immediately declare to the teaching professors any conflicts of interests (real or perceived) concerning any students in your labs (friends or relatives, etc.)
- Do not give exam "tips" from past exams or "tips" on any assignments that the teaching professors have not agreed to
- Provide clear expectations of grading criteria
- Maintain impartiality and consistency in grading

CODE OF CONDUCT FOR TEACHING ASSISTANTS

Responsibility: A Business 111/121 TA acts in a *responsible* manner.

- Arrive on time and fully prepared for all labs and meetings
- Use extra time in labs for supplementary material provided — do not end early
- Pursue excellence by keeping up with and maintaining accurate and relevant course content
- Provide timely and helpful feedback to students
- Be able to justify every mark you give — marking can not be delegated!
- Take responsibility for mistakes
- Refer all instances of student misconduct to the teaching professors

Code of Conduct for *Teaching Professors*
Core Ethical Values and Principles

As Business 111/121 Professors in the School of Business & Economics at WLU we recognize the role that we play in shaping the ethical direction of students in the program. Just as we have certain expectations of you in regards to how you conduct yourselves in the program, we also recognize that you have certain expectations of us. As such we pledge to adhere to the principles outlined below. Some of these principles have been adapted from Ethical Principles in University Teaching published by the Society for Teaching and Learning in Higher Education.

Respect: A Business 111/121 Professor treats others with *respect*.

- Treat others (students, staff, and other faculty) in the same manner as you would want to be treated

- Do not demean students (through put-downs or ridicule, etc.) in or out of the classroom

- Avoid derogatory comments regarding other instructors (TAs or professors) and students — "... avoid actions such as exploitation and discrimination that detract from student development"[1]

- Respect differing points of view, particularly when dealing with sensitive topics — "topics that students are likely to find sensitive or discomforting are dealt with in an open, honest, and positive way"[1]

- Respect the right of students to an optimal learning environment by ensuring that all students adhere to the B.B.A. Student Code of Conduct regarding classroom behaviour

- Begin and end class on time

- Respect students' privacy by maintaining confidentiality — "student grades, attendance records, and private communications are treated as confidential materials, and are released only with student consent, or for legitimate academic purposes, or if there are reasonable grounds for believing that releasing such information will be beneficial to the student or will prevent harm to others."[1]

- Demonstrate respect for colleagues "a university teacher respects the dignity of his or her colleagues and works cooperatively with colleagues in the interest of fostering student development"[1]

- Demonstrate respect for the institution — "in the interests of student development, a university teacher is aware of and respects the educational goals, policies, and standards of the institution in which he or she teaches"[1]

CODE OF CONDUCT FOR TEACHING PROFESSORS

Concern: A Business 111/121 Professor demonstrates *concern* for students.

- Display an interest in and concern for student development — "the overriding responsibility of the teacher is to contribute to the intellectual development of the student"[1]

- Be available to assist students in dealing with course material and concepts

- Ensure that the content of the course is consistent with the course outline, course objectives, and calendar description — "... communicate the objectives of the course to students, and select methods of instruction that... are effective in helping students to achieve the course objectives"[1]

- Ensure that the course contributes to student learning — "... ensure that course content is current, accurate, representative, and appropriate to the position of the course within the student's program of studies"[1]

- Develop competence in course content — "... maintain a high level of subject matter knowledge"[1]

- Be well prepared for every class

- Strive for excellence in teaching — give clear explanations, speak clearly and audibly, and display a passion that stimulates student interest in the subject matter of the course

Fairness: A Business 111/121 Professor treats students *fairly*.

- Avoid favouritism which could be created or perceived through close personal relationships with students — "to avoid conflict of interest, a teacher does not enter into dual-role relationships with students that are likely to detract from student development or lead to actual or perceived favouritism on the part of the teacher"[1]

- Provide clear expectations of the requirements of the course and grading criteria

- Make every effort to ensure teaching assistant impartiality and consistency in grading through the provision of appropriate marking guidelines and procedures — "... instructors are responsible for taking adequate steps to ensure that assessment of students is valid, open, fair, and congruent with course objectives."[1]

- Change assignments and test questions regularly so as not to create an environment that encourages academic misconduct

- Ensure that no student gains an unfair advantage over any other student by enforcing the S.B.E. and University Code of Conduct regarding academic integrity and misconduct

---

[1] H. Murray, E. Gillese, M. Lennon, P. Mercer, & M. Robinson, *Ethical Principles in University Teaching*. North York: Society for Teaching and Learning in Higher Education, 1996.

Course Structure

The Business 121 course will use a *blended learning* model. What this means is that we will be using both online/outside class and classroom learning together, along with the labs, to meet the objectives of the course. You will spend less time in class ... but before you get too excited, understand that this means that you will be responsible for learning the base 'threshold' material (called this because without its understanding it is difficult to progress further in the subject) outside of class. For the most part, your professors will expect that you will have done the required reading and assigned exercises on these concepts before class, and will move beyond this base material to integrate, apply and provide a richer understanding of the concepts in class. You will also be expected to engage in class vs just listen and take notes, as engagement has been proven to enhance learning.

The following table outlines the progression of topics covered in the course and most importantly the split of responsibility between online/outside class, classroom, and lab learning. A similar but more complete outline with due dates for assignments, etc. will be provided with the course outline/syllabus.

A diagram of the course model follows. It provides the framework for how the main topics in the course connect, to give you a more complete understanding of how a business works. We will use this course model as a base framework to build our understanding of the course material.

STRUCTURE OF THE COURSE

Week	Online/Outside Class	Class	Lab
1 (Jan. 3–6)	DISC Assessment (online)	Course Introduction	Lab Registration: January 5 and 6
2 (Jan. 9–13)	EQi (online) Business Models — GEL and BMC (lab manual)	Business Planning & Business Models	Teamwork & Leadership
3 (Jan. 16–20)	Communication (text) & Critical Thinking (lab manual)	Communication & Critical Thinking	Art of the Pitch & Individual Presentation Skills
4 (Jan. 23–27)	Understanding the Customer (text/online tests)	Marketing — Who is the Customer & What do they Want?	Critical Thinking & Case Analysis Tools
5 (Jan. 30–Feb. 3)	Creating Marketing Strategies (text/online tests)	Marketing — Reaching the Customer	Individual Student Pitches
6 (Feb. 6–Feb. 10)	Using Financial Information and Accounting (text/online tests)	Accounting — Cash vs Profit, Understanding Statements	Writing Skills & Business Model Canvas
7 (Feb. 13–Feb. 17)	Managing the Firm's Finances (text/online tests)	Finance — CVP Analysis, Debt vs Equity	Case Analysis w/Numbers
		Reading Week (Feb. 20–24)	
8 (Feb. 27–Mar. 3)		Midterm Exam Review/Prep	Catch-up & Midterm Review
9 (Mar. 5–Mar. 9)	Achieving World-Class Operations Management (text/online tests)	Operations & Sustainability	Negotiations Exercise
10 (Mar. 12–Mar. 16)	Managing Human Resources and Labour Relations (text/online tests)	Human Resources & EI	Effective Group Presentations & Case Practice
11 (Mar. 19–Mar. 23)		Labour Relations	Group Presentations
12 (Mar. 26–31)	Negotiating (lab manual)	Negotiating	Group Presentations
13 (April 2)		Final Exam Review/Prep	

Integrative Model of a Successful Business

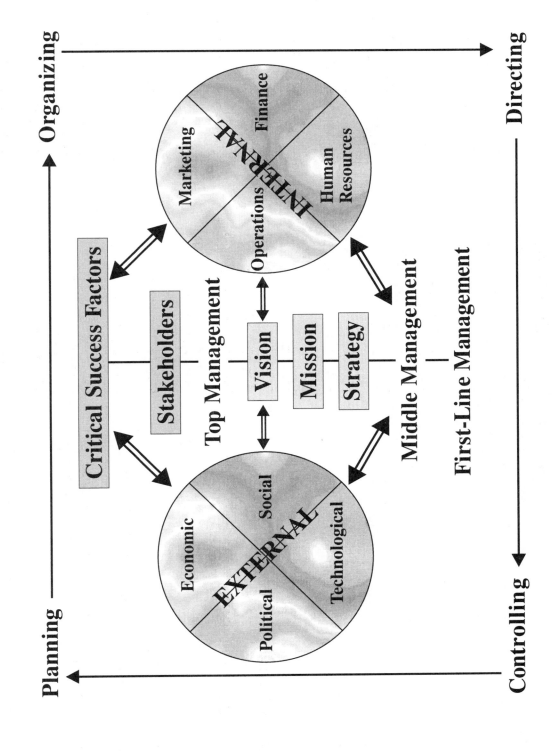

Week #1   Lab Registration & Assessments

Lab Registration

LABS START THE SECOND WEEK OF CLASSES.

Make sure you have properly registered at www.wlu.ca/sbe/bu121 according to the instructions announced in the first class. Registration will take place on January 5th for BBA and Double Degree students, and January 6th for non-BBAs.

EQi and DISC Assessments

You will be completing 2 online assessments for this course. You will also be required to hand in a reflection on both these assessments at the end of the term for marks. The purpose of these assessments is to give you some insight into yourself and how you respond to situations both individually and in a team, in order to help both you and your team increase your odds for success. Mark penalties will be assigned for assessments that are not completed prior to the deadlines given.

A 'coupon' entitling you to complete these assessments was shrink-wrapped with this lab manual. DO NOT THROW IT OUT! It must be handed in to your TA in your first lab.

BEFORE going to your first lab it is critical that you **complete the DISC assessment (through People Keys)** using the instructions provided on the course website. You will be required to take a printed copy of your completed DISC assessment report with you to the first lab. Marks will be deducted if this assessment is not completed by Sunday January 8th at 11:59pm.

Instructions for completing the second assessment — the EQi (through MHS Multi-Health Systems) will be provided in your first lab.

Week #2 / Lab #1

Class — Business Planning & Business Models

Readings from two books are attached to this week's section of the Lab Manual as they are required for class and will also form the basis for your first hand-in assignment:

- *Business Models Made Easy* by Don Debelak
    - Business Models — A Definition
    - The GEL Factors: Predicting Success
        - Finding a Great Customer Group
        - Making the Easy Sale
        - Building a Long Future
    - Evaluating Your Concept

- *Business Model Generations* by Alexander Osterwalder & Yves Pigneur
    - Definition of a Business Model
    - The 9 Building Blocks
    - The Business Model Canvas

Lab #1 — Teamwork & Leadership

IMPORTANT INSTRUCTIONS:

- It is expected that you will have completed, read, and reflected on the DISC Assessment that you did in Week #1 of the course.
- Be sure to download the assessment report, print and <u>bring it to the lab</u> (along with your signed *Statement of Academic Integrity* form).
- Complete both Keyword Exercises in the Detailed Keyword Analysis section of the DISC report, as well as Step 1 of the Action Plan (Step 2 is not necessary for this lab).

Business Models — A Definition

Chapter 1

Business Models– A Definition

From Wikipedia, the Internet's free encyclopedia

A business model (also called a business design) is the instrument by which a business intends to generate revenue and profits. It is a summary of how a company means to serve its employees and customers, and involves both strategy (what a business intends to do) as well as an implementation (how the business will carry out its plans).

THE BIGGEST PROBLEM WITH WRITING A BOOK TITLED *BUSINESS Models Made Easy* is that no single accepted definition of business models has really emerged. For decades terms like the *razor blade business model*, where you sell a product for a low value and cash in on the consumable sales, have been used for years. Other terms, like the *application service provider* (ASP), model were big in the dotcom era, where an ASP hosted complex software on its site and allowed customers to use it for a monthly fee.

But discussing those models doesn't get to the nature of what a business model really is. Another way to get at the definition of business model is to look at why people, particularly banks and investors, often mention business models—because it is easier to evaluate a business' potential with a business model than with a business plan. Most people can't articulate clearly what they feel is the business model, and often they just say they don't like the model when they see something in a business concept that they don't agree with. So the purpose of the business model concept for investors and bankers is a quick way to evaluate a business. People developing a business concept should apply the same reasoning—they need a quick and easy way to evaluate their concept to see if it will work, or to see how it can be modified in order for it to succeed.

Easy to Understand and Use

The purpose of the business model concept for investors and bankers is a quick way to evaluate a business.

Despite the lack of a consistent, recognized definition of business model, I've found that most of the people I've known, and most of the articles I've read discussing the business model concept deal with the following six elements when deciding if the company has a good business model. When all six of these elements are favorable, then you have a good business model. The Great Customers, Easy Sales, and Long Life (GEL) factor analysis, discussed in Chapter 4, offers a way for you to understand when your concept meets the favorable test for each of the six elements, and how to adjust your concept if it doesn't.

1. Acquire high value customers—favorable condition: without spending a lot of money.
2. Offer significant value to customers—favorable condition: having a significant competitive advantage.
3. Deliver products or services with high margins—favorable condition: with high quality and few opportunities for error.
4. Provide for customer satisfaction—favorable condition: service and training, if needed, provided by someone else.
5. Maintaining market position—favorable condition: market position is protected or a steady stream of new products or services can be maintained.
6. Funding the business—favorable condition: investments reasonable for market size and risk both for start-up costs and for market maintenance.

I like to consider the six key elements as being three green and three red lights. The first three points, acquiring high value customers, offering significant value, and delivering products and services at high margins are three positive elements you need to go ahead. You have them in place and you have the green lights. The last three points, providing for customer satisfaction, maintaining market position, and funding are areas where a business model can run into a red light. The business model stops working if product support is difficult, if you don't have a good method of maintaining your market position, or if the business model requires too much investment. So a great business model delivers big time on the green lights and avoids the red. Add the green lights and avoid the red and you have a "can't miss" business model.

Insight

Though you will understand business models after reading this book, most of the people you talk to will not, so as you are developing your model look for other companies that work under a similar model. Then when you are asked about your model tell people it is similar to that company's, and then explain your model.

A successful business model, however, is only the first checkpoint on the way to a good business plan. Once you have a model, the rest of your plan, management, marketing strategy, strengths, and weaknesses all still matter. So you need a good start with the model, followed by a thorough business plan that takes advantage of your model and helps create the management team and staff necessary to implement the plan. Then you have success. But everything still starts with a winning model.

You need a good start with the model, followed by a thorough business plan that takes advantage of your model and helps create the management team and staff necessary to implement the plan.

Green Lights

Acquiring High Value Customers

High value customers doesn't mean rich customers, but customers who

- ▶ Are easy to locate
- ▶ Allow you to charge a profitable price
- ▶ Are willing to try your product after minimal marketing expenses
- ▶ Can generate enough business to meet your sales and profit objectives

Customers don't necessarily need to be the end users of your product or service, they could be retailers, distributors, catalogs, or whoever you sell your product or service to. If your end users or distributors don't fit this profile, you still could be able to meet this requirement by attracting high value customers through partnerships or alliances with other companies in the market.

Offer Significant Value to Customers

People typically think in terms of competitive advantage related to features and benefits as significant value, but there are a number of ways you can create value besides maintaining a competitive advantage. They include providing:

*B*usiness today is nothing like it was 20 or even 10 years ago where product features were the prominent ways people added value to customers.

▶ Unique advantages in features and benefits;

▶ Better distribution through retail or distribution;

▶ More complete customer solutions through alliances with other companies;

▶ Lower pricing due to manufacturing efficiencies or pricing options; and

▶ Faster delivery, broader product line, or offering customers more options for customization.

Business today is nothing like it was 20 or even 10 years ago where product features were the prominent ways people added value to customers. The rise of the Internet and outsourcing, but most of all the increased willingness of companies to partner in creative ways to serve customers, has resulted in every industry creating innovation in business strategy. This gives you opportunities, but also makes it imperative that you stay on the creative edge to fend off competition.

Insight

It is very difficult for small businesses or entrepreneurs to compete against significantly larger businesses as a minimum of a 25 or even 50 percent advantage is necessary to succeed. A break-through product like a Garlic Twist, rather than a garlic press, has that advantage, but more than likely an improved garlic press won't. You can get by with less of an advantage if you face small competitors. One additional key to look for is that your customers immediately spot your advantage. Don't count on an advantage that is hard to notice.

Deliver Products or Services with High Margins

Better manufacturing costs due to overseas manufacturing is typically not the clear way to higher margins, as competitors will often match your costs in the end. Higher margins come from having a product that can be made from an improved process or by having high value features that provide significant value that allow you to charge more. But you can achieve high margins with other tactics including:

- Having a more efficient distribution channel
- Requiring less sales support and sales effort
- Having an industry-leading, lean manufacturing process
- Offering more auxiliary products or other opportunities for revenue without increasing sales costs

Delivering products or services with high margins seems like it is an obvious concern for every business. It certainly has been a concern for at least the 35 years that I've been in business. But it seems that the business models and business plans I've seen over the last few years do not have enough time spent on delivering high margin products and services despite its being a bedrock principle in every successful business model. That is a big mistake, as often your significant value can come out of your ability to achieve high margins.

Red Lights

Provide for Customer Satisfaction

This is the start of the business model red lights. The question is: Will it be difficult (and therefore expensive) to satisfy customers once they buy? Some of the aspects of a business that create high customer satisfaction costs include:

- Having good warranty policies
- Maintaining extensive technical support
- Easy installation either through simplicity of the product or by the assistance of a support staff
- Maintaining extensive customer service
- Interfacing easily with other equipment or dealing quickly with interface problems

In a sense, a business model determines resource allocation. An ideal model uses a company's resources to add customers and create customer value, which improves a company's market position and adds value to a company, and uses few resources to produce products and services and maintain customer satisfaction. Customer satisfaction costs, which occur after the sale, are red flags because the costs are typically high and don't produce revenue or profits. Maintaining customer satisfaction is only ideal when it results in your company adding value to the customer.

An ideal model uses a company's resources to add customers and create customer value.

8

As in all aspects of a business model, the fact that your type of product might have high customer service costs isn't a deal stopper; you just need to configure your business to put these costs on someone else, either with partnerships or alliances, or by restricting your sales to an aspect of the business that doesn't require high costs for customer satisfaction. For example, the business I started in 2005 sells diesel particulate traps, which are part of a diesel emission system. Dealing with a new product to truck and bus fleets requires lots of technical support, follow-up maintenance, and customer service. We have chosen to sell the filter only to system integrators that take on the costs of customer satisfaction of fleets. We still need to keep our integrators happy, but that is much easier to do as we have fewer customers and far fewer problems.

Maintaining Market Position

A good business model uses its resources to improve its market position, adding new products, features, and customers or expanding into new applications.

A good business model uses its resources to improve its market position, adding new products, features, and customers or expanding into new applications. A business cannot do that if it has to constantly fight for market position, either with price discounts to major customers, or by absorbing the costs of trading customers with competitors. Patent protection, brand names, customer loyalty, and unique value in the market are ways companies strengthen market position. But there are red flags to watch for that indicate a model could be in trouble, including:

▶ Two or three major customers buy most of your product

▶ Major potential competitors control the distribution network

▶ Technology changes rapidly and requires high-risk product development

▶ There are alternative technologies being developed to meet the same need

▶ You have well-funded potential competitors who could quickly move into your market

There is an old adage that people can't see the forest for the trees. Often entrepreneurs fall into that trap, looking at the details of their business without understanding the overall market landscape, and the features of that landscape can cause them trouble. Long term, your ability to hold market position is determined by the characteristics of the overall market. For example, I worked for a company in the semiconductor manufacturing business. New technology constantly was being developed, some that worked with our product and some that didn't. We were a small company, and guessing right on every technology change, something we had to do to hold market position, was just too difficult.

Funding the Business

Start-up costs, operating capital, personnel and overhead costs are just a small percentage of the funding requirements for any business. The question is whether or not the investments will have a high return, and whether or not the business can grow without substantial new investments. Drug companies might have a high initial investment for R&D in a new drug, but then after that investment is made a drug can be sold at a high profit for years. Service businesses, on the other hand, may require substantial investments for all expanded sales dollars. Red flags for a business model regarding investments include:

> ▶ ROI (return of investment) is less than 25 percent in the first three years
> ▶ Incremental production of products or services requires substantial additional investments
> ▶ Less than 50 percent of the investment required will be used in revenue-producing areas (sales and production)
> ▶ Investments have to be made prior to sales commitments
> ▶ Industry as a whole has a poor ROI or poor profitability

New entrepreneurs tend to think money will be hard to come by and often put together a business model that requires little money, outsourcing all production as an example, but then don't leave enough room in their pricing to generate profits. Money is available for the right plan and the right model. Always start with the investments you need for your most efficient business model. You'll find money available if your ROI is right and if you have financial leverage, which means your initial investment will allow you to double or triple sales without requiring any more funding.

You'll find money available if your ROI is right and if you have financial leverage, which means your initial investment will allow you to double or triple sales without requiring any more funding.

The GEL: Factors: Predicting Success

Chapter 4

The GEL Factors: Predicting Success

After a wild ride through the dotcom to dotbomb era, venture funding, angel investors, and business loans are back to normal levels. Everyone has learned a few lessons along the way, the most important being that business fundamentals always count. Businesses are analyzed today based on business fundamentals including a strong management team, a profitable business model, and a well-thought-out business plan.

The GEL Factors

The three main characteristics for producing success are what I refer to as the GEL factors (see Figure 1-1).

1. Having **G**reat customers
2. Sales are relatively **E**asy to make
3. The business will have a **L**ong life

A business will make a lot of money for a long time if it possesses all three GEL factors. To determine whether or not a business has these three points you need to evaluate customers, products, distribution networks, technical support, new product development, and production.

Reproduced from Don Debelak, *Business Models Made Easy*, (Newburgh, NY: Entrepreneur Press), Chapter 4.

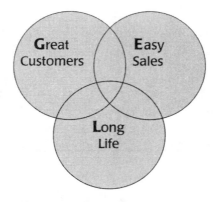

Figure 1-1. GEL: Overlapping Factors for Success

The GEL factor evaluation isn't a pass-fail test; it's to determine what's wrong with your business approach so you can repair it. Once you fine-tune your business so it delivers all the GEL factors, you will be able to write a great business plan.

How will you know if your business has these success points? That's what this first section of the book is all about—dissecting your business so you know you have great customers, easy sales, and long life. In reality, most new businesses won't have all the success elements in place at first. That's not a problem. This section will show you how to modify your business operation so it will really sizzle. Figure 1-2 details the analysis points of your GEL factor evaluation.

Starbucks—Brewing Success One Cup at a Time

Starbucks is a great example of a company with all the success factors. Its great customers are mid- to upper-income people who like to pamper themselves. There are a large number of those customers, they are easy to find by their neighborhoods and where they work, and they spend freely. Those customers provide plenty of value to the company because the dollar value of their sales is much higher than at traditional coffee shops, repeat business is great (like two to five times a week, and for some people two to three times a day), and the ongoing product support costs are very low as people consume the product.

G—Yes
E—Yes
L—Yes

GREAT CUSTOMERS	Characteristics	Number Ease of Finding Spending Patterns
	Value to You	$ Value of Sale Repeat Sales Ongoing Sales Support
EASY SALES	Value to Customer	How Important Competitive Advantage Price/Value Relationship
	Customer Acquisition Cost	Entry Points Sales Support Required Promotional Activities
LONG LIFE	Profit per Sale	Margins Up-Selling and Cross-Selling Selling Cost per Sale
	Investment Required	To Enter Business To Keep Market Share To Stay on the Cutting Edge

Figure 1-2. GEL Factors for a Successful Business

Starbucks also scores high in the easy sales criterion, starting with its value to its customers. The Starbucks "premium quality" image is important to its customers; its products are better than coffee from a coffee cart or a fast food chain; and its price, though higher than its competitors', is still a bargain for the "trendy and upscale" image their brand creates for its customers. In terms of acquiring customers, Starbucks started in Seattle, where it could afford the number of stores and the promotion it needed and its name recognition means it requires minimal ongoing promotional support.

As for long life, Starbucks meets all the profitability tests and has had little trouble holding onto its market share and expanding its store base. One advantage Starbucks had was a relatively low start-up cost. They only had two questions before opening. One was whether or not target customers would feel premium brands of coffee make them feel good about themselves, and second, how often those customers would come to Starbucks. Both of those questions could be answered at the test store that Starbucks opened in Seattle.

Kinkos—Tweaking the Concept

Kinkos started out as a copy center at major colleges and universities. To create recurring revenue it offered students copies of articles or papers that professors wanted to distribute to their classes. Kinkos would get a list of desired handouts from the professors, and then arrange for the rights to copy them and sell them to students. The idea was that Kinkos would have many products to sell to many students. As an additional service, Kinkos added computer workstations that students could use 24 hours a day.

G—No
E—No
L—Yes

This business approach had many elements for success. It provided a service professors wanted, it offered easy access to thousands of customers, and it produced a steady revenue stream.

There was just one problem: the work involved for each sale was too high. Kinkos needed just too many employees to execute its strategy for the fees students were willing to pay; the work was especially difficult when they made copies for just one class. This could have been the end of the story—except that Kinkos strategy of being open 24 hours a day had a side benefit: Kinkos started getting jobs for overnight production of copies of documents for businesses, plus other big orders like booklets for classes, presentations, court documents, legal documents for investors, and a whole range of other jobs that needed to be done at the last minute.

So Kinkos switched its business approach. It started locating its stores near large business centers, where there was always lots of last-minute rush business. All of a sudden Kinkos business model changed, focusing on businesses instead of students. The old model had students, who watched their money closely, as its target customers. The new model had as its target customers companies that would pay almost anything to get the rush job they needed done on time. Students thought a $20 purchase was big. Companies were happy spending hundreds and even thousands of dollars to get their documents done on time.

The results are clear. The new approach has a much better group of customers with critical needs that only Kinkos is addressing. The customers are easy to identify and happy to spend money to meet their needs. The new customer group is all it took to turn Kinkos into a profitable powerhouse.

Finding a Great Customer Group

Chapter 5

Finding a Great Customer Group

> reat customers are probably the most important element for a highly profitable business. They allow companies to make strong profits and enjoy steady sales increases. Great customers aren't necessarily the customers with the most money, but they're the customers who value what you offer and are willing to pay for it. More importantly, they're the customers who will keep buying from you repeatedly and their purchases are significant

I DON'T MEAN TO IMPLY BY THE TITLE OF THE CHAPTER THAT THERE'S ONLY one right group of customers. All customer groups buy many products and there is a different right customer group for every product. These may sound like some pretty stiff requirements, but in fact many businesses are able to attract and keep a great group of customers.

Rockbottom Brewery is a restaurant chain that is growing fast around the country. It promotes Rockbottom Beer; has moderately priced food; and specializes in events, entertainment, pool tables, contests, and other once-a-month activities.

G—No
E—No
L—Yes

Why is Rockbotton different? Its average price per dinner is $15 to $20 per person, including a drink or two. At that price, many people are not only willing to visit the restaurant, but ready to visit it regularly. Plus

Reproduced from Don Debelak, *Business Models Made Easy*, (Newburgh, NY: Entrepreneur **Press**), Chapter 5.

> ## Company Story—The Real Life Works Here but Not There
>
> Rainforest Café had a brief run of success in the late 90s in both high-traffic vacation or destination sites and upscale neighborhoods. At first the restaurants were all a success. But after a few years, Rainforest closed its restaurants that weren't at travel destination spots. What happened?
>
> Rainforest's target customer group is people who want to go to an upscale theme restaurant where the theme is more important than the food. At destinations, with a steady stream of new people, there were always enough customers. But away from destinations, people only occasionally wanted to visit a theme restaurant and there just weren't enough customers to keep buying its product.

Rockbottom always has something going on to appeal to the 20- to 35-year-old single crowd that frequently goes out for drinks and dinner.

In contrast, Rainforest's bill typically runs over $30 per person. That upscale price lowered the number of potential customers to the point that there just weren't enough to support the business at locations away from travel destinations.

G—Yes
E—Average
L—Yes

Six Key Factors for Evaluating Customers

		Desired	Excellent	Average	Poor
Customer Characteristics	Number	High			
	Ease of Finding	Easy			
	Spending Patterns	Prolific			
Customer Value to Company	$ Value of Sale	High			
	Repeat Sales	Many			
	Ongoing Sales Support	Low			

Figure 2-1. GEL Factor Customer Checklist

Number

Why It's Important

Businesses need a large enough customer base to cover their cost of running the business, meet income expectations, and have enough funds to keep sales momentum going with promotions and business expansions. Without a large enough potential customer group, you just won't have enough sales to cover these costs.

When It's a Key Concern

1. **Your product or service is inexpensive.** A low-priced product needs lots of customers to make money.
2. **Opportunities for repeat or add-on sales are limited.** If you need new customers every year, you need a big prospect pool.
3. **When customers can't find your business easily.** Customers look for some businesses in the Yellow Pages. If they don't look for your type of business, then you have to find them.
4. **People don't know about your type of product, business, or service.** They won't be looking for you if they don't know you exist.

Success Tip

Once you tightly define your customer group, check to be sure that there are successful businesses that appear to be targeting the same customer group. List what is similar about what the companies are offering and what is different. Pay particular attention to the price, the amount of repeat business, and the importance of the product to the customer. Be wary of customer groups that don't support successful businesses.

What Can Compensate

1. **You can present a compelling reason to buy.** You can get by with fewer prospects if your concept significantly meets a major customer desire.
2. **You can have a devoted distribution channel.** For example, people who buy map-related products are a small, widely scattered group of customers who go out of their way to find the few map stores that are in their area.
3. **You can be in places where your customers go.** A store that wants to sell ceramic tiles for home address numbers or garden plaques, for example, might thrive if located in a mall or town with a concentration of artisan stores and shops.

4. **You can be part of a network of organizations serving the same customer group.** You can promote effectively if you combine your efforts with other companies serving the market.

Ease of Finding

Why It's Important

You need to either easily locate customers or be easy for them to locate you. If it's hard to find customers, you may need to spend, spend, spend to find them and that cost might prohibit your success. For example, how does a company that sells small, in-home soda dispensers, similar to the ones in fast-food restaurants, find customers when only a small number of people will want the hassles of an in-home carbonated soda machine? Who are they and how can you find them?

When It's a Key Concern

Anytime that you can't depend on the following means of finding customers easily:

1. **Customers belong to clubs or associations related to your product.**
2. **There are trade or consumer magazines targeted at your customer group.**
3. **Customers can be identified through purchased lists.**
4. **Big events or trade shows target your customer group.**
5. **A distribution market serves your market.** Special woodworking shops or wild bird catalogs, for example, are targeted at customers who would otherwise be hard to find.
6. **Customers know where to look for you.** For example, people looking to go hunting in Montana look for lodges on the Internet or in hunting magazines.

Buzzwords

To be considered a *customer group*, people need to act in a similar manner. For example, people who cook dinner after eight hours of work are not a customer group. They'll behave differently depending on whether they have children, how many people they cook for, and whether or not they use prepared foods. A customer group would be working people who minimize their use of prepared food and are concerned about nutrition.

What Can Compensate

1. **Consolidate several products or services into a high-dollar purchase** that will justify spending lots of money to locate a few customers.
2. **Find potential customers through current customers.** A painter specializing in high-appeal party rooms knows that one person who loves to entertain knows many others who like to do the same, which can lead to referral business.
3. **Create a joint marketing campaign with other companies serving the same target group facing the same problem of finding customers.**
4. **Offer classes or seminars or attend trade shows to attract prospects.** A company that offers services to convert lawns into natural wildlife gardens might offer classes and demonstrations or start a club for people interested in a yard with natural fauna.

Success Tip

Confused customers never buy. Customers don't think the same way a salesperson does. Salespeople sell their product features, while customers worry about how a product will solve their problems or meet their desires. You'll always sell more if you gear your sales and marketing efforts toward showing the customers how they will meet their goals with your product.

Spending Patterns

Why It's Important

Some customer groups buy primarily on emotion and they will spend freely. Parents of young children may spend on impulse. Companies that want to be perceived as being leading-edge typically will spend money to protect their image. How customers spend impacts a company in two ways. The first is that customers who spend freely typically require less sales effort and customer service than customers who watch their money closely. The second is that customers who spend freely will often make bigger purchases, which simply results in more sales for less effort.

When It's a Key

1. **The sale is based on practical considerations rather than an emotional response.** People will almost always spend freely when it's an emotional purchase, such as a car, but they're always looking to cut costs for practical purchases.

2. The product is not a priority purchase for the customer. Customers who are reluctant will still always buy if it's a high priority for them.

3. You don't have the resources to provide an intensive sales effort. You can't shortchange the sales effort unless the customer is spending freely.

4. The product needs to be purchased only once. Unless your product is consumed and frequently purchased, you can afford only a limited sales effort for each sale and a limited sales effort won't sell customers who watch every penny.

How to Compensate

1. Find a way to translate your sale into an emotional purchase. Subway did a great job with its promotion of the student who lost over 100 pounds eating low-fat Subway subs. Giving people an easy way to lose weight stirs up powerful emotions.

2. Sell a complete solution. Find out what the customers feel is their goal when they buy your products or services and add products or services to help the customers achieve their overall goal.

3. Set sales policies to make the buying decision easy. Thirty-day trials, guaranteed returns, leases, and monthly fees versus a straight purchase are all ways to make the purchase decision easier for the customer.

4. Concentrate your efforts on big potential accounts. Most salespeople will tell you it's just as much work to sell $5,000 to a small company as it is to sell $200,000 to a big company.

5. Add a product or a service that your potential customer will look for. For example, people don't know where to look for invention marketing services. A firm might add prototype services, which its customers do look for in their Yellow Pages.

Success Tip

When you're having trouble locating customers, ask yourself what characteristics of customers make them strong candidates to buy your product. For the soda machine distributor, the people most likely to buy might be mid- to high-income people with more than three kids or people who have lots of kids around, like coaches. Those are people whom the company could find and sell to, so it would have a chance to succeed.

Dollar Value of Sale

Why It's Important

A high-dollar sale automatically creates a high-value customer. That means that a company can afford to devote resources to the customer, knowing that the sale will result in a profit. A company that supplies fuel stations for compressed natural gas vehicles may have an average sale price of $750,000. It can afford the sales support the customer needs to make a buying decision. On the other hand, a $5,000 to $8,000 industrial sale, especially to a small business, can be a dangerous price point, because the price still requires extensive sales support, but the size of the sale doesn't produce the necessary profits.

When It's a Key

1. **Sales support is required.** Sales of complex or technical items require an extensive sales effort, as do sales that are important for a company's operation and sales for which the final buying decision involves many people.
2. **Products are customized for each customer.** A person installing rock gardens needs to plan, select the right materials, and offer plenty of hand-holding support.
3. **The sales cycle is long.** Most families spend a lot of time thinking and planning before deciding to go ahead with a major home redecorating project. Many business-to-business sales start with an assessment of the available products, a preliminary request for budget approval, and then a final analysis by many people before a product is purchased.
4. **There are many competitors.** Your closing rate will typically be lower if you have many competitors, which means that you will have to make a large number of sales calls for every order you receive.

Buzzword

Closing rate is a term that states the percentage of prospects who give you an order. A 5 percent closing rate means that 5 percent of the prospects buy. Try to determine which type of prospects has the best closing rate for you and then concentrate on them.

5. **There are few opportunities for follow-up sales.** People put up vinyl siding only once in the time they own a home. They might, in contrast, buy a new entertainment system every three to four years.

How to Compensate

1. **Sell a turnkey solution.** A product that is integrated into a system requires a great sales effort, because the customer has a lot to worry about: in the end he or she is responsible for making sure the system works. Sell a solution that will not make the customer worry.

2. **Get the customers to come to you.** An average sales call can cost a company anywhere from $200 to $800. You can minimize that cost by having customers come to your location. Demonstrations, trainings, special events, and plant tours are all ways to attract customers to your location.

3. **Create an independent sales network.** Independent sales agents receive a commission on what they sell. Typically, companies have only minimal upfront fees with sales agents.

4. **Add product lines.** One way to increase the dollar value of each sale is to add complementary products so you have more items to sell. You can add your own new products or start to sell products from other companies.

The Market Niche

For the last 20 years, marketing has been about the *market niche* or, as the venture capitalists call it today, the space a company operates in. I don't mean to suggest in this chapter that the focus on a market segment or customer group (otherwise known as a *niche*) is not important. The goal of a business is to provide value to a customer; it can do that best by focusing on one group. You'll have a much easier time making money if you have a lot of free-spending, easy-to-find customers than if you try scratching out a living from a few, hard-to-find, tightwad customers. That's the point of the GEL analysis—finding a way to operate that will create a profitable business.

Repeat Sales

Why It's Important

Regular repeat sales are where companies can find really big profits. The sales costs are low, product support costs are usually low, and typically customers buy a standard product for which manufacturing costs are low. Companies can spend lots of money to get customers who will buy repeatedly and they can spend money to develop a strong relationship with those customers.

When It's a Key

1. **The dollar value of each sale is small.** It's difficult to drive down the cost of sales. It costs money to create a customer file, check credit, and monitor results even if a customer just calls you out of the blue to order.
2. **Customer service costs are high.** Selling to large customers, selling a product that interfaces with many other products, and selling a product with a large number of variations all typically require extensive customer service support.
3. **The purchase is a low-priority decision for customers.** It's difficult to get customers to make a purchase decision that they feel is a low priority. But it can still be worth the trouble to get the sale if it's an item people purchase regularly, such as office supplies, maintenance supplies, or telephone service.
4. **You have a small sales staff.** Customers making a major one-time purchase will be wary of a small company, because they will worry about after-sales service. But they will be happy to buy items they purchase regularly from a smaller supplier.

How to Compensate

1. **Create a more important purchase decision.** Ask how you can turn this purchase into one that will have a meaningful impact on a customer. For example, painters who create a memorable faux finishing look for a home will obtain much more business than a painter offering a straight paint job.

Success Tip

Controlling sales and marketing is a key to a successful business model. If you sell through distributors, sales and marketing costs—which include advertising, trade shows, direct mail, and brochures—should be no more than 20 to 22 percent of your sales revenue. If you sell direct to consumers, keep your costs below 30 percent.

2. **Find complementary ways to add value.** For the most part, what customers want is "no worries." Try to figure out what concerns a customer has about your type of purchase and then add services that make the decision "hassle-free."
3. **Create a low-cost sales plan.** You can keep sales costs low by selling on the Internet, through catalogs, through distributors and manufacturers' sales agents, at trade shows, or through another company.

4. **Expand the target market to a larger area.** If you can't get enough repeat business from your current market, you might need to expand to a bigger market. The bigger your target market, the more likely you'll find more customers eager to buy and your sales costs will be lower.

5. **Focus on big buyers.** Every market has big buyers, customers whose sales volume might justify your sales costs. If they don't, you need to reevaluate your business model.

Ongoing Sales Support

Why It's Important

When you sell office supplies, you don't need to offer much ongoing product support, which means that you get to keep most or all of the profit from each sale. But if you offer a lawn service that fertilizes lawns, you'll need more support. People will call up and check on whether or not a treatment is safe for pets or ask what to do if it rains right after the lawn is fertilized. All of these services cost money, and sometimes support costs can eliminate all the profits from a sale. Customers can represent high value to the company when they require little or no support, even if the profit margin per sale is low. The reverse is also true. An apparently profitable customer can quickly become a profit drain if support costs are high.

Pitfalls to Avoid

Most new companies badly underestimate the follow-up support required for products and services. Manufacturers find that people don't understand the simplest instructions and they break products despite clear warnings. Service providers find that customers change their minds about what they want or ask for one change after another. Find out what your product support costs will be from someone already in the industry.

When It's a Key

1. **Customers are buying an expected result instead of a defined product or service.** When people buy a food processor, for example, it's because they expect it will prepare some great exotic meals. Customers will complain if those meals don't come, even if the food processor works perfectly.

2. **Customer satisfaction depends on the application.** This is a common problem in business-to-business markets where customers have different applications. Some of those applications are bound to not work as well

as others and that will create follow-up costs.

3. **The product is new and users aren't familiar with its operation.** People will typically have trouble with any new device. With established products, customers will accept problems with comments of "That's just the way a product works" or they'll be able to find someone who can help them use it.

4. **Products are customized to a customer's application.** You're offering a beta unit when you're selling a customized product or service. Beta units have tons of kinks that can be worked out only in the field, which requires tons of product support.

Buzzword

Beta sites, *beta units*, and *beta customers* are terms you hear all the time with new companies or products. They simply mean test sites or test units. Companies often put products and services out at beta sites for 6 to 12 months to make sure the products or services work. It's not uncommon for support on beta units to exceed 25 percent of the sales price.

---

5. **Products interface with a number of other products.** Computer hardware and software products have only now, after two decades, started to interrelate well with each other, and those interface problems created product support costs.

How to Compensate

1. **Design products so that use is intuitive and "idiot-proof."** Do you read manuals? Probably not. You expect products to be intuitive. Most people wait until a problem develops—and then call technical assistance.

2. **Manage customers' expectations.** To a large degree, the supplier sets customers' expectations. If your advertising, sales presentations, and brochures all promise the world's greatest product, that's what customers will expect.

Success Tip

To determine just what expectations your customers have, ask your last 15 customers why they decided to buy from you, and what their expectations were. If those expectations are overly high, you have a major problem to correct. This is especially important for service providers, because customers can't see or touch what you're offering before buying.

---

3. Choose your customers carefully. Some customers have expectations you can't meet. Others have applications where your performance is marginal. Still others require ongoing support you can't afford.
4. Offer training programs at your location. Bringing the customers to your location is proactive, offers value to your customers, and is cost-effective for you.
5. Sell through a network that can provide service. Many industries—including power tools, lawn equipment, motorcycles, and industrial compressors—sell through a network of dealers that provide the service customers need.

Great Customers Exist Everywhere

Company Vignettes

Note to readers: I'll be tracking three companies—Dr. Spock Co., O'Naturals, and Jawroski's Towing and Service—in Chapters 5 through 7 to see how they compare on each GEL factor. The one point to notice is that a business needs all of the GEL factors for success.

There are six comparison factors related to great customers:

1. Number
2. Ease of finding
3. Spending patterns
4. Dollar value per sale
5. Potential for repeat sales
6. Ongoing sales support required

Dr. Spock Co.

Dr. Spock Co. provides parents advice on child rearing based on the works of Dr. Spock.

Parents of babies, especially parents who are professionals and in their 30s, appeared to the founders to be the right customer group. Their goal is to become the number-one spot that parents come to for baby advice, relying on the company's books, web sites, and pamphlets.

Evaluation on the basis of customers
1. Customers are older parents (28 years old and up); they are numerous. Rating +.

2. They are easy to locate through birth records, parenting shows, parenting magazine subscriptions, and purchases at child-oriented stores. **Rating +.**
3. This customer group is willing to spend money, and probably lots of money, for their children. It is not clear that customers value the advice of someone whose popularity peak was over 25 years ago (Dr. Spock). **Rating =.**
4. The dollar value of each sale will be modest, probably $10 to $50, so the company may lose money on the first sale. **Rating ?.**
5. Repeat sales could be strong, as children have new challenges as they grow older. Babies also go through stages very quickly, making it reasonable that customers will order every few months. **Rating +.**
6. The cost of ongoing customer support will be low. Information doesn't require warranty work or follow-up calls to be sure everything is working well. **Rating +.**

O'Naturals

O'Naturals is a chain of fast-food restaurants in New England that serve natural, organic foods.

Does fast food have to mean *fat* food? Not at O'Naturals, which is looking to gain a small part of the $20 billion natural food market. Its target customers are in wealthy New England towns that are populated by busy, highly educated, upper-income families.

Evaluation on the basis of customers
1. Although the market for natural foods is large, the number of customers interested in a natural/organic restaurant is unclear, even in the carefully chosen market. **Rating =.**
2. People preferring natural organic food should be relatively easy to find through their interest in food co-ops, subscriptions in organic food magazines, and their trips to farmers' markets and other health food–oriented businesses. **Rating +.**
3. The target customers appear to be committed to health foods and they spend extra money for their food of choice. But they are also probably willing to take extra time to prepare food themselves. **Rating =.**
4. The dollar sale value and profit per sale are modest, with a sale value of less than $7 per meal. **Rating ?.**
5. The number of repeat sales should be high, since O'Naturals is one of few natural-food restaurants and the only fast-food option for most of

its customers. If customers like the food, they should keep coming back. **Rating +.**

6. The ongoing customer support element of a restaurant is average. There's no sales follow-up required, but O'Naturals must ensure a pleasant dining experience, from good service to a clean restaurant, to keep customers happy. **Rating =.**

Jawroski's Towing and Repair

Jawroski's is a car repair and towing business in a fast-growing suburban area.

This business generates 25 percent of its revenue from towing, 40 percent from fleet repairs, and 35 percent from consumer drive-in traffic. The business does about $1.3 million per year in revenue and has been growing at a rate of 25 percent a year, with the growth of neighborhoods and businesses in the area. Most of Jawroski's towing business comes from vehicles that have broken down on a local major freeway.

Evaluation on the basis of customers

1. Almost everyone over the age of 18 has at least one car and many businesses have sizeable fleets. **Rating +.**
2. Customers couldn't be easier to locate. People who need a tow go looking for a business to help them. The businesses with vehicle fleets can be found easily through county and state business records, and almost every home has a car. **Rating +.**
3. People need their cars and they will pay to have them towed and repaired. They may not always appreciate their car repair services, but they definitely have to purchase the service when their vehicle needs it. **Rating +.**
4. Car repairs rarely run under $100, and towing costs of $75 to $100 are common. These are substantial sales, which means the company needs only a small number of sales each day. **Rating +.**
5. Repeat sales should be good if Jawroski's delivers quality service. Many people go way out of their way to go to a car repair shop where they've always gotten good service. **Rating +.**
6. Car repair shops don't have to work that hard to retain customers because people are leery of new shops. Car repair shops will keep their business as long as the shops give good service and keep current with technology changes. **Rating +.**

Many Ways to Skin a Cat

You've got stiff competition? Lucky for you there are still many methods you can use to build up a steady stream of business. I've listed here just a few of the tactics you can use.

1. Make part of your business a consumable product that clients have to buy repeatedly. Salt for water softeners, printer cartridges, and water for office coolers are all strong, consumable products.
2. Provide ongoing service. A lawn sprinkler system needs to be serviced in both spring and fall. Equipment suppliers to businesses frequently provide service contracts, both to produce ongoing revenue and to have the best chance of acquiring future business.
3. Sell a service rather than a product. Application service providers (ASPs) provide server-to-host software for their customers for a monthly fee, rather than selling software.
4. Spread your cost on a monthly basis, rather than requiring a major purchase. Leases, service contracts, and maintenance agreements all spread costs out over time. Customers are less likely to look for a new supplier if payments are low.
5. Provide incentives for increased use. Airlines do this with frequent flyer miles, as do grocery stores that give customers extra incentives when they reach certain purchasing milestones. For companies selling consumable industrial products, a popular tactic is to increase discounts for ongoing purchases.
6. Provide guaranteed trade-in value for upgrades. Allow companies to upgrade your products for a fee and give you a trade-in for current products. This is especially effective in software and fast-changing technologies.

Making the Easy Sale

Chapter 6

Making the Easy Sale

For almost everything they buy, your customers can choose from many products or services. Entrepreneurs understand this and realize that they have to have better value than their competition. But another fact often overlooked is that prospects buy only a small percentage of the products they could buy. You need to do more than just deliver better value than your competitors; you need to deliver better value than other companies supplying radically different products.

For example, an average worker looking for a way to relax might enjoy golf, fishing, boating, camping, resort vacations, hunting, or gambling. People don't have time to pursue all these activities and, to a large degree, the value they perceive for each activity will determine where they spend their money.

ENTREPRENEURS HAVE TWO PROBLEMS TO OVERCOME IF THEY WANT truly easy sales. First, they need to offer something that customers really want to select among literally thousands of choices. Two, they need a cost-effective method of finding and communicating with those customers.

Reproduced from Don Debelak, *Business Models Made Easy*, (Newburgh, NY: Entrepreneur Press), Chapter 6.

Company Story—Only One Winning Choice?

The battle was on for online research for academic papers and business papers. Originally it was a battle for college students, but students look for free downloads rather than ones they have to pay for. So, with the wrong target customer, both competitors changed course to succeed. Questia (*www.questia.com*) has 50,000 primary textbooks and 4,000 journal articles online and charges $19.95 a month or $99.95 per year for access to articles and books on its web site. Though it is a service for college students as well, the company mostly sells its service to businesses. Ebrary (*www.ebrary.com*) also started with college students and offered over 17,000 books online with searches free, but copying documents cost from 15 to 25 cents per page. Ebrary's original concept didn't last, as it couldn't generate enough money with its approach, and now it sells services to libraries, with over 900 current customers. What made their new approaches work while both companies' original model failed? They found customers who not only need their service (students also needed the service) but also they needed to be willing to pay for it (which is where selling to students failed). Both companies found a way to turn their failing model around into a profitable model that could sustain a business.

G—Yes
E—Yes
L—Yes

Six Key Factors for Evaluating Easy Sales

		Desired	Excellent	Average	Poor
Value to Customer	How Important	Important			
	Competitive Advantage	High			
	Price/Value Relationship	Low			
Customer Acquisition Cost	Entry Points	Many			
	Sales Support Required	Little			
	Promotional Activities	Low			

Figure 6-1. GEL Factor Easy Sales Checklist

Are You Important to Customers?

Why It's Important

Customers determine value by their standards and not by yours. Those standards have been evolving over the last few years to be more emotional than practical. Think of some of the great recent sales successes—Apple's iPod, Netflix, virtually all scrapbook products, and the restaurant chain Noodles. None of these offered a product or service that was truly important for customers. But customers wanted them because those items made them feel better. It was a reward for them; it said to others that they were important; it was to have fun; and it was to reinforce their own image of being a part of the smart crowd.

The marketing reality is that buying is dominated by what buyers feel are their top priorities.

Companies operate in the same way. They want to project a variety of images that could include being a "breakthrough company," "marketing-driven company," "quality-conscious company," and even "cost-conscious company." Businesses need to project an image to their employees, vendors, customers, and competitors, and the image they desire is important.

The marketing reality is that buying is dominated by what buyers feel are their top priorities. People may have only two or three priorities that they can worry about and those are the only ones that drive their buying decisions.

When It's a Key Concern

1. **When the product is sold through a distribution network.** If the product is important to customers, then brand loyalty will probably exist, and distributors will buy products that have a loyal customer base. New companies will have trouble breaking into the market when customers are brand loyal because they won't switch if the product is important to them.

2. **Practicality is more influential on the customer's buying decision than fun or emotion.** Customers with money in their pocket are willing to buy from anyone's products that add fun, but they stick with the tried and true when it is a practical purchase.

3. **Customers aren't confident of the purchasing process.** Confused buyers rarely buy. And confused buyers take the trouble to learn about a product or service only if the benefit is very important to them.

4. **Purchases can easily be delayed or postponed.** For example, most of the time a new CD player isn't a necessary purchase; people can take a long time before deciding to buy. You'll waste time chasing customers who

Pitfalls Alert

Most buyers, whether it's business customers or consumers, are worried about only their top two or three priorities. Many entrepreneurs make the mistake of not asking customers if buying their product or one like it is a priority decision. Because they fail to ask, they may mistakenly believe that they have a winner if people state they like their product or service idea, when in fact what the entrepreneur is offering doesn't meet a desire that's high on the customers' list of priorities.

keep delaying their purchase decision because the purchase isn't important to them.

5. **You have a limited number of contacts with any one customer.** You may get only one or two times to truly talk to a customer, and you need to be to selling something important to the customer if you want the customer to buy quickly.

How to Compensate

1. **Add an emotional context to the purchase decision.** Purchasing a new set of car tires is a practical decision. But Michelin added an emotional context to that decision when it showed a baby in its ads and promotions with the tag line "there's a lot riding on your tires."

2. **Create strong promotional programs to encourage immediate buying.** When your product or service isn't important by itself, you can often create a buying decision by making the buyer feel they will miss out if they don't buy right away.

3. **Use testimonials from industry experts or affiliations with other people trusted by customers.** Customers, both consumer and industrial, like to buy winning products, so testimonials can be a big asset.

4. **Target a segment of your customer group where your product or service is most important** rather than trying to sell to the broad market.

How Do They Act?

How can you really be sure that your product or service is important? One good barometer is the effort customers are already taking to try and solve the problem. There are many ways you can tell if customers have a strong desire for a certain product or service.

1. Great success for companies currently meeting that desire
2. High customer attendance at shows or seminars on the topic

3. High use of consultants and other services to deal with the issue
4. Heavy news coverage and stories
5. Buyers buying. People started buying bigger homes and SUVs and the market responded.
6. Success in other markets. A retail concept might take off in one area and then spread, such as Staples, starting on the East Coast and then moving into the Midwest.

Your Competitive Advantage

Why It's Important

Customers have options—they can almost always find another product to meet the same need as your product. If you're going to succeed, you must have a strong reason for people to buy your product or service over competing products or services. The following is a list of some of the areas where you can get a competitive advantage.

1. Better support of customers' self-image
2. Best performance
3. More complete solution
4. Top perceived value
5. First with the newest technology
6. Most visual appeal
7. Highest-quality product
8. Best-known product brand
9. Lowest pricing

When It's a Key Concern

1. **A distribution channel is involved in the product.** Distribution channels are more knowledgeable about the differences among products and they evaluate all of the product choices. They will evaluate your competitive advantage and won't buy if they feel your advantage is not strong enough.
2. **Competitors are established in the market.** Buyers feel more comfortable buying from companies they know. With established competitors, a strong advantage is the only way to get noticed.
3. **You have fewer resources than competitors.** Companies that can't compete with a marketing budget must rely on their product differentiation to sell products.
4. **Customers can quickly tell which product or service is best.** For exam-

> ## Pitfalls to Avoid
>
> One sure way to guarantee problems in selling your product is to offer the same benefits as everyone else. How many companies targeting businesses have as their primary benefit that they help customers save money? Thousands. Customers quickly learn to avoid messages when they've heard them before.

ple, you can just try out two scanners and see that one has better resolution than another.

5. **Buyers are willing to shop for the best product.** Some people visit 10 to 15 furniture stores before buying a sofa. They check out all the product features before buying.

How to Compensate

1. **Add features and/or form partnerships.** A competitive advantage is one tactic for getting buyers to notice you. Another option is to join forces with a partner to either sell a package of products or services together to offer a more complete solution to the customers.
2. **Focus more clearly on a smaller target customer group.** Try to look for customers where your product has distinct advantages and then focus on that group.
3. **Offer convincing proof.** You might do this with test results, testimonials, documented cost savings, or customer evaluations of competing products.
4. **Increase your use of visual images.** People are heavily influenced by first impressions, and the visual is a key to that first impression. Having the best-looking package or the best-looking product is a big advantage.
5. **Become a market focal point.** You can sponsor events, conduct classes, be a leader of association committees, or sponsor a trade show or special speaker.

Perceived Price/Value

Why It's Important

People have a strong sense of what something is worth to them, a value that is determined by their own criteria. If a family takes a vacation to Disney World and the total bill comes to $5,000, will they consider that a great value? Some people will consider it a bargain because of Disney World's atmosphere and excitement, while others will resent the high prices and think that they would have been better off taking a camping trip to the mountains for $500. When you consider the perceived value of your product or service, it doesn't matter what the product or service costs to provide or what value you feel it has. It only matters what the target customer perceives the value of your product or service to be.

Buzzword

Value-added is a phrase you'll hear both from bankers and venture capitalists. It refers to services or add-ons that make a product or a service more valuable to customers. Putting a spring on the bows of kids' glasses is a value-added feature, because it makes it more difficult for kids to break their glasses.

When It's a Key Concern

1. **Customers consider the product or service a discretionary purchase.** I see flowers all the time at downtown outdoor malls. I buy some for my wife when I think the price/value is right.
2. **There are many other options for purchasing.** You won't buy a CD if you think the price is too high, because you have both many other places to buy a CD and many other CDs you could buy instead.
3. **Your product isn't well-known or is unproven.** People will take a chance on buying a new product if they feel it's a better value than current products, but they won't try a new product if they feel it's overpriced.
4. **Your customers are cost-conscious or value-oriented.** Engineers, accountants, and thrifty people all evaluate their product choices closely.

Pitfall to Avoid

When establishing the perceived value for your product, don't ask people what they feel it is worth or what they would pay. Customers almost always state an amount that's much lower than what they actually will pay. Instead, have your customers rank your product or service along with five or six other similar products or services by value. Your perceived value will be close to the products ranked just above and just below your product.

How to Compensate

1. **Add high value elements or services.** Better-quality components, stainless steel versus plastic, or an enhanced atmosphere for a store will raise perceived value.
2. **Drop features or benefits for which the perceived value is low.**
3. **Find a cheaper way to produce your product or service.** If you can't add enough value, you may be able to cut your costs so that your perceived value is acceptable to customers.
4. **Totally overhaul your business approach.** You may not be providing enough value to your customers. Successful businesses frequently change their business concept three to four times before finding something that works.

Entry Points Available

Why It's Important

How many ways can people start to buy from you? Those are your entry points. The more entry points you have, the easier it will be for you to find and sell to customers.

Here's an example: A copier supplier could just sell or lease a product. That's two entry points. The supplier could also offer a 60-day trial or offer the product for rent. That's two more entry points. The company could also have a web site and offer its product through an office supply store as an incentive for buying a year-long office supplies contract.

Entry points apply to all businesses. For a manufacturer of consumer products, entry points include anywhere a person can buy the product from stores, catalogs, and Internet sites. For a retailer, the entry points include how people can access the stores: the number of doors, the foot traffic by the store caused by nearby retailers, and the number of people who drive by.

When It's a Key Concern

1. **Your market is highly competitive.** Often the company that makes the sale is the one that makes its product most available with a high number of entry points.
2. **Customers may elect not to buy your product or service.** Life insurance, water filtration systems, or special phone headsets are all products people can elect not to buy. You have the best chance of encouraging a buy-

ing decision by having the product available in many locations and in many different ways.

3. **The sale is to a customer that provides limited revenue opportunities.** These customers don't justify sales and marketing expenses, and your best chance of success of a sale is having your product available in many locations.

4. **People have a short buying process.** For example, if I'm going to buy a fishing rod, I wait until I'm getting ready to go fishing and then I buy one at the first store I come to.

How to Compensate

1. **Go into the customer's world.** You need to hold contests, host seminars, be active in associations, and, in effect, go where customers go.

2. **Form partnerships and alliances to expand your market presence.**

3. **Create a strong prospect follow-up program.** If your customers can't easily run across your products, you can stay after them. Contact management programs like Act or Goldmine help companies set up programs for periodic mailings and follow-up phone calls.

4. **Create an easy-to-sell entry point.** CD- and movie-buying clubs have just two entry points: customers can respond to a direct mail piece and join through the Internet. Those entry points are easy for the customer to use.

Sales Support Required

Why It's Important

A new home, a piece of production equipment, an annuity, and a new, enterprise-wide software package are the types of buying decisions that people make only after extensive sales support, which includes presentations, demonstrations, training, help with installation, and answering repeated calls.

Sales support presents two problems for companies. The first is that it requires a big and expensive sales organization. This cost is overhead and, especially for start-ups, it can represent an expense that can produce substantial deficits for the first year or two. The second reason is that sales support costs can end up being 25 to 40 percent of revenue: that expense can take a heavy toll on the bottom line.

When It's a Key Concern

1. **When you have a complex or unknown product.** You need to worry about support anytime the customer needs help making a buying decision.
2. **The sales dollars you can generate from each customer are low.** To succeed, the sales support must be limited based on your profit per sale.
3. **Your resources are limited.** Sales support costs money, sometimes lots of money, in terms of sales staff, demo products, sales materials, and training.
4. **Your customers are widely scattered.** Complex sales requiring lots of sales support sometimes also require multiple sales calls, which are especially costly when customers are scattered.
5. **The purchase is not a high priority for the customer.** Customers tend to put off complex sales; this tendency is even stronger when the purchase is not one of the top two to three priorities for the customers.

How to Compensate

1. **Take responsibility for the complete solution.** Guaranteeing a result that meets the customer's expectations minimizes the need for sales support.
2. **Offer a service rather than a purchase plan.** No worries—that's what the customer wants when a purchase is complex, confusing, or difficult. Instead of just selling a product that the customer needs to figure out how to use, you can also provide a service that does the job for the customer.
3. **Set up or use a distribution network.** One of the advantages of distribution networks is that they have more frequent contact with your customer than you do and they can offer sales support at a lower cost.

> ### Pitfall to Avoid
>
> Many companies take it for granted that distributors will push your product once they decide to sell it. That's simply not true. One of the reasons that distributors can build customer loyalty is that they are careful to only present customers with products or services in which they have confidence. When using distributors, be sure you take the time to train them so they will push your product aggressively.

4. **Offer high sales compensation.** If you have a tough sale, you need the best salespeople, and you can get them only with generous compensation. Look for experienced salespeople with a history of high earnings.
5. **Enlist the aid of industry experts as part of your marketing team.** They can overcome customer confusion, skepticism, and worry—the big three reasons that a sale becomes difficult.

Promotional Activities Required

Why It's Important

Promotional activities are another item that can be a prohibitive expense. Retail stores in offbeat locations can spend money on big events, advertising, attendance at trade shows, or direct-mail campaigns. Other stores will pay the expensive rent of a mall to bring in customers. On the other hand, some businesses have low promotional expenses; some can operate out of homes and simply call on the four big customers in their area. A group of ex-Lockheed engineers, for example, started a product design business with just one customer, Lockheed. They had no promotional budget. High promotion costs result in more overhead, higher prices, and generally a riskier business concept.

When It's a Key Concern

1. **Customers are difficult to locate.** You need to promote aggressively when you can't buy a list of customers, don't have events where customers gather, or can't team up with other suppliers serving the same market.
2. **You can't be sure when a customer is going to buy.** Which business this year will be buying new office partitions for an employee expansion? You can spend lots of money when you don't know which customers to concentrate on.

3. **Low to moderate pricing and average sale value.** The more customers to whom you need to promote your product or service in order to generate a profitable sales level, the more you need to be concerned about promotion expense.
4. **You need to create a new brand or product against established competition.** Getting brand recognition takes a long time, especially if competitors have an entrenched customer base.
5. **You have a new category of product or service.** The toughest job of promotion is when people aren't even aware that your brand or service is available.

How to Compensate

1. **Establish a recurring revenue stream from each customer.** A monthly service produces more sales than a one-time product sale.
2. **Add new products or services that customers need.** Many companies have their own product line but are also distributors for other manufacturers. Companies will also be sales agents for other companies.
3. **Develop tools to attract customer interest early in their buying process.** Classes, seminars, and informational web sites are all ways to find customers well before they're ready to buy.
4. **Create extremely effective promotional materials or visual images.** We live in a visual age, and I've found that people are four to five times more likely to remember your product or service if you associate a powerful visual image with it.

Success Tip

The best visual images don't focus on your product, but instead on the solution or result for the customer. This helps customers relate the product to their situations. A picture of a kitchen cabinet doesn't connect with a customer, but a glistening remodeled kitchen does. Your visuals should reflect the result customers want when they buy your product.

5. **Have a distinctive product or service feature that makes your company memorable.** You can cut significantly the number of exposures customers need before buying if you have one unique, dramatic feature or benefit.

Easy Sales Are Hard to Come By

Company Vignettes

There are six comparison factors related to easy sales:

1. How important the purchase is to customers
2. How strong your competitive advantage is
3. How customers perceive your price/value relationship
4. How many sales entry points you have
5. How much sales support is required
6. How many promotional activities you'll need

Dr. Spock Co.

Dr. Spock Co. provides parents with advice on child rearing based on the works of Dr. Spock.

The entire premise behind Dr. Spock Co. is that raising children is extremely important to a certain segment of professional parents. That importance is the motivator that drives the business.

Evaluation on the basis of easy sales:

1. Children are important to all parents and bringing up children well is important to a large segment of professional parents of infants. **Rating +.**
2. Customers' perception of Dr. Spock's competitive advantage over newer authority sources is unclear. **Rating ?.**
3. Customers may not see Dr. Spock as having a strong price/value relationship unless they first value Dr. Spock's advice. **Rating ?.**
4. The company should be able to have a large number of entry points, especially if they get their pamphlets distributed by doctors. **Rating +.**
5. Sales support of users will be low because of Dr. Spock's name recognition to certain customers and because the purchase price is relatively low. **Rating +.**
6. Promotional activities will be needed, especially as the customer base will change each year, but the promotional activities will still be low due to brand name recognition of its targeted customers. **Rating +.**

O'Naturals

O'Naturals is a chain of fast-food restaurants in New England that serve natural, organic foods.

O'Naturals founders developed a stronger position for customer value because they started with what they felt was an unmet customer need: healthy fast food. O'Naturals has to deal with two aspects regarding customer value. The first is whether healthy food is important to O'Naturals' customers. The answer is clearly yes. The second is whether or not fast food is important to people who want healthy meals. The jury is certainly out on this second point.

Evaluation on the basis of easy sales:

1. In terms of importance to the customers, healthy food alone rates a +, but healthy fast food is at best an even choice. **Rating =.**
2. O'Naturals clearly has a competitive advantage over other fast-food restaurants and an advantage in terms of speed over other healthy food restaurants or eating at home. **Rating +.**
3. The customers' view of the O'Naturals price/value relationship depends on how much they value service speed. People willing to take the time to eat healthy food may not place a premium on saving 15 minutes a day at a fast-food restaurant. **Rating =.**
4. O'Naturals has only a few restaurants and the number of entrees they can offer will be limited because they're a fast-food restaurant. **Rating ?.**
5. Sales support will be important for O'Naturals as it will need to reinforce on each customer visit that it's serving healthy food. The positive point for O'Naturals is that it should be inexpensive to offer that support, with placards on the table and information in the restaurant. **Rating +.**
6. Promotional activities will be expensive for O'Naturals. While word-of-mouth advertising might work for dedicated healthy eaters, promotion will probably be needed for people with only a mild interest in healthy foods. **Rating ?.**

Jawroski's Towing and Repair

Jawroski's is a car repair and towing business in a fast-growing suburban area.

Jawroski's will be judged by how effectively the employees solve the customers' problems, the quality of their service, and how their price compares with the competitors. If they do well by those three criteria, customers will keep coming back and word-of-mouth advertising will carry the business.

Evaluation on the basis of easy sales:

1. Car repair is obviously important: if your car is not working, you need it fixed. **Rating +.**

2. Jawroski's has built its competitive advantage around its high-test equipment and its ability to repair cars right the first time. This is important to its fleet customers and people in its nearby upscale neighborhoods. All of Jawroski's competitors are smaller shops with less technology. **Rating +.**

3. Jawroski's customers value getting results above all else, so they perceive that Jawroski's has a strong price/value relationship. **Rating +.**

4. Jawroski's number of entry points is limited, but the company's ideal location on a busy street compensates. **Rating +.**

5. Jawroski's sales support is simply giving good service so that cars work. Jawroski's high-technology garage and the owner's commitment to keeping his employees well-trained give Jawroski's all the sales support it needs. **Rating +.**

6. Jawroski's depends on its location for promotion. But it can also generate low-cost promotions in the neighborhood by sponsoring sports teams, allowing high school organizations to hold car washes on its site, and doing inexpensive neighborhood mailings. **Rating +.**

The Buying Binge

ADC Telecommunications is one of the market leaders in fiber optic technologies for the telecommunications and computer industries. In the late 1990s and early 2000s, ADC purchased several companies that provided products that were complementary to its own. ADC was able to cut its cost of acquiring customers dramatically in several ways because of a bigger product line.

G—No
E—Average
L—Yes

1. Add entry points, especially in equipment markets. ADC's customers require many products to achieve a solution to their needs. By expanding its product line, ADC improved the chances that a customer would call for at least one product.

2. Cut sales support costs for each product line. Customers are looking for a complete integration solution. A broader product line allows ADC to consolidate its whole product line into its training and demonstration programs.

3. Make promotional programs more effective. The more complete your solution, the more your messages and promotional programs will interest potential customers.

Building a Long Future

Chapter 7

Building a Long Future

ALONG FUTURE DEPENDS ON MONEY: HOW MUCH YOU NEED TO invest, how much you make on every sale, and how much you need to stay in business. The most important factor is probably profits from every sale, but even profitable companies can be waylaid if they need too much investment. Even a business with a great concept can have unpredictable costs, such as an unexpected lawsuit, a sudden price increase from a key vendor, or high promotional expenses in response to an aggressive competitor. A business can also find itself faced with unexpected investments required to meet a competitive market. A business ideally set up for long life has margins high enough to absorb unexpected costs and requires just modest investments to adjust to market and competitive changes.

Company Story—Nothing Comes Easy

GiftCertificates.com had a simple business concept. It would be a Web site where people could easily buy gift certificates from a wide variety of retailers. The company set up 4,000 corporate clients and partnerships with 700 merchants, including major retailers like Bloomingdale's. The company had high upfront costs setting up, but

G—Yes
E—Yes
L—No

Reproduced from Don Debelak, *Business Models Made Easy*, (Newburgh, NY: Entrepreneur Press), Chapter 7.

that was to be expected. The problem was having high margins in the face of competitive pressures and high ongoing investment to hold onto the business.

The first problem was smaller competitors offering the same package of services for lower prices. GiftCertificates.com responded by buying out two of the bigger competitors, GiftSpot.com and GiftPoint.com, acquisitions that brought the company's debt load up to $90 million. Next the company had to worry about big portal sites like AOL and Yahoo! Locking the big sites into GiftCertificates.com would be difficult when AOL and Yahoo! could offer the same service if GiftCertificates.com is successful. The company has responded by repeatedly going back to the market for additional capital to promote itself. But can GiftCertificates.com survive? Their only chance is to hold onto market share by heavy and repeated expenditures to buy off competitors, promote the site to potential customers, and keep its predominant position as an incentive gift supplier to 70 percent of the *Fortune* 500 companies.

Six Key Factors for Evaluating Long Life

		Desired	Excellent	Average	Poor
Profit per Sale	Margins	High			
	Up-Selling and Cross-Selling	Much			
	Ongoing Product Costs	Low			
Investment Required	To Enter Business	Low			
	To Keep Market Share	Low			
	To Stay on the Cutting Low Edge	Low			

Figure 7-1. GEL Factor Long Life Checklist

Healthy Margins

Why It's Important

Healthy margins with adequate sales are by far the number one indicator of a healthy company. When I started in business right out of college, I could never understand why finance people had so much power in a company.

After all, I thought, they don't do anything constructive. But I've since learned that I was wrong. Since companies often survive on a profit of 2 to 5 percent on sales, a few percentage points difference in margin can make all the difference in the world between making and losing money. Controlling margins is one of the most effective ways to determine just how successful a company will be.

When It's a Key Concern

1. **Healthy margins are always a key concern.** What about the old adage that we'll make up for a low margin with high volume? Baloney. Wal-Mart doesn't have low margins. They have low prices because they have the buying volume to drive down the prices they pay. The fact is that the strategy of low margins and high volume is a risky strategy. You incur large upfront costs to generate high volume, and if the demand shifts even slightly those high costs will be a huge anchor on your profitability.

How to Compensate

1. **Add more value.** Companies that match each other's pricing typically end up losing money. The better approach is to find out what customers really want and then provide that.
2. **Cut major costs.** A company with a sustainable advantage in costs is almost impossible to defeat.

Success Tip

Service companies and retail stores have costs that they should evaluate constantly. A maternity shop may decide to only keep one size of each garment on the floor with offsite warehousing to keep down inventory costs. Service companies may have high rent, which represents a cost problem, or they may have too many of their employees in administrative positions, raising their costs of doing business.

3. **Find another method of distribution.** Sometimes low margins are caused by distribution costs. For example, if you sell to a wholesaler that sells to a distributor that sells to a retailer you'll only be receiving a fraction of the final retail price. It's not always clear that one or more of these steps in the distribution chain is adding that much value in getting the products to customers.
4. **Choose another customer group.** You need to find someone who finds

more value in your products or service than your current customer group.

5. **Lower your overhead structure.** Overhead is a heavy burden for every company, and you need to check it periodically, whether it's rent, phone bills, or computer reports, to keep costs in line.

Up-Selling and Cross-Selling

Why It's Important

Building customer trust is time-consuming and expensive. Once you have it, each subsequent sale is easier to make than the previous sale. This is one of the main reasons that people use manufacturers' representatives and distributors. They have already built a bond with customers. Additional sales to an existing customer base are much easier to make than sales to new customers. Businesses that can cross-sell or up-sell have a much better chance of improving their profits per customer.

Buzzwords

Cross-sell refers to selling another type of product to the same customer. For example, a cross-sale for a retailer of upscale audio equipment might be big-screen TVs or a car audio system. An up-sale is adding features to an already existing purchase. A TV retailer, for example, would consider a "surround sound" stereo system to be an up-sell because it is an upgrade of a TV purchase.

When It's a Key Concern

1. **A purchase is rarely made.** People buy a refrigerator once every 10 years. An appliance store can make much more money if they can add significantly to the customer's purchase with an up-sell or cross-sell. The extra sale has to be made on the spot since the customer might not come back for another 10 years.

2. **The sales costs are high relative to the purchase price.** All products or services have a certain value to the customer that limits what you can charge. The amount might not cover your sales costs unless you can increase your profit by selling additional items to most customers.

3. **Future customer contact is unlikely.** When you call to order a product from a TV commercial you are unlikely to call that company again.

4. **The purchase is a low priority.** Customers are often responsive to an up-

sell or cross-sell when they are making what is for them a high priority purchase, but not when it is a low priority.

How to Compensate

1. **Add a consumable component to your sales mix.** Water softener manufacturers deliver salt and put it into water softeners. Software companies charge a monthly lease fee for software and others have a monthly maintenance fee. This will keep customers in constant contact with you, allowing more opportunities for up-selling or cross-selling.

2. **Sell private-label products.** Find products that complement yours or are a natural up-sell or cross-sell and then arrange to sell them under your name. This is especially effective if the private-label product is a consumable product.

3. **Combine ongoing with one-time services.** An air conditioning service company for industrial buildings might include yearly cleaning of the vents, shut-down and start-up services, and even air quality monitoring services.

4. **Restrict your sales to high-yield customers.** You can't afford to try and sell to every potential customer. Find the customers that you can sell to profitably and then just forget about the others.

Ongoing Product Costs

Why It's Important

A supplier of playground equipment to children's day care centers knows that his customers have steady turnover, and the supplier needs to expect numerous follow-up calls and inquiries over the life of the equipment. Garden shops know that trees it sold that die within 12 months will have to be replaced. Computer equipment manufacturers know that changes in computer hardware and software will necessitate follow-up support for their equipment. In every case, the supplier may need to provide service at no charge to the customer, but the service is certainly not free to the supplier. Too many ongoing costs per sale can certainly kill a company's profits.

When It's a Key Concern

1. **There is turnover among people using your product.** An advertising agency will have high costs if the main contact at its customers keeps changing. The agency will need to offer more personal contact, more

Success Tip

Entrepreneurs tend to be optimists and they frequently wear rose colored glasses when someone brings up a potential negative for their business. Don't ignore problems. Instead, try and talk to other people in your business at trade shows or association meetings and see what types of costs they are incurring. It's likely your costs will be similar. You might not like the answer, but at least you'll be prepared.

sales presentations, and more no-charge demonstration work to ensure they don't lose the account.

2. **Your product or service interfaces with many other products or services.** You may need to offer new connections, or you might need to integrate your equipment to new products offered by other manufacturers after the customer has already purchased your product.

3. **The market you compete in has rapid changes.** Changes in the market typically mean your customers may be using your product in different ways. They'll be contacting you for updates on how to use your products, and you may need to provide adjustments to the products or services you've provided.

4. **Customers don't have the knowledge to adjust for or correct small problems.** When something small goes wrong with a lawnmower most homeowners know how to fix it. Customers don't know what to do when unfamiliar with a product.

5. **Your product or service replaces a well-known product.** Established products typically have all of their kinks worked out and they run smoothly for customers. Customers expect a new product to work just as smoothly, which rarely happens with a new product.

Pitfalls to Avoid

Ongoing product support doesn't have to be free. You can charge for it and make a profit. I feel one of the biggest mistakes companies make is to try to provide a minimal level of support that only irritates the customer. Those companies would be much better off giving customers exactly what they want and charging for it.

How to Compensate

1. **Set your customers' expectations.** Don't act as if your product or service is "Drop and Run" (you sell it and never come back) if in fact you know the customer will need a fairly large amount of ongoing product support.

2. **Create online or ongoing training and service.** Let the customer know up front that you have ongoing training and service programs. Have the staff in place to execute those programs, and plan on these expenses in your budget and the price of your offering.

3. **Plan product upgrades that track industry changes.** Hewlett-Packard is a good example of a company that anticipates industry changes and has the product upgrades available right when their customers need them.

4. **Make accessibility to solutions easy for customers with problems.** Have solutions to problems prepared in advance that you can send to customers with problems. Many people will fix a problem themselves if you tell them how to do it.

Big Steps Often Work

One of the big problems many companies have when dealing with cost issues and particularly margin issues is that they think incrementally. That may work to tweak a business just a few margin points, but you should also consider big radical moves. I worked with a $30 million company that sold products to the dental industry. The company made money most years, but the profits were always modest. The company had a large administrative staff, big marketing and R&D departments, and three manufacturing plants.

Looking at the customer base the company found that about 40 percent of its customers were very loyal. The rest of the customer base had varying degrees of loyalties, but the last 20 percen, were not only not loyal, they were expensive to sell to as they required lots of product support. The company's strategy was to cut nonmanufacturing office personnel by 80 percent and just sell to its loyal and semi-loyal base. Sales dropped about 25 percent, but profits went up over 800 percent. Incremental thinking would never have come to this conclusion. Consider your business from all angles to find solutions to profitability problems.

Costs of Entering the Market

Why It's Important

Start-up costs include manufacturing costs, setting up the company, and launching a marketing and sales campaign. The main concern most people have is having enough money to launch the business. But from a GEL factor perspective it's not just how much money—after all, companies raise hundreds of millions of dollars in initial investments—it's how much money the investment will make. Ideally you want the annual market sales potential to be at least 10 times the amount of the investment required. Otherwise you have to question whether or not the investment is worth the risk of the business failing.

When It's a Key Concern

The amount of investment versus the market potential is always key, but in some cases it is of critical importance.

1. **You have an untested business concept.** New business concepts have plenty of kinks and a business's chance of success is in doubt if the upfront investment is high and you can't be sure when the business will turn a profit.
2. **The product life cycle is short.** A short product life cycle means that a company has to get its investment back in a big hurry, which can be hard to do with a big initial investment.
3. **You don't have access to significant resources.** You and your inner circle

> ### Pitfall to Avoid
>
> Too often new entrepreneurs assume that competitors will just keep on operating the way they always have even if they lose market share to the new entrepreneur. Unfortunately, competitors do respond, sometimes decisively, when a new entrepreneur takes business.
>
> Businesses need a feature that gives them a sustainable advantage, one that competitors can't easily duplicate, in order to succeed.

of initial investors have to provide a significant share of the start-up capital. If you are low on funds, pick a project that only requires a modest upfront investment.
4. **You have a major competitor.** You'll need to provide twice as much service for the same price as the big competitor because customers are just as skeptical of newcomers as they are comfortable with a major supplier.

How to Compensate

1. **Partner up with major players.** Cut your investment by partnering with another company and using its resources. You might have a partner handle all of your administrative functions, use their sales force, or simply use the partner's name for credibility.
2. **Pre-sell contracts to major prospects.** You will reduce your risk if you convince three or four customers to sign a contract before you make the

initial investment. Distributors, retailers, and buyers will often place an order if you offer the right incentives and have an innovative product or service.

3. **Quickly corner a segment of the market.** With a big upfront investment you want to avoid a lengthy period waiting for sales. One tactic is to focus on a small part of the market to generate a solid, though small, sales base.

4. **Have an innovative promotional or sales strategy.** You can set up sales, distribution, or promotional programs to lock up customers, such as selling a product based on a monthly service charge rather than a standard sales price.

5. **Outsource high-cost operations.** Manufacturing, promotion, and staffing require the biggest upfront costs, and these functions can be outsourced to other companies. You can also share administrative costs and overhead expenses by sharing office space.

Costs to Hold Onto Market Share

Why It's Important

The company story box at the beginning of this chapter was about GiftCertificates.com. Buying market share for six months is great if the edge you generate will sustain itself afterward with a much lower promotional level. If it won't, the company will have trouble surviving. Buying market share with lower prices is typically a short-lived strategy because competitors will respond with their own low prices. The same is true with promotions and sales effort. The competitors can match you and then your only recourse is to try and outspend your rivals.

When It's a Key Concern

1. **Customers don't perceive differences between products.** Levi's held major market share in the jeans market for years with heavy promotion. Then their promotional efforts slowed down, and they immediately lost market share.

2. **Large, established competitors are already in the market.** Big companies have their own promotional war chest that you have to compete against to get noticed.

3. **Alternative low-cost marketing methods (events, shows, association and user groups) are not viable.** Customers have a keen interest in some

product categories, such as wedding dresses, or Internet marketing, and they will come to events and notice new market entrees. If you don't have the strong interest, you will need a strong promotional budget to hold market share.

Success Tip

Alternative marketing tactics work best when a product or service is new and unusual. You don't, however, have to have a radically new segment to use this tactic. Garden stores that offer classes in English rock gardens are offering a slight twist that will generate customer interest. Paint and home improvement stores are taking the same tack with faux finishing classes, merchandise, and displays.

4. **You can't gain an advantage with sales and/or distribution tactics to minimize promotional costs.** Offering the highest commissions, setting up franchises or distributorships, signing exclusive agreements with key distribution outlets, and signing up customers to long-term contracts are all options to minimize promotional expenses.

5. **Marketing and promotion costs are high.** Marketing to teenagers is expensive. Advertising on TV or in teen-oriented magazines costs lots of money as does sponsoring rock bands or other events.

How to Compensate

1. **Find more effective ways to differentiate your product.** Find one important desire of your customers and then create a feature or benefit that customers can easily notice.
2. **Compete only in segments where your product is differentiated.** Stop trying to sell to markets where your costs are high and competition stiff because prospects can't see your advantage.
3. **Form partnerships to offer a better customer solution.** Customers love to

Buzzwords

Features are the specific tasks or image your product or service offers. Benefits are why those features are important to the customer. An automatic transmission on a car is a feature. The benefit is that people don't have to shift gears manually. Benefits are more important than features, because customers actually buy a solution, which in this case is an easy-to-drive car. So think in terms of solutions rather than features when you are trying to differentiate your company from the competition.

buy a "plug and play" solution—something works immediately. Once you understand the solution the customer wants, you'll find that there are plenty of potential partners available.

4. **Go out of the box with your name and promotion strategy.** Companies now use billboards on vehicles that drive around to promote their business to reach customers more cost-effectively. Another popular tactic is street marketing teams that are sent to an event to promote a new product cost-effectively.

5. **Refocus on a smaller market segment that you can afford.** Companies have to be sure they get a return on the money they spend, and sometimes that means they have to go after a small market where their promotional efforts will have an impact.

Costs to Stay on the Cutting Edge

Why It's Important

Nothing succeeds like having the newest, best products and services that everyone wants. The demand for the product brings you the promotional recognition you need without having to pay for it. If you are not on the cutting edge, not only are you at a distinct disadvantage when selling every customer, but you also are faced with the need for a much higher promotional budget. Cell phones are a good example. When they first came out there were just a few competitors with state-of-the-art products, and those companies had very small promotional and advertising budgets. They didn't need to advertise because people knew about the products from magazines and newspaper stories. Today consumers don't differentiate cellular phones that well, and companies have to advertise heavily.

When It's a Key Concern

1. **Customers are gadget or new technology lovers.** These customers know what's happening in the market, and they won't stay with you even one week if someone else introduces the latest gadget.

2. **Customers rely on cutting-edge products for status.** Salespeople, business executives, and others always want the latest electronic gadget so they look like they are on the cutting edge.

3. **New technology significantly reduces costs or raises productivity.** This means customers will quickly switch to a new supplier with improved features in order to gain those savings.

4. **Current technology has well-known deficiencies.** Diesel truck technology has two big deficiencies: they are big-time polluters, and they have low gas mileage. Truck owners immediately look at new products that can minimize those problems, providing they have a minimal cost.

5. **Rapid product or service changes occur in the industry.** This applies to most markets today. The pace of product change and improvement has never been higher.

How to Compensate

1. **Become tightly affiliated with a segment of the target market.** You can't stay on the cutting edge of development if you don't have a great understanding of your customers' current and upcoming needs.

2. **Use a customer advisor group to keep ahead of the market trends.** Meeting with key customers or prospects three to four times a year will help you keep a firm grasp of what customers want.

Pitfalls to Avoid

Many executives feel they don't need customer input. That's true when a company knows:

1. What solution every customer wants.
2. The customer's priorities for each aspect of the solution.
3. All the upcoming changes from products or services the solution interacts with.
4. New and emerging trends in the customer's world that will impact their solution.

Nobody can know all this all the time. You need customer input.

---

3. **Use outside product design sources.** Some companies have a relationship with outside inventors. Explain to the outside sources, inventors, or product designers about your upcoming needs and offer to pay a royalty on any products they develop that are introduced.

4. **Focus spending on product development.** If the cutting edge is where your company belongs, you are often far better off spending your efforts developing new products or services than you are spending money setting up a well-oiled administrative staff.

Great Model Fundamentals Require Discipline

Company Vignettes

This time, we'll compare these factors:

1. The health of margins
2. The amount of up-selling and cross-selling available
3. The size of ongoing product support
4. The cost to enter the business
5. The cost to keep market share
6. The cost to stay on the cutting edge

Dr. Spock Co.

Dr. Spock Co. provides parents advice on child rearing based upon the works of Dr. Spock.

The publishing industry has large fixed costs in producing the first unit, and then low costs to produce more copies. The situation is much better in e-publishing where there are no upfront print costs. The nice point of Dr. Spock's concept is that while the upfront costs are high, future costs should be modest as the company should generate up-sells and cross-sells.

Evaluation of Dr. Spock's potential for long life:

1. Dr. Spock will have high margins for everything they sell once they overcome their upfront costs. **Rating +.**
2. People who adopt the Dr. Spock approach are likely to buy many products and services as their child goes through their early years. **Rating +.**
3. One nice aspect of the publishing costs is that there are few ongoing sales costs except returns. Many of Dr. Spock's products and services will be sold over the Internet where return costs will be low. **Rating +.**
4. The upfront investment is high but certainly justified based on the Dr. Spock brand name and the large potential market. **Rating +.**
5. Funding to hold market share, based on the company's evaluation of the acceptance of Dr. Spock, should be relatively low. **Rating +.**
6. Dr. Spock won't need to spend money to stay on the market edge as children and their needs don't change. The company's only significant spending, if they choose to do it, would be research showing that the Dr. Spock method is still relevant. **Rating +.**

O'Naturals

O'Naturals is a chain of fast-food restaurants in New England that serve natural organic foods. Many fast-food restaurants have struggled over the years because the profit per sale is low. After all, one of the dominating benefits of fast food is low prices. Restaurants depend on volume, and volume at every meal. Fast-food restaurants try cross-selling and up-selling with upsizing and desserts, but they only add modestly to sales. All three costs are a problem at fast-food chains as it is tough to compete with McDonalds.

Evaluation of O'Naturals potential for long life:

1. Margins at fast-food restaurants like O'Naturals are significantly lower than traditional restaurants. **Rating ?.**
2. Cross-selling at a restaurant is usually associated with selling more food, which is not likely with a customer base of people who watch what they eat. One smart option O'Naturals is pursuing is family meals to take home—similar to the Boston Market offer. **Rating =.**
3. Follow-up costs are extremely low at a restaurant as the people consume the product. **Rating +.**
4. The initial investment is high, but like Dr. Spock, it is justified by the significant size of the market. **Rating +.**
5. Funding to hold market share is probably out of reach of most start-up companies if the natural fast-food restaurant concept takes off. The company's position can usually be salvaged by selling out to a well-funded company. **Rating =.**
6. The investment required for new food entrees or the occasional remodeling is small, but promoting those changes is high. **Rating ?.**

Jawroski's Towing and Repair

Jawroski's Towing and Repair is a car repair/towing business in a fast-growing suburban area. One thing consumers soon learn is that there is always lots of maintenance that can be done on a car, and customers have to get the repair work done right. That is great for Jawroski's, as they have lots of possibilities for selling more services. Jawroski's has a high upfront investment with its high-tech diagnostic equipment, but once it's in, ongoing costs are modest.

Evaluation of Jawroski's potential for long life:

1. Auto repair shops typically have strong margins as long as their mechanics can complete work in a timely manner. **Rating +.**
2. Up-selling and cross-selling are naturals with mechanics who both want

to sell more services but also want customers to be aware of other problems in case the car suffers another quick breakdown. **Rating +.**

3. Jaworski's has to be careful to control its service quality and to control customers' expectations of the work performed in order to keep follow-up sales costs down. **Rating =.**

4. It's expensive to open up a car repair facility, but the cost is justified by the market size and the high profit margins of an auto repair facility. **Rating +.**

5. Funding to hold market share is usually not a problem for car repairs because consumers like to use a shop either near their home or where they work. There is a danger in losing fleet business, but Jawroski's has a big head start there as it already holds the business and has an excellent reputation. **Rating +.**

6. Auto repair shops have to invest to stay on the cutting edge, but the expense is usually minimal as all the major companies offer training classes and assist shops in getting equipment needed for the new cars they introduce. **Rating +.**

Don't Level the Field

eWork Markets (*www.eworkmarkets.com*) is a dotcom company that started from a $10,000 investment and has grown to serve over 17,000 clients with almost 100 employees. eWork Markets is an Internet matchmaker between consulting firms and end users, which include Fortune 500 companies like Texaco and Hasbro. At first glance eWork doesn't seem to be much different than GiftCertificates.com. They have competition from Guru.com and other sites that connect consultants and companies and endless promotion seemed to be in their future.

G—Yes
E—Yes
L—Yes

But eWork realized that they would only succeed by staying on the cutting edge. They realized that firms had hundreds of consultants to choose from, but that they didn't always know the right firm to choose. eWorks stands out from competition by developing Internet-based tools and standards that helped companies select the right consultant for the right price for their firm. eWork succeeded with one of marketing's basic lessons: customers will locate you when you give them exactly what they want. Follow eWorks' approach for success. Don't try to out-promote the competition. Instead offer what prospects perceive to be a better package of services.

Evaluating Your Concept

Chapter 8

Evaluating Your Concept

THE REASON I'VE HEARD MOST FROM BUSINESS OWNERS FOR NOT doing a business plan is that things change too fast and a business plan is obsolete after just a few months. The business owners have a point. Plans do constantly change.

But the fact that things change is the very reason business owners need to do GEL factor analysis frequently. Whether they end up writing a plan is not as important as doing an analysis. I recommend you take a close look at your business concept, see its flaws, and then correct them as your business changes.

The big advantage of this approach is that flaws you find in your business concept can be corrected before they cost you any money. Those entrepreneurs writing a plan before doing a GEL factor analysis will probably eventually make the same changes that an entrepreneur doing a GEL factor analysis will make. But they'll make them only after they've learned by failing—a lesson that can be very expensive.

There are three steps involved in evaluating your concept:

1. Fill in your checklists.
2. Readjust your strategy.
3. Do the final tally.

Company Story—Not Always the First Choice

EC Outlook of Houston, Texas, has been chosen as one of *Inbound Logistics Magazine*'s Top 100 Logistics IT Providers, one of *Upside Magazine*'s Hot 100 companies, and one of *Computerworld*'s top 100 emerging companies to watch. EC Outlook provides e-business connectivity solutions—and today it's thriving.

> G—Yes
> E—Yes
> L—Yes

EC Outlook is succeeding, but it's actually on its fourth business model concept. The company demonstrates the wisdom of the old adage, "If at first you don't succeed, try, try again." EC Outlook's technology is a solution for the problem of connecting companies, with widely varying internal software, through e-marketplaces and e-transactions. EC Outlook's solution is a translation package that converts files from varying formats into a format a communication partner can read.

EC Outlook's first idea was to sell its products to big companies. But that sale, and subsequent product support, was too complicated and expensive. Plan 2 was to provide conversion services and software to small companies. In this case, the amount of effort to sell small customers was too much for the revenue generated by the sales. The third choice was to sell a service to large companies that would convert incoming and outgoing data to and from small and mid-sized vendors that didn't have conversion capabilities. This was a big sale and relatively easy, as it eliminated a big problem for big companies: how to seamlessly connect to small and mid-sized vendors that have minimal technology capability. This model was successful for the company and it allowed it to move to a fourth business model, where it both provides conversion service and sells its conversion products.

EC Outlet's experience is typical of new start-ups: they frequently need to change their business model in order to succeed. The trick is to find the right model without spending a lot of money. Hopefully this chapter will help you make the changes you need without exhausting your resources.

Fill in Your Checklists

The first step in evaluating your concept is to fill in the checklists at the end of this chapter. As you're filling in these checklists, don't look at them as a matter of pass or fail. They're a starting point for fine-tuning your business concept, for adjusting the model to make it more effective. The next section of the chapter covers how to make adjustments when necessary. You may need to go through the checklist process several times, so you have permission to copy the checklists for those multiple uses. Remember: these checklists are used to help you create a winning strategy for your firm. Grading your model too high will only hurt you in the long run.

		Desired	Excellent	Average	Poor	Compensating Tactics Yes	Compensating Tactics No
GREAT CUSTOMERS							
Customer Characteristics	Number	High					
	Ease of Finding	Easy					
	Spending Patterns	Prolific					
Customer Value to Company	$ Value of Sale	High					
	Repeat Sales	Many					
	Ongoing Sales Support	Low					
EASY SALES							
Value to Customer	How Important	Important					
	Competitive Advantage	High					
	Price/Value Relationship	Low					
Customer Acquisition Cost	Entry Points	Many					
	Sales Support Required	Little					
	Promotional Activities	Low					
LONG LIFE							
Profit per Sale	Margins	High					
	Up-Selling and Cross-Selling	Much					
	Ongoing Product Costs	Low					
Investment Required	To Enter Business	Low					
	To Keep Market Share	Low					
	To Stay on the Cutting Edge	Low					

Figure 8-1. GEL Factor Checklist

The GEL factor checklist will give you an initial assessment of your concept. Objectively evaluate each point on the chart and check the box. For any of the key determinants in the business model evaluation in which your model rates a grade of "average" or "poor," consider compensating tactics.

		List Compensating Tactics	**Effectiveness**		
			1	**2**	**3**
GREAT CUSTOMERS					
Customer Characteristics	Number				
	Ease of Finding				
	Spending Patterns				
Customer Value to Company	$ Value of Sale				
	Repeat Sales				
	Ongoing Sales Support				
EASY SALES					
Value to Customer	How Important				
	Competitive Advantage				
	Price/Value Relationship				
Customer Acquisition Cost	Entry Points				
	Sales Support Required				
	Promotional Activities				
LONG LIFE					
Profit per Sale	Margins				
	Up-Selling and Cross-Selling				
	Ongoing Product Costs				
Investment Required	To Enter Business				
	To Keep Market Share				
	To Stay on the Cutting Edge				

Figure 8-2. Compensating Tactics

The Compensating Tactics checklist is a chart where you can list ways to compensate for the weak points of your business—any key element rated as "average" or "poor." A "poor" element needs one or more highly effective compensating tactics; an "average" element might get by with a mildly effective tactic or even without any compensating tactic.

I recommend that you do a little brainstorming exercise before filling out this chart. List at least four to five possible compensating tactics for each element where you rate your performance "average" or "poor." Next, let those tactics set for two to three days. Then, look at them again and try to list two to three other tactics you could use. Finally, wait another two days and chose the tactics you might consider using.

Success Tip

Most businesses I've worked with can't effectively implement more than three compensating tactics. You need to choose your tactics carefully, both in terms of what concerns you want to address and in terms of which tactics will have the most impact on your business. Consult with at least three or four customers to help you choose the right tactics. They will know which tactics will best help you overcome weaknesses in your business model.

		Winner	Average	Corrected	Concern
GREAT CUSTOMERS					
Customer Characteristics	Number				
	Ease of Finding				
	Spending Patterns				
Customer Value to Company	$ Value of Sales				
	Repeat Sales				
	Ongoing Sales Support				

Figure 8-3. Preliminary Evaluation Form (continued on next page)

		Winner	Average	Corrected	Concern
EASY SALES					
Value to Customer	How Important				
	Competitive Advantage				
	Ongoing Sales Support				
Customer Acquistion Cost	Entry Points				
	Sales Support Required				
	Promotional Activities				
LONG LIFE					
Profit per Sale	Margins				
	Up-Selling and Cross-Selling				
	Ongoing Product Costs				
Investment Required	To Enter Business				
	To Keep Market Share				
	To Stay on the Cutting Edge				

Figure 9-3. Preliminary Evaluation Form (continued)

The Preliminary Evaluation form provides an easy way for you to rate how you stand in regard to each element of the successful business model criteria. The "Concern" column is for weak elements of your business model where you can't implement a compensating tactic or where you can't be sure your compensating tactic will work. Of course you'd like all of your check-marks to be in the "Winner" column, but I've never seen a concept have a winning rating in every category. But you definitely want your checkmarks to be clustered down the left side of the columns of this chart.

I believe that, in order to succeed, three of the six categories must be dominating winners and the other three must be average, at worst.

Must Have Winners		
Customers—Ease of Finding	_____Yes	All must be checked Yes or the model is flawed.
Value to Customer—Price/Value Relationship	_____Yes	
Profit per Sale—Margins	_____Yes	
Must Not Be a Concern		
Customers—Spending Patterns	_____No	All must be checked No or the model is flawed.
Customer Value to Company—Ongoing Sales Support	_____No	
Investment Required—To Keep Market Share	_____No	

Winners	Concerns
1._____	1._____
2._____	2._____
3._____	3._____
4._____	4._____
5._____	5._____
6._____	6._____
7._____	7._____
8._____	8._____
9._____	9._____

Winners need to outnumber concerns by three to one in order to proceed.

Figure 8-4. Final Evaluation Form

Readjust Your Strategy

I've found you can correct problems in your business model by evaluating four areas of your business strategy:

1. Change target customers.
2. Change the value to customers.

Pitfalls to Avoid

One of the biggest negatives I've ever heard from a venture capitalist about entrepreneurs is that they are "married to their idea"—which translates into "The entrepreneurs aren't going to listen to advice or make the changes necessary to make their business succeed." The chances of creating the ideal business model right from the start are slim. It's crucial for your success to evaluate and adjust your concept.

3. Change the sales/distribution strategy.
4. Change how the product/service is produced.

You may need changes in one area or you may decide to change all four. Try to make as few adjustments as possible, however, since a change in one area could create unanticipated concerns in other categories. For example, a change in your target customer could create a dramatic negative shift in your company's value proposition to customers.

Change Target Customers

You might need to look for new target customers for a wide number of reasons, including the following:

- ▶ You can't find enough of them.
- ▶ They don't spend freely.
- ▶ Your product isn't important enough to them.
- ▶ They are hard to acquire.
- ▶ They require too much sales support.

You simply cannot change a customer group's behavior, perceptions, or tendencies.

Change the Value/Importance to Customers

If you have the right customer group and the customers just aren't buying, you can do any or all of the following:

- ▶ Add features and/or services.
- ▶ Become a solution.
- ▶ Increase your competitive advantage.

The secret to figuring out how to change value and/or importance to customers is to understand what customers really want; the reasons why they buy. You need first-hand customer input; you cannot just pull together what you feel customers want. This is especially true for establishing a competitive advantage. You have an advantage only if you are offering features or solutions that count with the customers.

A simple way to get this information is to make up six to eight product or service offerings with different features and with varying progress toward a solution. You may need to do brochures for each product or service. Then ask customers these questions:

1. What was your first consideration when you evaluated each product?
2. What product would you rank first? Why?
3. What product would you rank last? Why?
4. What features/services would you like to see added?
5. What features/services would you like to see dropped?

Change Sales/Distribution Strategy

Sales and distribution strategy is probably the most important characteristic of any marketing program. It's also the category where you have far and away the most options. I've listed next some of the major problems you can correct with sales and distribution and some of the corrective measures you can take. Some of these problems can also be addressed with product feature changes.

1. **Customers are hard to locate.** Correction—sell through other companies or distributors that have already located these customers.
2. **Customers require high sales or ongoing product support.** Correction— sell through dealer networks or set a franchisee network to provide the support required.
3. **Customers don't perceive your product or service as being important.** Correction—sell through other manufacturers or set up a network where a total solution is provided.
4. **Customers make a slow decision.** Correction—sell through a network where your product is part of a more important choice.

Buzzword

"Distribution" is a term that people typically think of as being a sales channel, such as selling through distributors to retailers. But it really means any method you use to get your product to customers. For example, a business that holds seminars for inventors and then sells its products and services at those seminars has a distribution strategy—its seminars. Franchises, store location, and selling through other stores are all distribution strategies.

Change How the Product/Service Is Produced

In some cases, your model might have costs that are too high, resulting in margins that are just too low. For example, a software consulting service could have a complete staff, which is a high-cost option, or it might only have a few project managers on staff and then hire the independent contractors it needs for each job, which is a lower-cost option. Manufacturers in the United States frequently move production to lower-cost manufacturing outlets, either elsewhere in the country or overseas.

Do the Final Tally

Once you've made the final tally, you simply need to go back to the section, "Filling in Your Checklists." Recheck your score to be sure it is high enough. Once it is, wait at least one week and go over your business model again. With a fresh look you might be able to get a few more ideas on how your model could be further improved. Check your business model score at least every six months. You'll find out new things from the marketplace that might help you further refine your model.

Spending Rises Exponentially

I've found over the past 30 years that there is one business fact no one likes to discuss. That fact is that as your concept, solution, or tactic moves away from the ideal, your spending to make that tactic effective increases at what appears to be exponential rates. That is, if an ideal tactic takes $10 to implement, then even a modestly less ideal tactic takes anywhere from $50 to $100 to implement with equal effectiveness.

The tendency for many people is to gloss over deficiencies in their model and throw in compensating tactics. You should be cautious about compensating tactics, as it's difficult for any company to implement more than two or three of them effectively. A better solution is to keep reworking your business concept until you have one that better meets the successful business model criteria. My experience is that compensating tactics will, at the very best, be only half as effective as changing the model so that it meets the success criteria.

Definition of a Business Model

14

Def_ Business Model

A business model describes the rationale of how an organization creates, delivers, and captures value

The starting point for any good discussion, meeting, or workshop on business model innovation should be a shared understanding of what a business model actually is. We need a business model concept that everybody understands: one that facilitates description and discussion. We need to start from the same point and talk about the same thing. The challenge is that the concept must be simple, relevant, and intuitively understandable, while not oversimplifying the complexities of how enterprises function.

In the following pages we offer a concept that allows you to describe and think through the business model of your organization, your competitors, or any other enterprise. This concept has been applied and tested around the world and is already used in organizations such as IBM, Ericsson, Deloitte, the Public Works and Government Services of Canada, and many more.

This concept can become a shared language that allows you to easily describe and manipulate business models to create new strategic alternatives. Without such a shared language it is difficult to systematically challenge assumptions about one's business model and innovate successfully.

We believe a business model can best be described through nine basic building blocks that show the logic of how a company intends to make money. The nine blocks cover the four main areas of a business: customers, offer, infrastructure, and financial viability. The business model is like a blueprint for a strategy to be implemented through organizational structures, processes, and systems.

The 9 Building Blocks

The 9 Building Blocks

☐ Customer Segments

An organization serves one or several Customer Segments.

☐ Value Propositions

It seeks to solve customer problems and satisfy customer needs with value propositions.

☐ Channels

Value propositions are delivered to customers through communication, distribution, and sales Channels.

☐ Customer Relationships

Customer relationships are established and maintained with each Customer Segment.

17

5 Revenue Streams

Revenue streams result from value propositions successfully offered to customers.

6 Key Resources

Key resources are the assets required to offer and deliver the previously described elements...

7 Key Activities

...by performing a number of Key Activities.

8 Key Partnerships

Some activities are outsourced and some resources are acquired outside the enterprise.

9 Cost Structure

The business model elements result in the cost structure.

18

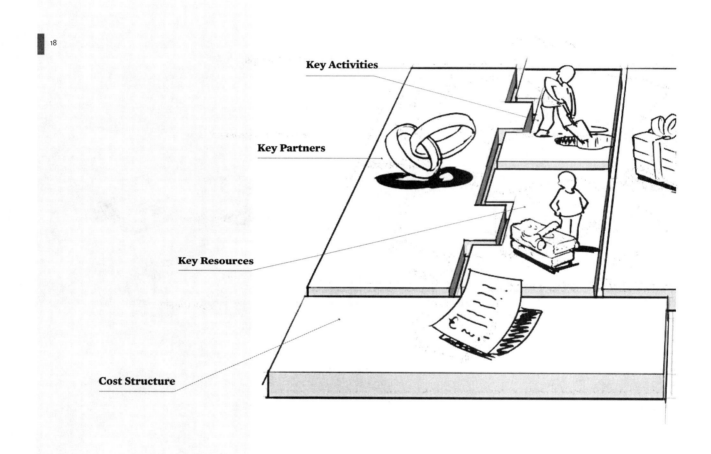

Key Activities

Key Partners

Key Resources

Cost Structure

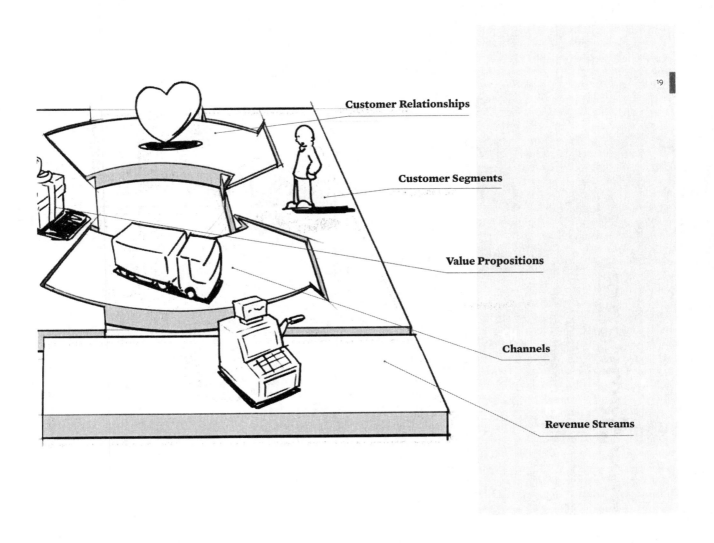

19

Customer Relationships

Customer Segments

Value Propositions

Channels

Revenue Streams

1

Customer Segments

The Customer Segments Building Block defines the different groups of people or organizations an enterprise aims to reach and serve

Customers comprise the heart of any business model. Without (profitable) customers, no company can survive for long. In order to better satisfy customers, a company may group them into distinct segments with common needs, common behaviors, or other attributes. A business model may define one or several large or small Customer Segments. An organization must make a conscious decision about which segments to serve and which segments to ignore. Once this decision is made, a business model can be carefully designed around a strong understanding of specific customer needs.

Customer groups represent separate segments if:

- *Their needs require and justify a distinct offer*
- *They are reached through different Distribution Channels*
- *They require different types of relationships*
- *They have substantially different profitabilities*
- *They are willing to pay for different aspects of the offer*

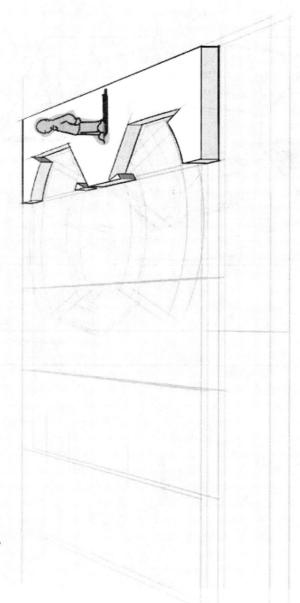

For whom are we creating value?
Who are our most important customers?

There are different types of Customer Segments. Here are some examples:

Mass market

Business models focused on mass markets don't distinguish between different Customer Segments. The Value Propositions, Distribution Channels, and Customer Relationships all focus on one large group of customers with broadly similar needs and problems. This type of business model is often found in the consumer electronics sector.

Niche market

Business models targeting niche markets cater to specific, specialized Customer Segments. The Value Propositions, Distribution Channels, and Customer Relationships are all tailored to the specific require- ments of a niche market. Such business models are often found in supplier-buyer relationships. For example, many car part manufacturers depend heavily on purchases from major automobile manufacturers.

Segmented

Some business models distinguish between market segments with slightly different needs and problems. The retail arm of a bank like Credit Suisse, for example, may distinguish between a large group of customers, each possessing assets of up to U.S. $100,000, and a smaller group of affluent clients, each of whose net worth exceeds U.S. $500,000. Both segments have similar but varying needs and problems. This has implications for the other building blocks of Credit Suisse's business model, such as the Value Proposi- tion, Distribution Channels, Customer Relationships, and Revenue streams. Consider Micro Precision Systems, which specializes in providing outsourced micromechanical design and manufacturing solutions. It serves three different Customer Segments — the watch industry, the medical industry, and the industrial automation sector — and offers each slightly different Value Propositions.

Diversified

An organization with a diversified customer business model serves two unrelated Customer Segments with very different needs and problems. For example, in 2006 Amazon.com decided to diversify its retail business by selling "cloud computing" services: online storage space and on-demand server usage. Thus it started catering to a totally different Customer Segment — Web companies — with a totally different Value Proposition. The strategic rationale behind this diversification can be found in Amazon.com's powerful IT infrastructure, which can be shared by its retail sales operations and the new cloud computing service unit.

Multi-sided platforms (or multi-sided markets)

Some organizations serve two or more interdepen- dent Customer Segments. A credit card company, for example, needs a large base of credit card holders and a large base of merchants who accept those credit cards. Similarly, an enterprise offering a free news- paper needs a large reader base to attract advertisers. On the other hand, it also needs advertisers to finance production and distribution. Both segments are required to make the business model work (read more about multi-sided platforms on p. 76).

2

Value Propositions

The Value Propositions Building Block describes the bundle of products and services that create value for a specific Customer Segment

The Value Proposition is the reason why customers turn to one company over another. It solves a customer problem or satisfies a customer need. Each Value Proposition consists of a selected bundle of products and/or services that caters to the requirements of a specific Customer Segment. In this sense, the Value Proposition is an aggregation, or bundle, of benefits that a company offers customers.

Some Value Propositions may be innovative and represent a new or disruptive offer. Others may be similar to existing market offers, but with added features and attributes.

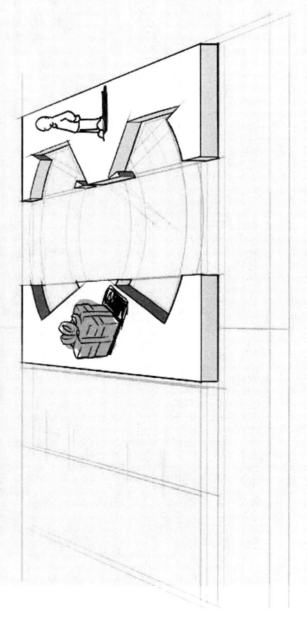

What value do we deliver to the customer?
Which one of our customer's problems are we helping
to solve? Which customer needs are we satisfying?
What bundles of products and services are we offering
to each Customer Segment?

A Value Proposition creates value for a Customer Segment through a distinct mix of elements catering to that segment's needs. Values may be quantitative (e.g. price, speed of service) or qualitative (e.g. design, customer experience).

Elements from the following non-exhaustive list can contribute to customer value creation.

Newness

Some Value Propositions satisfy an entirely new set of needs that customers previously didn't perceive because there was no similar offering. This is often, but not always, technology related. Cell phones,

for instance, created a whole new industry around mobile telecommunication. On the other hand, products such as ethical investment funds have little to do with new technology.

Performance

Improving product or service performance has traditionally been a common way to create value. The PC sector has traditionally relied on this factor by bringing more powerful machines to market. But improved performance has its limits. In recent years, for example, faster PCs, more disk storage space, and better graphics have failed to produce corresponding growth in customer demand.

Customization

Tailoring products and services to the specific needs of individual customers or Customer Segments creates value. In recent years, the concepts of mass customization and customer co-creation have gained importance. This approach allows for customized products and services, while still taking advantage of economies of scale.

"Getting the job done"

Value can be created simply by helping a customer get certain jobs done. Rolls-Royce understands this very well: its airline customers rely entirely on Rolls-Royce to manufacture and service their jet engines. This arrangement allows customers to focus on running their airlines. In return, the airlines pay Rolls- Royce a fee for every hour an engine runs.

Design

Design is an important but difficult element to measure. A product may stand out because of superior design. In the fashion and consumer electronics industries, design can be a particularly important part of the Value Proposition.

Brand/status

Customers may find value in the simple act of using and displaying a specific brand. Wearing a Rolex watch signifies wealth, for example. On the other end of the spectrum, skateboarders may wear the latest "underground" brands to show that they are "in."

Price

Offering similar value at a lower price is a common way to satisfy the needs of price-sensitive Customer Segments. But low-price Value Propositions have important implications for the rest of a business model. No frills airlines, such as Southwest, easyJet, and Ryanair have designed entire business models specifically to enable low cost air travel. Another example of a price-based Value Proposition can be seen in the Nano, a new car designed and manufactured by the Indian conglomerate Tata. Its surprisingly low price makes the automobile affordable to a whole new segment of the Indian population. Increasingly, free offers are starting to permeate various industries. Free offers range from free newspapers to free e-mail, free mobile phone services, and more (see p. 88 for more on FREE).

Cost reduction

Helping customers reduce costs is an important way to create value. Salesforce.com, for example, sells a hosted Customer Relationship management (CRM) application. This relieves buyers from the expense and trouble of having to buy, install, and manage CRM software themselves.

Risk reduction

Customers value reducing the risks they incur when purchasing products or services. For a used car buyer, a one-year service guarantee reduces the risk of post-purchase breakdowns and repairs. A service-level guarantee partially reduces the risk undertaken by a purchaser of outsourced IT services.

Accessibility

Making products and services available to customers who previously lacked access to them is another way to create value. This can result from business model innovation, new technologies, or a combination of both. NetJets, for instance, popularized the concept of fractional private jet ownership. Using an innovative business model, NetJets offers individuals and corporations access to private jets, a service previously unaffordable to most customers. Mutual funds provide another example of value creation through increased accessibility. This innovative financial product made it possible even for those with modest wealth to build diversified investment portfolios.

Convenience/usability

Making things more convenient or easier to use can create substantial value. With iPod and iTunes, Apple offered customers unprecedented convenience searching, buying, downloading, and listening to digital music. It now dominates the market.

3

Channels

The Channels Building Block describes how a company communicates with and reaches its Customer Segments to deliver a Value Proposition

Communication, distribution, and sales Channels comprise a company's interface with customers. Channels are customer touch points that play an important role in the customer experience. Channels serve several functions, including:

- *Raising awareness among customers about a company's products and services*
- *Helping customers evaluate a company's Value Proposition*
- *Allowing customers to purchase specific products and services*
- *Delivering a Value Proposition to customers*
- *Providing post-purchase customer support*

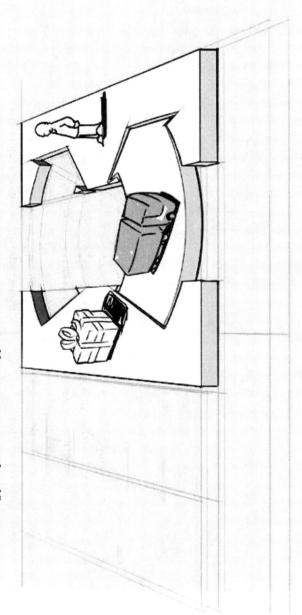

Through which Channels do our Customer Segments want to be reached? How are we reaching them now? How are our Channels integrated? Which ones work best? Which ones are most cost-efficient? How are we integrating them with customer routines?

Channels have five distinct phases. Each channel can cover some or all of these phases. We can distinguish between direct Channels and indirect ones, as well as between owned Channels and partner Channels.

Finding the right mix of Channels to satisfy how customers want to be reached is crucial in bringing a Value Proposition to market. An organization can choose between reaching its customers through its own Channels, through partner Channels, or through a mix of both. Owned Channels can be direct, such as an in-house sales force or a Web site, or they can be indirect, such as retail stores owned or operated by the organization. Partner Channels are indirect and span a whole range of options, such as wholesale distribution, retail, or partner-owned Web sites.

Partner Channels lead to lower margins, but they allow an organization to expand its reach and benefit from partner strengths. Owned Channels and particularly direct ones have higher margins, but can be costly to put in place and to operate. The trick is to find the right balance between the different types of Channels, to integrate them in a way to create a great customer experience, and to maximize revenues.

Channel Types

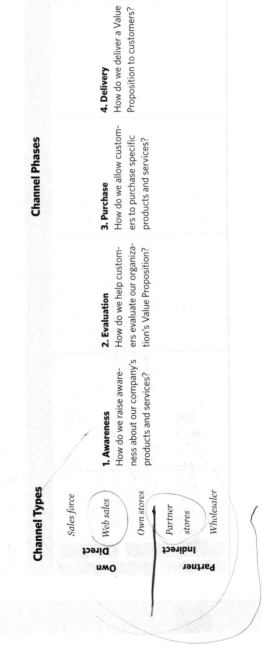

Own — **Direct**: Sales force, Web sales
Own — **Indirect**: Own stores
Partner — **Indirect**: Partner stores, Wholesaler

Channel Phases

1. Awareness
How do we raise awareness about our company's products and services?

2. Evaluation
How do we help customers evaluate our organization's Value Proposition?

3. Purchase
How do we allow customers to purchase specific products and services?

4. Delivery
How do we deliver a Value Proposition to customers?

5. After sales
How do we provide post-purchase customer support?

83

4

Customer Relationships

The Customer Relationships Building Block describes the types of relationships a company establishes with specific Customer Segments

A company should clarify the type of relationship it wants to establish with each Customer Segment. Relationships can range from personal to automated. Customer relationships may be driven by the following motivations:

- *Customer acquisition*
- *Customer retention*
- *Boosting sales (upselling)*

In the early days, for example, mobile network operator Customer Relationships were driven by aggressive acquisition strategies involving free mobile phones. When the market became saturated, operators switched to focusing on customer retention and increasing average revenue per customer.

The Customer Relationships called for by a company's business model deeply influence the overall customer experience.

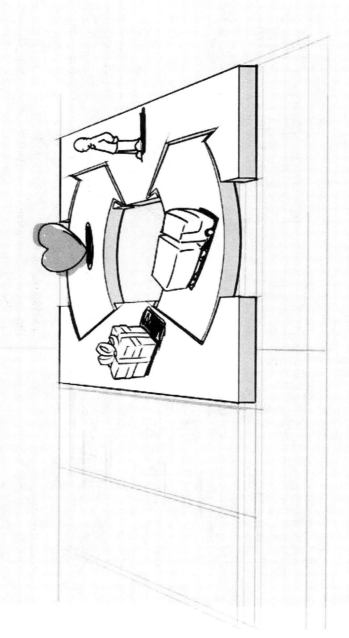

What type of relationship does each of our Customer
Segments expect us to establish and maintain with them?
Which ones have we established? How costly are they?
How are they integrated with the rest of our business model?

*We can distinguish between several categories of
Customer Relationships, which may co-exist in a
company's relationship with a particular
Customer Segment:*

Personal assistance

This relationship is based on human interaction.
The customer can communicate with a real customer
representative to get help during the sales process or
after the purchase is complete. This may happen on-
site at the point of sale, through call centers, by e-mail,
or through other means.

Dedicated personal assistance

This relationship involves dedicating a customer
representative specifically to an individual client. It
represents the deepest and most intimate type of
relationship and normally develops over a long period
of time. In private banking services, for example, dedicated bankers serve high net worth individuals. Similar
relationships can be found in other businesses in the
form of key account managers who maintain personal
relationships with important customers.

Self-service

In this type of relationship, a company maintains no
direct relationship with customers. It provides all the
necessary means for customers to help themselves.

Automated services

This type of relationship mixes a more sophisti-
cated form of customer self-service with automated
processes. For example, personal online profiles give
customers access to customized services. Automated
services can recognize individual customers and their
characteristics, and offer information related to orders
or transactions. At their best, automated services can
stimulate a personal relationship (e.g. offering book or
movie recommendations).

Communities

Increasingly, companies are utilizing user communities
to become more involved with customers/prospects
and to facilitate connections between community
members. Many companies maintain online communities that allow users to exchange knowledge and
solve each other's problems. Communities can also
help companies better understand their customers.
Pharmaceutical giant GlaxoSmithKline launched a
private online community when it introduced *alli*, a
new prescription-free weight-loss product.

GlaxoSmithKline wanted to increase its understanding of the challenges faced by overweight
adults, and thereby learn to better manage customer
expectations.

Co-creation

More companies are going beyond the traditional
customer-vendor relationship to co-create value with
customers. Amazon.com invites customers to write
reviews and thus create value for other book lovers.
Some companies engage customers to assist with the
design of new and innovative products. Others, such
as YouTube.com, solicit customers to create content
for public consumption.

Customer Segments

1

The Customer Segments Building Block defines the different groups of people or organizations an enterprise aims to reach and serve

Customers comprise the heart of any business model. Without (profitable) customers, no company can survive for long. In order to better satisfy customers, a company may group them into distinct segments with common needs, common behaviors, or other attributes. A business model may define one or several large or small Customer Segments. An organization must make a conscious decision about which segments to serve and which segments to ignore. Once this decision is made, a business model can be carefully designed around a strong understanding of specific customer needs.

Customer groups represent separate segments if:

- Their needs require and justify a distinct offer
- They are reached through different Distribution Channels
- They require different types of relationships
- They have substantially different profitabilities
- They are willing to pay for different aspects of the offer

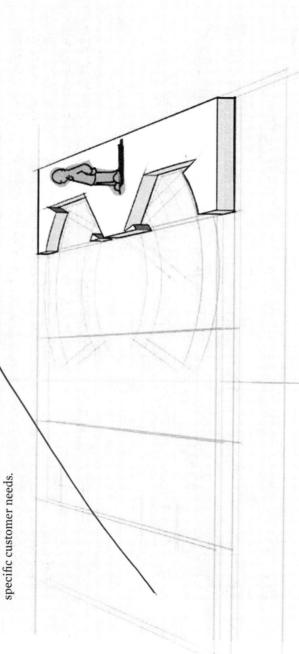

For what value are our customers really willing to pay? For what do they currently pay? How are they currently paying? How would they prefer to pay? How much does each Revenue Stream contribute to overall revenues?

There are several ways to generate Revenue Streams:

Asset sale

The most widely understood Revenue Stream derives from selling ownership rights to a physical product. Amazon.com sells books, music, consumer electronics, and more online. Fiat sells automobiles, which buyers are free to drive, resell, or even destroy.

Usage fee

This Revenue Stream is generated by the use of a particular service. The more a service is used, the more the customer pays. A telecom operator may charge customers for the number of minutes spent on the phone. A hotel charges customers for the number of nights rooms are used. A package delivery service charges customers for the delivery of a parcel from one location to another.

Subscription fees

This Revenue Stream is generated by selling continuous access to a service. A gym sells its members monthly or yearly subscriptions in exchange for access to its exercise facilities. World of Warcraft Online, a Web-based computer game, allows users to play its online game in exchange for a monthly subscription fee. Nokia's Comes with Music service gives users access to a music library for a subscription fee.

Lending/Renting/Leasing

This Revenue Stream is created by temporarily granting someone the exclusive right to use a particular asset for a fixed period in return for a fee. For the lender this provides the advantage of recurring revenues. Renters or lessees, on the other hand, enjoy the benefits of incurring expenses for only a limited time rather than bearing the full costs of ownership. Zipcar.com provides a good illustration. The company allows customers to rent cars by the hour in North American cities. Zipcar.com's service has led many people to decide to rent rather than purchase automobiles.

Licensing

This Revenue Stream is generated by giving customers permission to use protected intellectual property in exchange for licensing fees. Licensing allows rightsholders to generate revenues from their property without having to manufacture a product or commercialize a service. Licensing is common in the media industry, where content owners retain copyright while selling usage licenses to third parties. Similarly, in technology sectors patentholders grant other companies the right to use a patented technology in return for a license fee.

Each Revenue Stream might have different pricing mechanisms. The type of pricing mechanism chosen can make a big difference in terms of revenues generated. There are two main types of pricing mechanism: fixed and dynamic pricing.

Brokerage fees

This Revenue Stream derives from intermediation services performed on behalf of two or more parties. Credit card providers, for example, earn revenues by taking a percentage of the value of each sales transaction executed between credit card merchants and customers. Brokers and real estate agents earn a commission each time they successfully match a buyer and seller.

Advertising

This Revenue Stream results from fees for advertising a particular product, service, or brand. Traditionally, the media industry and event organizers relied heavily on revenues from advertising. In recent years other sectors, including software and services, have started relying more heavily on advertising revenues.

Pricing Mechanisms

Fixed "Menu" Pricing		**Dynamic Pricing**	
Predefined prices are based on static variables		Prices change based on market conditions	
List price	Fixed prices for individual products, services, or other Value Propositions	*Negotiation (bargaining)*	Price negotiated between two or more partners depending on negotiation power and/or negotiation skills
Product feature dependent	Price depends on the number or quality of Value Proposition features	*Yield management*	Price depends on inventory and time of purchase (normally used for perishable resources such as hotel rooms or airline seats)
Customer segment dependent	Price depends on the type and characteristic of a Customer Segment	*Real-time-market*	Price is established dynamically based on supply and demand
Volume dependent	Price as a function of the quantity purchased	*Auctions*	Price determined by outcome of competitive bidding

33

6

Key Resources

The Key Resources Building Block describes the most important assets required to make a business model work

Every business model requires Key Resources. These resources allow an enterprise to create and offer a Value Proposition, reach markets, maintain relationships with Customer Segments, and earn revenues. Different Key Resources are needed depending on the type of business model. A microchip manufacturer requires capital-intensive production facilities, whereas a microchip designer focuses more on human resources.

Key resources can be physical, financial, intellectual, or human. Key resources can be owned or leased by the company or acquired from key partners.

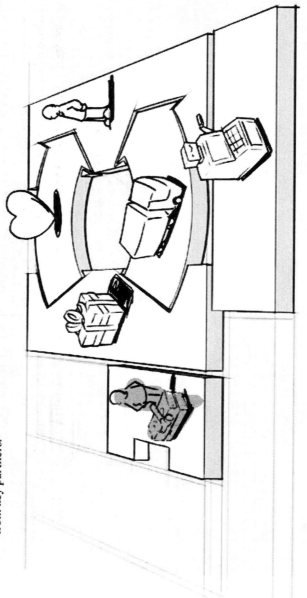

What Key Resources do our Value Propositions require? Our Distribution Channels? Customer Relationships? Revenue Streams?

Key Resources can be categorized as follows:

Physical

This category includes physical assets such as manufacturing facilities, buildings, vehicles, machines, systems, point-of-sales systems, and distribution networks. Retailers like Wal-Mart and Amazon.com rely heavily on physical resources, which are often capital-intensive. The former has an enormous global network of stores and related logistics infrastructure. The latter has an extensive IT, warehouse, and logistics infrastructure.

Intellectual

Intellectual resources such as brands, proprietary knowledge, patents and copyrights, partnerships, and customer databases are increasingly important components of a strong business model. Intellectual resources are difficult to develop but when success-

fully created may offer substantial value. Consumer goods companies such as Nike and Sony rely heavily on brand as a Key Resource. Microsoft and SAP depend on software and related intellectual property developed over many years. Qualcomm, a designer and supplier of chipsets for broadband mobile devices, built its business model around patented microchip designs that earn the company substantial licensing fees.

Human

Every enterprise requires human resources, but people are particularly prominent in certain business models. For example, human resources are crucial in knowledge-intensive and creative industries. A pharmaceutical company such as Novartis, for example, relies heavily on human resources: its business model is predicated on an army of experienced scientists and a large and skilled sales force.

Financial

Some business models call for financial resources and/or financial guarantees, such as cash, lines of credit, or a stock option pool for hiring key employees. Ericsson, the telecom manufacturer, provides an example of financial resource leverage within a business model. Ericsson may opt to borrow funds from banks and capital markets, then use a portion of the proceeds to provide vendor financing to equipment customers, thus ensuring that orders are placed with Ericsson rather than competitors.

7

Key Activities

The Key Activities Building Block describes the most important things a company must do to make its business model work

Every business model calls for a number of Key Activities. These are the most important actions a company must take to operate successfully. Like Key Resources, they are required to create and offer a Value Proposition, reach markets, maintain Customer Relationships, and earn revenues. And like Key Resources, Key Activities differ depending on business model type. For software maker Microsoft, Key Activities include software development. For PC manufacturer Dell, Key Activities include supply chain management. For consultancy McKinsey, Key Activities include problem solving.

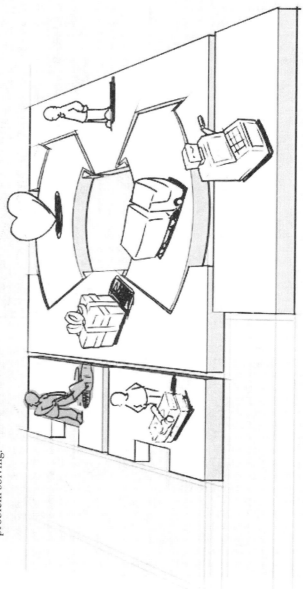

What Key Activities do our Value Propositions require? Our Distribution Channels? Customer Relationships? Revenue streams?

Key Activities can be categorized as follows:

Production

These activities relate to designing, making, and delivering a product in substantial quantities and/or of superior quality. Production activity dominates the business models of manufacturing firms.

Problem solving

Key Activities of this type relate to coming up with new solutions to individual customer problems. The operations of consultancies, hospitals, and other service organizations are typically dominated by problem solving activities. Their business models call for activities such as knowledge management and continuous training.

Platform/network

Business models designed with a platform as a Key Resource are dominated by platform or network-related Key Activities. Networks, matchmaking platforms, software, and even brands can function as a platform. eBay's business model requires that the company continually develop and maintain its platform: the Web site at eBay.com. Visa's business model requires activities related to its Visa® credit card transaction platform for merchants, customers, and banks. Microsoft's business model requires managing the interface between other vendors' software and its Windows® operating system platform. Key Activities in this category relate to platform management, service provisioning, and platform promotion.

What Key Activities do our Value Propositions require? Our Distribution Channels? Customer Relationships? Revenue streams?

Key Activities can be categorized as follows:

Production

These activities relate to designing, making, and delivering a product in substantial quantities and/or of superior quality. Production activity dominates the business models of manufacturing firms.

Problem solving

Key Activities of this type relate to coming up with new solutions to individual customer problems. The operations of consultancies, hospitals, and other service organizations are typically dominated by problem solving activities. Their business models call for activities such as knowledge management and continuous training.

Platform/network

Business models designed with a platform as a Key Resource are dominated by platform or network-related Key Activities. Networks, matchmaking platforms, software, and even brands can function as a platform. eBay's business model requires that the company continually develop and maintain its platform: the Web site at eBay.com. Visa's business model requires activities related to its Visa® credit card transaction platform for merchants, customers, and banks. Microsoft's business model requires managing the interface between other vendors' software and its Windows® operating system platform. Key Activities in this category relate to platform management, service provisioning, and platform promotion.

Who are our Key Partners? Who are our key suppliers? Which Key Resources are we acquiring from partners? Which Key Activities do partners perform?

It can be useful to distinguish between three motivations for creating partnerships:

Optimization and economy of scale

The most basic form of partnership or buyer-supplier relationship is designed to optimize the allocation of resources and activities. It is illogical for a company to own all resources or perform every activity by itself. Optimization and economy of scale partnerships are usually formed to reduce costs, and often involve outsourcing or sharing infrastructure.

Reduction of risk and uncertainty

Partnerships can help reduce risk in a competitive environment characterized by uncertainty. It is not unusual for competitors to form a strategic alliance in one area while competing in another. Blu-ray, for example, is an optical disc format jointly developed by a group of the world's leading consumer electronics, personal computer, and media manufacturers. The group cooperated to bring Blu-ray technology to market, yet individual members compete in selling their own Blu-ray products.

Acquisition of particular resources and activities

Few companies own all the resources or perform all the activities described by their business models. Rather, they extend their own capabilities by relying on other firms to furnish particular resources or perform certain activities. Such partnerships can be motivated by needs to acquire knowledge, licenses, or access to customers. A mobile phone manufacturer, for example, may license an operating system for its handsets rather than developing one in-house. An insurer may choose to rely on independent brokers to sell its policies rather than develop its own sales force.

9 | *Cost Structure*

The Cost Structure describes all costs incurred to operate a business model

This building block describes the most important costs incurred while operating under a particular business model. Creating and delivering value, maintaining Customer Relationships, and generating revenue all incur costs. Such costs can be calculated relatively easily after defining Key Resources, Key Activities, and Key Partnerships. Some business models, though, are more cost-driven than others. So-called "no frills" airlines, for instance, have built business models entirely around low Cost Structures.

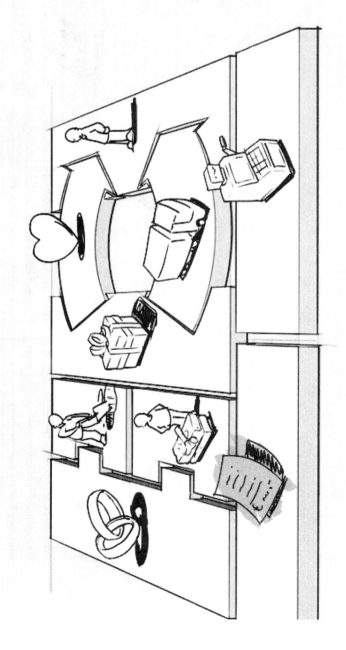

What are the most important costs inherent in our business model? Which Key Resources are most expensive? Which Key Activities are most expensive?

Naturally enough, costs should be minimized in every business model. But low Cost Structures are more important to some business models than to others. Therefore it can be useful to distinguish between two broad classes of business model Cost Structures: cost-driven and value-driven (many business models fall in between these two extremes):

Cost-driven

Cost-driven business models focus on minimizing costs wherever possible. This approach aims at creating and maintaining the leanest possible Cost Structure, using low price Value Propositions, maximum automation, and extensive outsourcing. No frills airlines, such as Southwest, easyJet, and Ryanair typify cost-driven business models.

Value-driven

Some companies are less concerned with the cost implications of a particular business model design, and instead focus on value creation. Premium Value Propositions and a high degree of personalized service usually characterize value-driven business models. Luxury hotels, with their lavish facilities and exclusive services, fall into this category.

Cost Structures can have the following characteristics:

Fixed costs

Costs that remain the same despite the volume of goods or services produced. Examples include salaries, rents, and physical manufacturing facilities. Some businesses, such as manufacturing companies, are characterized by a high proportion of fixed costs.

Variable costs

Costs that vary proportionally with the volume of goods or services produced. Some businesses, such as music festivals, are characterized by a high proportion of variable costs.

Economies of scale

Cost advantages that a business enjoys as its output expands. Larger companies, for instance, benefit from lower bulk purchase rates. This and other factors cause average cost per unit to fall as output rises.

Economies of scope

Cost advantages that a business enjoys due to a larger scope of operations. In a large enterprise, for example, the same marketing activities or Distribution Channels may support multiple products.

97

The nine business model Building Blocks form the basis for a handy tool, which we call the *Business Model Canvas*.

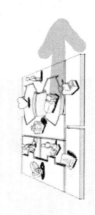

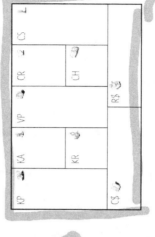

The Business Model Canvas

This tool resembles a painter's canvas — preformatted with the nine blocks — which allows you to paint pictures of new or existing business models.

The Business Model Canvas works best when printed out on a large surface so groups of people can jointly start sketching and discussing business model elements with Post-it® notes or board markers. It is a hands-on tool that fosters understanding, discussion, creativity, and analysis.

The Business Model Canvas

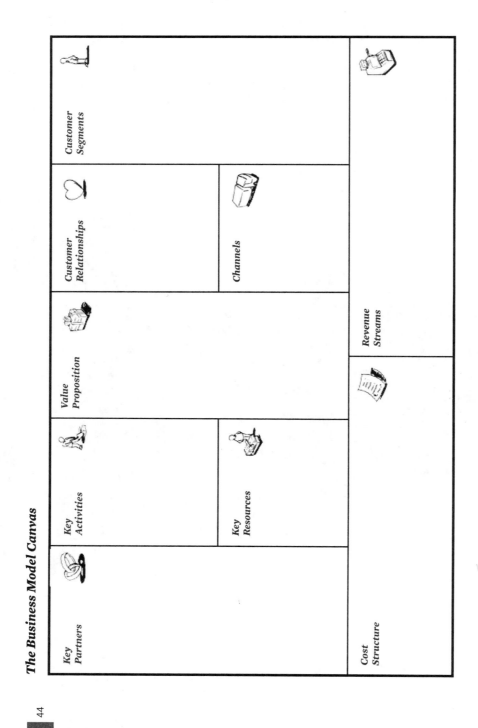

45

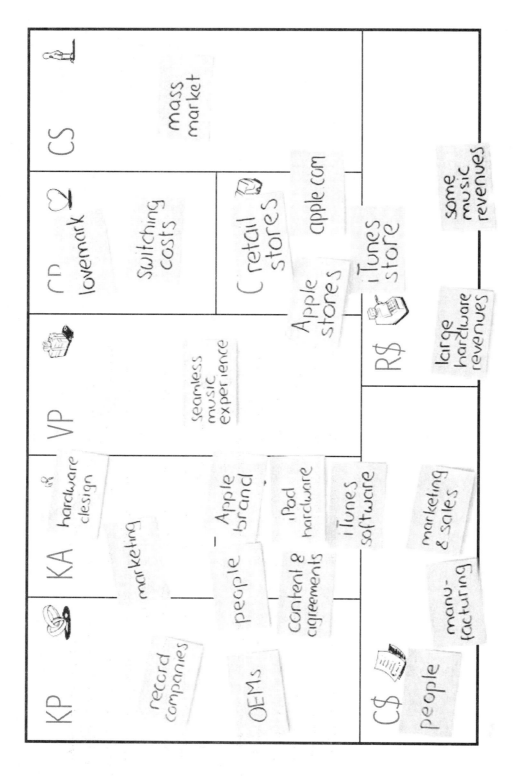

Example: Apple iPod/iTunes Business Model

In 2001 Apple launched its iconic iPod brand of portable media player. The device works in conjunction with iTunes software that enables users to transfer music and other content from the iPod to a computer. The software also provides a seamless connection to Apple's online store so users can purchase and download content.

This potent combination of device, software, and online store quickly disrupted the music industry and gave Apple a dominant market position. Yet Apple was not the first company to bring a portable media player to market. Competitors such as Diamond Multimedia, with its Rio brand of portable media players, were successful until they were outpaced by Apple.

How did Apple achieve such dominance? Because it competed with a better business model. On the one hand it offered users a seamless music experience by combining its distinctively designed iPod devices with iTunes software and the iTunes online store. Apple's Value Proposition is to allow customers to easily search, buy, and enjoy digital music. On the other hand, to make this Value Proposition possible, Apple had to negotiate deals with all the major record companies to create the world's largest online music library.

The twist? Apple earns most of its music-related revenues from selling iPods, while using integration with the online music store to protect itself from competitors.

Week #3 / Lab #2

Class — Critical Thinking

Selected readings from the following book are included in this week's section of the Lab Manual as they are required for class this week and will form the basis for part of next week's lab:

- *Critical Thinking for Business Students* by Linda Dyer
  - o What is Critical Thinking?
  - o Claims
  - o Evidence
  - o Underlying Assumptions
  - o Causal Claims
  - o Techniques of Persuasion

Lab #2 — Art of the Pitch & Individual Presentation Skills

In preparation for this lab:

- Read *Speak More Effectively* by Dale Carnegie
- Review the marking rubric for the Pitch assignment

What Is Critical Thinking?

- what are
- how find
- how test / challenge
- how build persuasive argument

Critical thinking is an approach to reading, thinking, and learning that involves asking questions, examining our assumptions, and weighing the validity of arguments.

Sometimes questioning our beliefs about what we read comes naturally, but other times we may accept ideas and statements uncritically. Critical thinking can be developed as a frame of mind — a set of strategies that we will use as we determine whether or not to believe what we read or hear. In learning about critical thinking, we make these strategies explicit. If we can become aware of the activities of critical thinking, we will be able to use them consciously to think effectively and make intelligent decisions, both professionally and in our personal lives.

Critical thinkers are self-aware, curious, and independent. They introspect on their own thinking processes; they work at knowing their own biases and can name the strategies they are using when they make judgments (self-aware). They explore beneath the surface of issues by challenging ideas that seem to be obvious, trying out new approaches, and seeking new viewpoints to extend their knowledge (curious). They listen to the ideas of others and learn from them, but then they use that learning to develop their own informed opinions, to understand the full range of their options, and to make their own judgments (independent).

"You're so critical!"

When we use the word *critical* in our ordinary conversations with acquaintances, we often mean negative or judgmental. Actually, the word comes from the Greek word *kritikos*, which means to question, analyze, or make sense of something. This is the way we shall be using the term. Sometimes critical thinking will lead us to reject a conclusion; other times we will decide to accept an idea as valid. But in either case, we will have subjected the issue to careful thought. So critical thinkers are not necessarily negative; rather, they try to assess the truth about a given matter.

Critical thinking about business

Many people claim that this is the age of information. We are bombarded with information when we watch television programs, read newspapers, and explore the Internet. In recent times, information about the world of business often has appeared to hold centre stage. The dominant discourses are economic performance and the productivity of companies, global markets, financial investment, consumer awareness, changing career paths, and unemployment. This explosion of interest in business started in the mid-1980s. Two decades later, Simba

---

Reproduced with permission from Linda Dyer, *Critical Thinking for Business Students*, 2nd edition (Concord, ON: Captus Press Inc., 2011), Chapter 1.

Box 1.1: Best-selling business books in North America

1. *Boom, Bust and Echo: Profiting from the Demographic Shift in the 21st Century* by David K. Foot with Daniel Stoffman (Stoddart, 2000).
This book makes predictions about economic markets and social life in Canada based on demographics — the relative number of children, twenty-somethings, middle-aged, and elderly people in our society.

2. *Flow: The Psychology of Optimal Experience* by Mikhail Csikszentmihalyi (Harper Perennial, 1991).
When we are fully engaged in a challenging activity that we truly love, we enter a state of "flow" in which we are most productive and happiest. With examples of surgeons, musicians, and many other case histories, the author's ideas speak to the pursuit of happiness at work.

3. *Freakonomics: A Rogue Economist Explores the Hidden Side of Everything* by Steven D. Levitt and Stephen J. Dubner (William Morrow, 2005).
An unconventional scholar and a journalist apply economic theory to popular culture — their topics include drug-dealing, the socio-economics of naming children, and cheating among teachers and sumo wrestlers.

4. *Getting to Yes: Negotiating Agreement Without Giving In* by Roger Fisher, William Ury, and Bruce Patton (Penguin Books, 1991).
The authors describe "principled negotiation" as a way to achieve agreement in the workplace. First published in 1981, it is now classic reading for sales representatives and business people who need to manage conflict.

5. *Getting Things Done* by David Allen (Penguin, 2002).
Allen, a management consultant and executive coach, provides insights about how to manage workflow and enhance productivity. The system has a devoted following, and "GTD" enthusiasts say that it has changed their lives.

6. *Good to Great: Why Some Companies Make the Leap...and Others Don't* by Jim Collins (Collins Business, 2001).
Collins describes how a moderately successful company can become a great one by a careful focus of their strategies, employees, and corporate culture. This was probably the most successful business book in the first decade of the 2000s.

7. *In Search of Excellence: Lessons from America's Best-Run Companies* by Thomas J. Peters and Robert H. Waterman (Harper, 1982).
The authors present case studies of successful companies and extracts eight principles for business success. The book was enormously influential and, although it has critics, many claim that its message has stood the test of time. One of the authors, Tom Peters, has become a management "guru".

8. *Now, Discover Your Strengths: How to Build Your Strengths and the Strengths of Every Person in Your Organization* by Marcus Buckingham and Donald O. Clifton (Free Press, 2001).
Rather than trying to improve your weakness, the authors suggest, you should focus on your strengths to maximize your performance, enhance your confidence, and have a satisfying work life.

Box 1.1 continued

9. *Outliers: The Story of Success* by Malcolm Gladwell (Little, Brown & Company, 2008).
    The author explains that innate talent is not the most important cause of extraordinary success. Family, culture, and the "10,000 hour rule" are some of the less-obvious factors that contribute to a person's success. Gladwell is well known for translating academic theories into vivid, user-friendly anecdotes.

10. *Who Moved My Cheese? An Amazing Way to Deal with Change in Your Work and in Your Life* by Spencer Johnson and Kenneth Blanchard (Putnam, 1998).
    This 96-page business parable features two mice and two men who must learn to deal with organizational change. There are more than five million copies in print, and the book is frequently bought by managers for distribution to their employees.

Information, a company that does market research on the publishing industry, estimated that $2.2 billion worth of books about business were being sold globally each year. It is frequently suggested that the huge market for these books stems from business managers' struggles to compete effectively with rival companies. **Box** lists some classic best-selling business books in North America.

In recent years, the market for trade books about business has declined. The 2001 collapse of the Texas energy-trading company Enron, the worldwide financial crisis of 2007–2010, and public reaction to similar business scandals may have contributed to the decreased interest in the writings of management gurus and retired executives. On the other hand, these events excited widespread debate about business ethics, the social responsibility of corporations, executive pay, and trust in the institutions of business. Online commentary on these matters enjoys unremitting growth. In addition, business magazines, seminars, workshops, and consultant reports, all contribute to the burgeoning business literature with which managers and other interested parties must cope.

The sheer volume of this information can be intimidating; critical thinking skills can play a vital role in helping us to sift through the multitude of ideas. Simply asking "Where have I heard this idea before?" helps us to deal with information overload. Critical thinkers recognize that the same idea can appear in radically different forms, and they search for commonalities among diverse texts. They discard the terminological chaff and conserve the enduring kernels of truth in the current understanding of how businesses work.

It is also said that this is the age of the expert. We count on experts to tell us how to look for a job, how to invest for our retirement, how to deal with difficult people at work, how to shop wisely. Our reliance on expertise extends beyond the boundaries of the workplace; we're given expert advice on nutrition, keeping fit, gardening, raising children, caring for aging parents, etc. The problem is that, all too often, experts disagree. Their ideas contradict one another. "For every theory dragging companies one way, there are two other theories dragging it in another," complain John Micklethwait and Adrian Wooldridge (1996: 16), two vocal critics of the business literature. How do we decide what to believe? If the business experts were infallible, there would be little need for critical thinking skills. But they are not. So we need to develop procedures we can use to assess the truth or validity of the differing ideas and conclusions the experts proffer.

Buyer beware

Many best-selling books written by business experts claim to deliver simple recipes for success that are based on a rich supply of anecdotes about successful executives and companies. They are often well written, entertaining, and optimistic in outlook. But *caveat emptor* — let the buyer beware. The ideas are not necessarily reliable, valid, or scientifically sound. The popularity of the books may say more about the effectiveness of the authors' and publishers' marketing techniques, or about the insecurity of the managers who buy the books, than about the worthiness of the books' contents. In the words of business scholar, Larry Cummings, best-selling business books are "frequently among the most dangerous because they are so well done (that is, well done in a marketing and journalistic sense), and therefore they are easily read and so believable. They are likely to influence the naive, those who consume them without critically evaluating their content" (Pierce & Newstrom, 1996: 22). A critical thinker does more than passively accept the ideas of others, even including the ideas of business experts.

As students of business, it is obvious that we need to think critically about the business discourse to improve our understanding of, and performance in, the world of commerce. Note, however, that critical thinking about business has a wider application. The values of business are permeating non-business spheres such as health care, politics, education, and the world of art and culture. The spread of business values is sometimes explicit, sometimes implicit, sometimes almost surreptitious. Government representatives, university administrators, hospital directors, police chiefs, boards of artistic and community organizations, all give voice to the pressure to revamp their activities to make them "run like a business", embracing values such as profitability, marketing, and competition. How valid is this generalization of business ideas to the not-for-profit sectors? What are the implications of extending the values of business into other spheres? It is important that we are able to ponder these issues and so to understand and evaluate the major role that the world of business plays in all aspects of our lives.

The sponge

Many writers about thinking skills use the idea of a "sponge" to demonstrate a procedure we should avoid when reading or listening to others. A sponge, whether it is the underwater marine animal or the pad lying beside the kitchen sink, simply sits there and soaks up liquid. A reader who acts like a sponge simply soaks up information. Of course, it is necessary to absorb knowledge about the world, particularly when you are learning about a new field. In your first marketing course, for example, you need to absorb the basics of marketing theory. Right now, you are "soaking up" some of the fundamentals of critical thinking. This is a necessary, though quite passive, exercise. It is preliminary to the next step — evaluating and judging critically ideas in marketing or other fields of business. This is the stage we must try to attain. Being a critical thinker means going beyond the level of being a passive sponge.

Dimensions of critical thinking

The critical thinking process can be divided into five major parts. First, critical thinking is purposeful — when we use these thinking strategies, we are trying to settle a problem, develop an answer to a question, or decide on appropriate action. It behooves us, therefore, to ensure that our thinking is directed at a significant and useful purpose and that we can state clearly the points at issue. This is the subject matter of the second chapter of this handbook, in which we focus on the **central claims** of business texts.

A second dimension looks at the quality of the data and reasons that are available to support claims. Are sufficient reasons provided? Is the information accurate? These and other questions that examine the **quality of the evidence** are presented in Chapter 3.

We also consider that claims and the evidence selected to support them are powerfully shaped by our basic assumptions or viewpoints. Can we identify the points of view that underlie the stated beliefs and evaluate their strengths and weaknesses? Can we turn our critical thinking focus onto our own **underlying assumptions and values**? Chapter 4 of the handbook looks at these notions.

Next, we pay special attention to inferences about cause and effect. In the field of business, many claims suggest prescriptions and formulae such as, "If you do X in your firm, then Y will be the result," or, "If employees are not given enough A, then they will become B." In Chapter 5, we will see that these are **causal claims**, and we will address the complex issue of judging the validity of causal inferences.

The fifth dimension to be considered here is the way in which ideas are expressed in order to persuade readers and listeners. As critical thinkers, we must consider carefully the way in which key concepts are presented, how contradictory evidence is managed, and in general, how words can sway our judgments. These ideas are presented under the broad heading, **Techniques of Persuasion**, in Chapter 6. The final chapter summarizes how the dimensions of critical thinking come together in writing a persuasive essay.

Consider an example

Let us now look at a brief text to which we might want to apply our critical thinking skills. There has been much concern recently about the underground economy, the notion that there are many transactions that occur among people who buy and sell goods and services "under the table" to avoid paying the applicable taxes. The following is a comment on the issue that we can evaluate critically:

> "I'd pay my taxes," says Richard, a Montreal landscape gardener and snow-removal contractor, "but they are too high and I get so little for them. I used to give receipts and accept cheques; I charged and paid GST and PST, and I declared all my income. People would offer to pay me cash under the table to avoid the GST and PST, but I said no. After a while, though, I asked myself what I was getting for all these taxes and decided that it really wasn't worth it. All these overpaid civil servants pushing paper until they get their fat, indexed pensions. All I get out of it is potholed roads, a failing

health-care system, and giving welfare cheques to people who can but don't work. I have to scramble to get business and to satisfy difficult customers; and not even a good pension at the end. Anyway, I was losing customers to competitors who don't charge tax and probably don't declare their income either. I have food to buy for my family and credit card bills to pay. These things keep going up. I have no choice. I have to survive. If tax rates were lower, I'd pay my taxes and declare all my income. But the current set-up? No way!"

Richard's views are not exceptional. According to research by the Fraser Institute, an economic think tank, the underground economy now represents between 5 and 20 percent of GDP. It used to be smaller, but the expansion of small business and tax levels, and especially the introduction of the GST, over the past few decades have caused it to grow. Governments recognize this too. Today, lost taxes probably cost the federal and provincial governments something in the order of $30 to $40 billion. Governments' response is more stringent enforcement, as if this will solve the problem. But this misses the point. The answer is not heavy-handed enforcement of the tax law. It is expensive to hire government spies to chase down tax evaders. The answer, according to a director of the 70,000 member Canadian Taxpayers' Federation in Ottawa, is to reduce the tax burden to a level that people will judge to be fair. This will eliminate the incentive to cheat. High taxes force people to cheat. If taxes were lower, people would not resent complying.

As you read the text, several questions may occur to you as you decide whether or not the writer has made a good case for lowering taxes.

1. How relevant are Richard's household expenses to his argument that he should not pay taxes? In general, does the anecdote about Richard affect the persuasiveness of the author's conclusion?

2. Is tax reduction better than enforcement? Will compliance really increase if taxes are reduced?

3. If compliance does increase, will this make up for the loss caused by a lower tax rate?

4. What is the effect of phrases like "potholed roads", "fat, indexed pensions", and "government spies"?

5. Why does the author say that more stringent enforcement "misses the point"?

6. Who are the people who are likely to join the Canadian Taxpayers' Federation? What is the effect of noting that there are 70,000 members?

7. What do you think is the position of the author of this piece? In fact, who is the author and what is his/her background?

8. In your own opinion, what are the reasons that people evade taxes? Which, if any, of them are morally justified?

These are the types of questions a critical thinker raises. When you have applied your critical thinking skills to a piece like this, you may decide, in the end, to accept wholeheartedly the views of the author, to accept them cautiously and with specific reservations, to seek out further information before deciding one way or the other, or to reject the ideas outright. Whatever the outcome, you will have clearly defined reasons for your position.

Critical thinking and effective communication

Another important outcome of developing your critical thinking skills is that you can improve your own arguments when you write or speak. You will know how to state your views clearly and provide appropriate justification for them. You will be able to avoid fallacies in reasoning, explore your own underlying assumptions, and deal effectively with evidence that runs counter to your views. In general, you will develop further your appreciation for the use of *language*. Careful attention to words can make our writing not only clearer, but more persuasive. Throughout our discussion of critical thinking skills, we will find that they translate quite neatly into guidelines for effective communication.

Claims

The first thing we must do, if we are to evaluate an argument, is to identify the author's *claim*. A claim is the major conclusion of a piece of writing that the author is trying to persuade you to accept. It is pointless to criticize a thesis if you are unable to say clearly what the author's claim is.

Sometimes the central claim is explicitly stated and is easy to find. At other times, the job of finding the central claim is a greater challenge because it is implicit in the author's statements; that is, it is not stated outright. If the latter is true, you will have to state the claim in your own words. In a short article, the claim may appear at the very beginning of the piece. It sometimes appears in the title or as a headline of a newspaper article. The central claim may also be placed near the end of the article as a conclusion.

Certain words or phrases may indicate that the author is about to state a claim. They include words such as *therefore, thus, in summary, I believe that, clearly, in short, the data show that, as a result, in fact,* and synonyms of these words. If you are having trouble finding the claim, it may be helpful to look for these *cue words*, read the phrases that immediately follow them, then decide what seems to be the main idea of the article. It is important to ensure that your statement of the claim is *fair* — that you have not distorted the author's meaning. After taking the time to evaluate a claim in depth, you don't want the author to respond: "Actually, you've missed my point. That's not what I said!"

Most of the other statements in the article will be *evidence*, the examples and reasoning that are presented to support the claim, since it is normally on the basis of evidence that we decide whether or not to accept the claim. We will discuss evidence in some detail in another chapter. At this point, we simply note that a claim is not an example, a definition, or a statistic. It is usually a broader issue, addressed at a greater level of abstraction than the evidence. For example, let's say that you read a passage that reports an anecdote about the case of a company that took a retailer to court for selling counterfeit versions of their trademark products. In the same passage is the statistic that an estimated 39% of the software in Canadian computers was not legally purchased. Neither of these pieces of information is the claim; rather, the claim is the more general statement that pirated merchandise is a big problem for manufacturing firms. The anecdote and statistic are evidence provided in support of the claim.

Uncontested claims

Given our focus on questioning and evaluation, we might wonder whether there are any situations where we might accept a claim without examining the evidence. Should we accept *any* claim without challenge? In fact, shouldn't we probe and question *all* the information that

Reproduced with permission from Linda Dyer, *Critical Thinking for Business Students*, 2nd edition (Concord, ON: Captus Press Inc., 2011), Chapter 2.

authors present? Let us reiterate that critical thinking does not mean negative thinking. When we read or hear a claim, we may indeed decide to accept it as unproblematic. If we tried to question every single sentence that we read or heard, we would be paralyzed. Here are some conditions in which people may accept a claim without challenge, even if no evidence is provided in its support.

1. We usually do not contest claims that are consistent with our own experiences and observations, things that we have actually seen, heard, or touched: *The roads are congested with traffic between 4 and 6 pm*. Similarly, we accept claims that relate to subjective experiences: *I like the taste of black olives* or *Golf is my favourite sport*.

2. Some claims appear to be facts that are independent of interpretation — *Quebec is larger than Nova Scotia*. Events that happened are often not questioned: for example, when we read a newspaper report of a train accident or an announcement of a merger between two firms, we tend to accept this type of claim as true. These events are not uncommon and well within the realm of possibility.

3. Areas in which there is agreement among experts, or strongly supported general claims that are common sense, are often uncontested. Knowledgeable and intelligent people are in general agreement that *You cannot physically be in two places at one time*. Business scholars agree that *Frederick Taylor has often been called the father of modern management*.

4. Technical or mathematical claims are usually accepted without challenge. We do not question that debits equal credits in double-entry accounting or that a megabyte is 0.0009765625 of a gigabyte.

Of course, accepting something as unproblematic *now* does not mean that we must *always* continue to accept it as unproblematic. For example, even agreement among experts can be a transitory phenomenon. As new information arises, we are free to re-examine the situation and challenge claims that we no longer believe to be true. Box 2.1 presents an example of a once-unproblematic claim that was re-examined in later years.

Contestable claims

When a claim does not fall into one of the categories described above, we need to question its truth or falsity using our critical thinking strategies. Authors may present claims that are not commonly accepted knowledge. For example, claims that *People who have excelled in the academic world make poor entrepreneurs* or that *Having a mandatory retirement age decreases a country's productivity and economic progress* are contestable claims. Political commentaries and editorials in the newspaper are a rich source of contestable claims. It is important to note that readers and listeners find contestable claims to be much more interesting and significant than claims that can stand without challenge. Contestable claims often introduce new ideas that awaken curiosity and cause people to think about things in new ways. If everything we read was an unproblematic claim, it would be dull reading indeed.

On occasion, you may see a contestable claim presented as if it were a fact, as in *The fact is that close supervision is totally inappropriate in the modern workplace*; or in *There is no doubt that a sizeable increase in tuition is necessary to improve the quality of university education*. Simply labelling a claim as fact, however, or saying that it is beyond doubt, does not mean that it

114

Box 2.1: An uncontested claim becomes problematic

Henri Fayol, a French industrialist, developed a profile of the manager in 1916. "Managers," said Fayol, "plan, organize, coordinate, and control." Fayol's claim entered the general vocabulary of business and was accepted as unproblematic — his profile of managers was described in practically all introductory text books in business, and was routinely taught in business courses for undergraduates. There seemed to be general agreement among experts that this was an accurate characterization of managers.

Almost sixty years later, a challenge arose to Fayol's claim. Henry Mintzberg, a professor of management at McGill University, conducted a number of research studies in which he observed managers closely as they did their work. As a result, he published an article in the *Harvard Business Review* (1975) entitled, "The Manager's Job: Folklore and Fact".[1] The article begins, "If you ask managers what they do, they will most likely tell you that they plan, organize, coordinate, and control. Then watch what they do. Don't be surprised if you can't relate what you see to these words" (p. 163). Mintzberg proposed that Fayol's classic claim was merely myth or folklore. His aim in this article was to "break the reader away from Fayol's words and introduce a more supportable and useful description of managerial work" (p. 164). Rather than being a systematic and thoughtful planner, the manager has a job characterized by rapid pace, a variety of brief and discontinuous activities, and little time or inclination to reflect. Rather than planning broad strategies for the firm, based on aggregated, documented reports, managers prefer telephone calls, impromptu meetings, even hallway gossip.

Mintzberg made a new claim — that the manager's job was best described in a series of 10 roles. These included interpersonal roles (such as figurehead and leader), informational roles (including the collection and dissemination of information), and decisional roles (such as entrepreneur and disturbance handler).

Challenging Fayol's claim certainly rang bells with many managers. In a retrospective commentary, Mintzberg reports that a common reaction to his article was, "You make me feel so good. I thought all those other managers were planning, organizing, coordinating and controlling, while I was busy being interrupted, jumping from one issue to another, and trying to keep a lid on the chaos."

Note

1. H. Mintzberg, "The Manager's Job: Folklore and Fact", *Harvard Business Review*, March/April 1990, pp. 163–76. [The article first appeared in *Harvard Business Review*, July–August, 1975.]

---

is an uncontested claim. Bosses, neophyte employees, and "old-hand" employees may have very different reactions to the claim about close supervision. Parents, students, professors, university administrators, and government officials may have varying opinions on the possible outcomes of a tuition increase. Neither claim, then, is independent of interpretation. Thus, unlike the examples in #2 above, both claims generally would be classified as contestable claims.

When making contestable claims, authors must provide evidence to justify their positions, and our job as critical thinkers is to examine and evaluate the justification. The quality of the reasoning and evidence (which will be covered in the next chapter) is what leads us to accept, or reject, contestable claims. Contestable claims cannot stand on their own. Without evidence, discussing contestable claims will rapidly degenerate into "my opinion against yours". In a related vein, we frequently hear the notion that "Everybody's opinion is of equal value" or "I have a right to my own opinion." Subjective opinions do have their place, of course, but little progress will be made in understanding the business world and how it works if we fail to see the crucial difference between simply stating that something is true and providing relevant and solid reasoning for our statements.

An example

Read the following passage and decide what the author's claim is.

> "Self-praise is no praise at all." This was one of my grandmother's maxims. It is not socially acceptable to brag about yourself and your accomplishments, she said. Ladies and gentlemen do not boast.
>
> But Grandma did not live in today's competitive work environment. Modesty is worse than useless at a job interview when dozens of my fellow-students are vying for the job I want. I'd be a fool not to tell the recruiter about the excellent paper I wrote about Activity-Based Costing, and how much I've learned about his company by surfing the Internet. And after I get the job, if I don't tell my boss how well my project is going, or the great skills I'm picking up at night school, who will? How will she know that I'm the one deserving of the big year-end bonus? Team-work is hot these days, and it's so easy to get lost in a crowd. I've got to let the right people know how many great ideas and long hours of work I contributed to the team effort. In short, it's a dog-eat-dog world, and if I want to get ahead, I've got to have the loudest bark.

You should have noted the cue words, *in short*, at the end of the passage. The claim is not stated explicitly, but the author's main point can be summarized as "Self-praise is necessary for career advancement." An alternative wording could be "Modesty is inappropriate in a competitive work environment," or "Bragging leads to success at work," or some similar formulation. It would not be appropriate to say that the claim was "It's a dog-eat-dog world," or "I've got to have the loudest bark," or even "Grandma was wrong." While these are colourful comments, they are not intelligible outside of the context of the passage, and none of them provides a good summary of the author's major point.

The rest of the paragraph contains the writer's reasoning and evidence presented in support of the claim.

Presenting claims

We have said that a good statement of the author's claim is the first step to evaluating it critically. When stating a claim, we try to present the essence of what the author is saying in an accurate and concise manner. Occasionally, we can find a sentence or phrase in the author's own words that is a good statement of his or her claim; more often, we must paraphrase and summarize elements of the text to state the claim clearly and efficiently.

While a claim is often stated as a sentence, especially when the text is short (like a newspaper article or the passage above), there are other ways of presenting claims. For longer texts, where a single sentence will not suffice, authors may provide a **list of important concepts** and a series of propositions about how these concepts are related. The claim may also be presented graphically as a diagram or drawing — a **concept map**. Concept maps are a compact way of summarizing complex material and can make the author's claims very memorable. A picture, the saying goes, is worth a thousand words. Concept maps may be simple boxes-and-arrows figures that highlight the main issues and show relationships. They may look like tree diagrams, geographical maps, or other creative images that summarize the author's main point. **Box 2.2** offers some tips in developing your own concept maps.

Box 2.2: Concept maps

The exercise of developing your own concept maps can help you to learn and remember the material you read for your courses. This is especially true when your concept maps contain images that are meaningful to you. In addition, concept maps can be an efficient and effective method of communicating the claims you make in your own reports to your readers.

Pictures have become more and more central to people's understanding of the world around them. Beginning in the mid-nineteenth century, the then-new technology of the photograph led to an explosion of reproductions of pictures and images in posters, advertisements, books, newspapers and later, television. The historian Daniel Boorstin has labelled this phenomenon the "Graphic Revolution".[1] Some social observers believe that images are taking over from words as the primary medium of communication today.

We can conclude, then, that graphic representation of concepts and claims has become increasingly important for communication with the average reader. In fact, the cognitive processing needed to develop the concept map is an aid to our own understanding and memory.

Here are some tips to help you develop your own concept maps:

1. In making your concept map, start with a list of the main ideas to be represented. These may be headings or subheadings from the text. If headings are not provided, try to decide what words would be the most effective summary of each section of the text. It is important that you stick to single words or short phrases.

2. The structure of your map may be boxes and arrows, pictorial representations, timelines, a tree-and-branch organization, overlapping circles, or a variety of other formats. You do not need to pick a structure in advance, just let it develop naturally as you proceed with your thinking about the concepts and the relationships among them.

3. Remember that your concept map may be highly individual — its evolution depends on the images, symbols, and graphics that are most meaningful to you. You will find that certain conventions are intuitive — arrows, for example, usually denote cause-and-effect linkages; circles or other boundaries are used to group related ideas. You will develop your own conventions over time. Colour and shapes may be used judiciously: for instance, blue oval for advantages and red rectangle for disadvantages.

Box 2.2 continued

4. If you intend to use your concept map as an illustration in your own written report, make sure that it is well labelled and that the significance of the images you chose is clearly described in the text.

The strength of a concept map is its ability to summarize concisely large amounts of information. The concept map should never be more than one page. Having a few well-chosen words is much better than cluttering the map with excess words. Your goal is that a single glance will evoke ideas that may have been expressed in several pages of written information. This can be especially useful when you need to review material before an examination or oral presentation.

Note
1. D. Boorstin, *The Image* (New York: Harper & Row Publishers, 1961).

Writing effectively

Critical thinking about claims has implications for your own writing. Since a clear understanding of the claim is so important to readers, make sure that when you are the author you present your main ideas with clarity and emphasis. Put the claim near the beginning or end of your report, and use the cue words discussed above (e.g., *in conclusion, therefore, the data show that*) so that there can be no confusion as to what your claim is. The title of your text, and subheadings, where necessary, should make your logic transparent to the reader. Make your titles work for you. As a heading, *Section Three* is much less useful than *Executive Pay Should Be Public Knowledge*. In longer reports, you may find concept maps to be helpful in emphasizing your main points. Use pictures and other vivid images to make your claims clear and memorable for your readers.

Evidence

We have defined a *claim* as the central idea that the author of a piece of writing is trying to persuade you to accept. An author who makes a claim usually offers reasons *why* you should accept it. *Evidence* is any statement that is a response to the question: Why is this true? It may consist of statistics, details of past events, anecdotes, written accounts, previously established claims, or other statements and reasoning that provide support for the claim. In the absence of evidence, a claim is merely an unsubstantiated opinion; the more contestable or controversial the claim, the more important that it be bolstered by solid evidence.

Finding the evidence

Evidence helps us to form judgments about claims. Just as it is crucial to identify the claim, we must locate the evidence before we can evaluate an argument. An *argument* is the combination of a claim and the evidence for it. Note that this differs from the common use of the word "argument" to mean "disagreement or contention". In a longer piece of writing, there will be several arguments — claims and evidence — that the author presents. Certain *cue words* indicate that the author is about to present a piece of evidence. Look out for phrases like *because, as a result, in the first place, in the second place, for example, in addition, given that, studies show, for the following reasons*, and similar phrases. Read the following passage, and locate the claim and evidence provided. The sentences are numbered to aid our analysis.

> Students today are more knowledgeable than they were a decade ago (1). In the first place, good early education plays an important role in this situation (2). Because of the prevalence of daycare, children leave home earlier, learning earlier to communicate with others and develop academic skills (3). For example, children in daycare are taught to read stories, write words and solve simple math problems even before they enter elementary school (4). In addition, teachers today are more highly educated than in the past (5). Most high school teachers hold at least a Bachelor's degree, and most university teachers have PhDs (6). At all levels, people receive training in teaching during their degree programs (7). Compared with the past, therefore, teaching is more effective nowadays (8). Finally, advances in high technology provide students with a number of chances to expand their knowledge (9). I read in the newspaper that more than 80% of Canadians have access to the Internet at home (10). Nowadays, students can use readily accessible, powerful Internet search engines to learn much more information about their courses or other interests in a convenient and efficient way (11).

Here, the central claim, *Students are more knowledgeable than they were a decade ago*, is stated explicitly and appears both at the beginning and the end of the passage. Why does the author

Reproduced with permission from Linda Dyer, *Critical Thinking for Business Students*, 2nd edition (Concord, ON: Captus Press Inc., 2011), Chapter 3.

think this? Several pieces of evidence are provided to answer our *Why is this true?* question. Notice the cue words such as *in the first place*, *for example*, *in addition* and *finally*, which precede the evidence. The evidence offered has to do with early learning in daycare (sentences 2–4), the skills of teachers (sentences 5–8) and the availability and power of Internet search engines (sentences 9–11).

Notice that each piece of evidence has to be explained — in fact, each is treated like a subordinate claim which itself needs to be supported. The broad, evidential statement about technology use, for example, is supported by more detailed evidence about the prevalence of Internet access and its use by students.

Quality of evidence

Of course, the mere presence of evidence is not automatic proof that the claim is acceptable. Evidence may be strong and substantial or weak and shaky. It is rare that we can be absolutely certain, beyond the shadow of doubt, about the evidence for any claim. Our job becomes one of evaluating whether the supporting evidence is of high quality and makes the claim highly probable, or whether it is of low quality, making the claim highly dubious. There are a number of ways in which we can test the quality of the evidence.

Accuracy

The first and most important characteristic of good evidence is its accuracy. Obviously, if you know that the information provided in justification is false, it undermines, if not negates, the claim. The problem is that accuracy can be impossible to judge without an independent and infallible source of information; usually we simply do not know whether the evidence provided is accurate. We could set out to verify the information by doing research of our own; more often we use *proxies* or other cues to decide whether the information is accurate. One such cue is whether or not the author makes other obvious errors. Even "trivial" errors, like grammar and spelling mistakes, or inaccurate quotations, undermine confidence in the author's reliability and make the argument less persuasive. Other cues that suggest accuracy relate to the precision of the evidence and our judgment about the source of the information (see below).

Precision

Good evidence is appropriately precise. If we hear that a mutual fund made 9.2% last year, we are more convinced by this precise number than if we were told that it did "quite well" or even "almost 10%". Saying that the turnout at a sports event was "rather low" is less effective than saying that only 63 people attended. Overuse of ambiguous and abstract words such as *a great deal, many, often, a high probability, few, usually*, and so on is indicative of low precision. Using numbers and providing direct quotations of what people actually said are the common ways of increasing the precision of our evidence. As we noted above, precision is sometimes used as a proxy for accuracy. Saying that 63 people attended suggests that we actually counted heads or ticket stubs, and that creates the impression of accuracy.

Box 3.1: Numbers and credibility

Isn't it odd that people are so impressed by numbers? Accountants, economists, psychologists, and their ilk take ordinary events and behaviours and translate them into numbers — and then their descriptions seem to acquire a special mystique. Just because activities are expressed in a quantitative language, people find them more convincing than when they are stated in simple prose.

Why such faith in the power of numbers? It is difficult to say, but part of the explanation may be that numbers are commonly associated with science. According to philosopher Abraham Kaplan, our excessive regard for numbers is a legacy of the nineteenth century, when advances in measurement led to great strides being made in the physical sciences.[1] Kaplan cites Lord Kelvin, who wrote: "When you can measure what you are speaking about, and express it in numbers, you know something about it; but when you cannot measure it, when you cannot express it in numbers, your knowledge is of a meagre and unsatisfactory kind." Quantitative measurement — numbers — in this view is the essence of scientific progress. Still today, as in the 19th century, science is generally believed to be the key to understanding the truth about our world, and thus the basis for improvements in human life and endeavours.

Note

1. A. Kaplan, *The Conduct of Inquiry* (New York: Harper & Row Publishers, Inc., 1963).

On the other hand, it is possible to be too precise. Appropriate levels of precision vary in different fields. It would be absurd for an accountant who is filling in his time sheet to say that he spent 17 hours, 9 minutes, and 34.6 seconds on a particular project, although someone in the field of athletics, say, a sprinter might measure his running speed in hundredths of a second. A manufacturer would not list a product weight as 8.4162 kilograms; that level of precision might, on the other hand, be quite appropriate for an experimental chemist. Over-precision, like under-precision, can detract from the credibility of our evidence. **Box 3.1** offers an explanation as to why numbers are associated with accuracy.

Sufficiency

To be persuasive, an author must present sufficient evidence to support a claim. In the field of business, it is unlikely that any claim can be substantiated by a single piece of data. If you had a single personal experience with a rude cashier last week, this incident alone would not be sufficient to support the claim that retail customer service has deteriorated markedly. Just how much evidence is sufficient, however, varies with the importance of the claim and the potential damage that would occur if the claim is incorrect. For instance, a teacher might ask three students whether her slides are readable from the back of the classroom. A team of researchers might sample 40 firms to determine what business practices make firms successful. Data from thousands of people would be necessary before politicians could claim that there must be a major change in laws governing health care.

When the evidence is not sufficient to support a claim, we say that the author is guilty of the *fallacy of hasty generalization*. A *fallacy* is defined as an "erroneous, but frequently persuasive, way of being led from a reason or circumstance to a conclusion." If we jump to a conclusion based on insufficient evidence, we are engaging in fallacious thinking.

Representativeness

Let us say that an author was making a claim about the reaction of Canadians to cutbacks in government services. The author teaches at a university, so he interviews students about their attitude to cutbacks and uses these interviews as the basis for his claim. Can this be considered good evidence? No. The problem is that university students tend to be younger than Canadians in general; they also may be more educated and have less disposable income. The evidence they provide is not *representative* of all Canadians. As a rule, the variety in the sources of evidence should match the variety in the population relevant to the claim. If an author is claiming that a certain company is abusive of employees and a terrible place to work, but the only people who consented to be interviewed were people who had quit or been fired, her data may not be a fair sample. It is not representative of those employees who have continued to work happily at the firm and her claim is undermined.

The *fallacy of hasty generalization* is also relevant to unrepresentative evidence. We should not be persuaded by evidence that does not come from a fair sample of information. For example, the accuracy of a forecast provided by a polling result depends on the sample that generates the result (see **Box 3.2**).

Authority

Typically, we don't have first-hand knowledge of the evidence when we write. Even experts have first-hand knowledge of only a small sample of experience. Every one relies on the experience of others. The question is, which others? When people have special training and professional credentials, or considerable experience in a particular area, we call them *authorities* and pay close attention to the evidence they provide. When writers cite business scholars and experienced business people, this lends authority to their arguments. The currency of the source is important. Apart from the classics in any subject, current writing is usually more authoritative than older sources, particularly in rapidly changing fields where new discoveries are important.

In addition, authority is context-dependent. A legal argument needs, first and foremost, authoritative legal sources, while scientific writing will cite the evidence produced by other scientists. On the other hand, we should be less persuaded when a film star endorses a particular diet regime or a sports hero is used to convince us of the usefulness of buying car insurance; in both cases, the endorsers are providing evidence outside their area of expertise. This is termed the *fallacy of false appeal to authority*, which we commit when we accept the testimony of someone who has no expertise in the relevant area. Sadly, advertisers know how easy it is for us to succumb to this fallacy!

Another fallacy that is related to the source of the evidence is the fallacy of *argumentum ad populum* which, loosely translated, means "appeal to the people". The mere fact that many people accept a belief is not in itself evidence that the belief is correct. This fallacy has also

---

Box 3.2: Political polls and representativeness

Can political polling predict election results? Often it can. Political polls are interesting for another reason — there is an immediate and definitive confirmation of the prediction. Polling, therefore, is one of the few areas in which researchers can determine just how representative their evidence is. If the information collected by the pollsters is drawn from an unrepresentative sample of the population, the poll results will be misleading.

A classic case occurred during the U.S. presidential election of 1936. The editors at the *Literary Digest* (a news magazine) mailed 10 million postcards to voters asking them who they planned to vote for — Alf Landon or Franklin Roosevelt. Of the two million responses they received, the votes were overwhelmingly in favour of Landon. A fortnight later, Roosevelt won by the largest landslide in American history. Why had the poll been so misleading? The *Digest* developed its mailing list using telephone directories and lists of car owners. Unfortunately, this created a sample with a bias in favour of the wealthy; only richer people could afford cars and telephones in those days. Poorer people were more likely to vote for Roosevelt as his political platform stressed jobs for the unemployed.

In the same election, another poll predicted the result accurately. This poll was an early success of George Gallup,[1] who had used a more representative sample. Yet even the famous Gallup polls have proved erroneous; their poll in 1948 predicted that Thomas Dewey would win the presidential election over Harry Truman. One of the explanations for their failure was that their sampling procedure under-represented people who lived in cities and over-represented people from rural areas. Since it was largely city people who favoured Truman, the number of their votes was under-estimated by Gallup's poll.

Note

1. To learn more about the history of the Gallup polls, see <http://www.gallup.com/corporate/1357/corporate-history.aspx>.

---

been called the *bandwagon effect*. If a manufacturing manager claims that adopting a "Six Sigma" program would be good for the company just because "everybody is on the Web these days", he may be falling prey to the fallacy of *argumentum ad populum*, especially if he has no independent basis for the belief apart from the knowledge that others are doing it. He is also presuming, perhaps erroneously, that other firms exercised good judgment when they decided to adopt the Six Sigma program.

Clarity of expression

The significance of the evidence should be clearly stated. A common failing is that authors provide information as evidence, but they are not explicit about what this information signifies. Often it is the use of tables, figures, charts, or graphs that creates this problem. In our discussion of precision above, we noted that quantitative data can be quite persuasive. Data must always, however, be interpreted for the reader. Numbers do not speak for themselves. Consider the following table:

Firm	Grievance rate	Absence rate	Firm performance
1	8.2	3.97	2.7
2	3.2	3.00	6.1
3	6.5	2.71	4.6
4	7.4	2.38	3.3
5	2.6	1.84	4.9

Quite precise, but what does it mean? The author should summarize the table, explaining the meaning of the numbers and telling us clearly that he interprets the numbers as showing that unhappy employees, defined as those who file grievances and are absent relatively often, undermine the performance of the firm. Once the evidence is expressed with clarity, the table begins to take on some meaning, and we can then see how it might bolster the author's claim that good people-management improves business success. So, too, should direct quotations be clearly interpreted when they are offered in evidence.

A sample analysis

Let us look again at the passage above that claims that students today are more knowledge-able than they were in the past. Here is a sample response that evaluates the quality of the evidence presented and discusses whether, on the whole, the reader is persuaded by the argument.

Accuracy I have independent information that suggests that some aspects of the data are accurate. For one thing, I have heard on TV about government initiatives to make daycare more affordable for the increasingly large number of dual-career couples and single parents, so perhaps that means that more children are indeed attending daycare compared with 10 years ago. On the other hand, I have no means of judging the accuracy of the statements about what kids actually learn in daycare. Second, my uncle is a teacher, and a few years ago he went back to school to do a graduate diploma so that he could continue in his career. In general, it is well known that teachers have increasingly been required to seek higher education in order to obtain the positions they want. However, I am unable to evaluate the accuracy of the comment that teachers are trained in teaching more frequently than they used to be 10 years ago. And as far as computers go, there is no question in my mind that nowadays more people have computers and Internet connections; the falling prices and conversations with my friends and acquaintances make this obvious to me. In summary, my evaluation of accuracy is mixed. I need to find other clues before I'd be willing to accept the evidence as accurate in its entirety.

Precision The information is fairly general. The author talks about *the prevalence of daycare*. It would have been more convincing if I had been given a percentage of children in daycare now, compared with a percentage 10 years ago. Also, *most high school teachers* is not precise. Even the statistic that *more than 80% of Canadians have access to the Internet at home* should have been more precise. There are no specific quotes presented. To my mind, the low precision detracts from the argument. In fact, if more precise numbers had been given throughout, it might have encouraged me to believe that the author had done careful research, which would create a more positive evaluation of *accuracy* as well.

Sufficiency Three different pieces of evidence are presented. For a text of this length, this might be deemed sufficient, especially since the claim does not have important policy implications. In other words, the truth or falsity of the claim may make for lively Sunday dinner conversations, but it is unlikely to affect education policies or practices. So I am satisfied that three pieces of evidence are sufficient for this claim.

Representativeness The types of evidence are quite varied, including evidence about how people learn in early childhood as well as when they are older students. Evidence includes both the content of knowledge (the three Rs, Internet information and teachers' knowledge of their disciplines) and the process of gaining knowledge (teaching skills, the convenience and efficiency of the Internet). I might have expected to see some comparison of the school curricula then and now, but in general I am moderately satisfied with the diversity, or representativeness, of this evidence.

Authority I don't know who the author of this piece is, or what are his or her qualifications and expertise. Nor are any other authorities actually mentioned in the text. At one point, the author says that he or she *read in the newspaper* a particular bit of evidence, but does not even mention which newspaper it was. It might have been a respected publication like *The Globe and Mail* or it might have been a neighbourhood weekly where the contributors may be less careful of their facts. It might even have been a computer news publication that might be biased in favour of overstating the percent of computer ownership. The absence of any controlled scientific research detracts from the authority. The opinions of an experienced teacher might also have helped, but as it stands, the text has very low authority. If there had been more authoritative information, it might also have helped to convince me that the evidence is *accurate*.

Clarity of expression The text is easy to read because the reasons are quite clearly expressed. The points are laid out in simple sentences with the claim explicitly stated at the beginning and the evidence summarized at the end.

Overall, my reaction to this argument is mixed. While the evidence appears to be sufficient, representative, and clearly expressed, I remain uncertain about the accuracy, especially since the precision and authority are so weak. The author needs to do more work if she or he is to convince me that I should accept the claim based on this evidence.

Other objections

As you read the analysis above, you may have objected to yet another aspect of the argument. If you believe that children learn just as much at home with a parent or nanny as they learn in a daycare, or that however early kids are taught, by eight years of age there is no difference in knowledge, then the increasing use of daycare will not be deemed *relevant* to the claim. If you think that most of the time on the Internet is spent playing online games, down-loading movies, or networking with friends, then you will not accept that widespread use of technology is *relevant* to increased knowledge among students. If you believe that people's greater expertise is unrelated to how well they can communicate with lay-persons, then the advanced degrees of today's teachers will not be seen as *relevant*. All these issues of relevance are related to your **underlying assumptions**, which is the topic of the next chapter.

Effective writing

When we study an issue and report our findings, we should present our argument in the form of a claim and supporting evidence. For complex arguments, each piece of evidence may be treated in turn as if it were a claim, and further, more detailed evidence is presented in explanation. Provide your readers with the wherewithal to determine whether your evidence is sound. Citing the sources of your evidence allows your readers to judge the *authority*, and so the *accuracy* of the information. (Of course, we also cite the sources because it is essential, when we use other people's ideas, to give credit where credit is due). Your readers will judge the authority of your views as a writer, too, since the selection of inappropriate or inaccurate sources reflects on the writer's judgment. Remember that one of the purposes of writing is to join the authority chain as well, if only in the eyes of the reader. If the claim is controversial, you must recognize this and not assume that one piece of evidence is *sufficient*. As well, note that when more than one authority must be cited, the selection of experts must be *representative*. Even if the readers cannot themselves describe the range of serious views, they can see quickly enough whether your selection of evidence has the appearance of being fair. Recall, too, that appropriate *precision* and *clear* statements of the significance of your evidence are crucial. Avoid the over-use of abstract, ambiguous words in your writing.

Underlying Assumptions

Consider the following case:

> Mammon Corporation spent over two million dollars on management consultants during the years 2002–2004. Much of the money was spent on business process re-engineering; several business units were eliminated and hundreds of employees lost their jobs through downsizing. A journalist writing about Mammon's performance claimed that the money spent on the consulting engagements had been wasted. Why? In reviewing the firm's annual report, she noted that profits reported in 2005 were no higher than they had been in the previous three years.

If we translate this case into our critical thinking terms, we can state it this way:

> Claim: Mammon Corporation wasted money on re-engineering consultants.

> Evidence: Over two million dollars was spent, but profitability has stayed about the same.

Are we persuaded by the journalist's claim that the money was wasted? Only if we agree that the 2005 profitability figures are *relevant* to the claim. In other words, do we agree that the 2005 profits *should count as evidence* that money was wasted? The general principle that connects the claim to the evidence is, "If money is spent to improve a business, but profits do not go up the next year, the money has been wasted." This principle is an *underlying assumption*. It is a logical link that fills the gap between the evidence and the claim.

Some readers may decide that the journalist's underlying assumption is sound. Re-engineering is a painful and costly process, and if the payoff for the firm is minimal, then indeed the money was wasted. Other readers may question the assumption. Perhaps there *was* a significant improvement in performance, but economic conditions in the industry were much worse in 2005. If Mammon had not engaged in re-engineering, it might be in receivership today. Keeping profits from falling is excellent performance under such conditions! Perhaps the money spent on financial packages for departing employees reduced profits this year, but since this was a one-time extraordinary charge, we might expect that future profits will be much higher if the re-engineering decision were correct.

As critical thinkers, we must find and state the author's underlying assumptions. What are the suppositions upon which the argument is based? What must we believe if we are to see the evidence as relevant to the claim being made? Subjecting underlying assumptions to careful scrutiny is an important step in the critique of a text. Even when the evidence is of good quality — accurate, precise, clearly expressed, authoritative, sufficient, and representative, the argument is not acceptable if the underlying assumptions are questionable.

Reproduced with permission from Linda Dyer, *Critical Thinking for Business Students*, 2nd edition (Concord, ON: Captus Press Inc., 2011), Chapter 4.

Why are they "underlying"?

We said earlier that underlying assumptions are usually found in the "gap" that separates claims and evidence. But why does this gap exist? Shouldn't authors be more careful to show exactly why every piece of evidence is relevant to the claim? Why are underlying assumptions generally *implicit* instead of *explicit*? In other words, why are assumptions "underlying"? The answer is that once a person's assumptions about a certain topic are formed, they are the foundation of everything she thinks, says, and does on that topic. They are deeply ingrained and taken for granted. It is quite rare that she would think consciously about the assumption. It simply becomes part of her tacit belief system — as natural as walking and breathing. This taken-for-grantedness of our assumptions is true for all of us.

For example, a common assumption in our society is that children should learn how to read and write. Basic education is valued. Even when we complain about the school system, we do not wonder whether or not literacy is a good thing — its value is taken for granted. This assumption is the foundation of many debates about child labour. An activist might claim that consumers should boycott factory goods like carpets and shoes that come from the labour of children in certain Third World countries. His or her evidence is, "Children work long hours in these factories, and have neither the time nor the freedom to go to school — they remain illiterate." The activist does not usually add, "And being literate is a good thing." This underlying assumption is taken for granted by both the activist and his readers or listeners.

So there is nothing wrong, really, with having unstated underlying assumptions. Authors who leave them out are not necessarily hiding them or trying to fool us. They are just taking them for granted as we all do. The only problem is that different people have different assumptions, reflecting different values. Other assumptions represent matters of fact — beliefs about reality — and they may be quite wrong or, at least, debatable. (We will return to value and reality assumptions in a later section). So uncovering assumptions and making them explicit is an important step in evaluating any argument. The process allows us to judge whether the evidence is relevant or appropriate support for the claim, and so, whether we should accept the claim. Needless to say, we tend to pay most attention to an author's underlying assumptions when they conflict with our own point of view! It is an important discipline, however, to examine assumptions explicitly even when we agree with the author's claim.

How to find underlying assumptions

In essence, we find underlying assumptions by looking at what people write, then making guesses about what they must believe in order to have written that. We look for the gap between the evidence and the claim by asking: *What must be true if the claim is to follow from this evidence? What general principle might link this particular claim to this particular evidence?* Sometimes it is useful to put oneself in the role of the writer. *What beliefs might I expect from this type of person?* For example, if you were role-playing a CEO (downsized worker, consultant, shareholder), what would you think about the evidence about consultants being a waste of money for Mammon Corporation? Other times, it is useful to be a devil's advocate: *Could someone believe this evidence and still disagree with the claim? Why?*

Sometimes finding underlying assumptions is easy because the gap between evidence and claim is a small one. At other times, however, the gap is large and pinning down the assumptions is quite difficult. When an author is very knowledgeable about a complex topic, she may leave large gaps in her logical connections between claims and evidence. She may be taking it for granted that her readers are also very familiar with the topic. Furthermore, when a person feels strongly about a claim, his emotions may overtake the logical presentation of his ideas and reasoning, and large gaps between evidence and claim may result.

Consider the following example:

> I was listening to a radio talk show that was dealing with the topic of the North American Free Trade Agreement, trying to assess the aggregate benefits and costs to Canadians in the 10 years since NAFTA was signed in 1989. One participant maintained that free trade had proved to be a very bad idea. He described an experience that, in his view, demonstrated conclusively the problems of free trade. Here's the evidence he presented (summarized and paraphrased):
>
> > My favourite shoes have always been Clark's Wallabees. You know Clark's — the British shoe company. I've worn those shoes all my life; they are so comfortable. Some years ago, however, they disappeared from the shelves. I couldn't find them anywhere. Finally, a shoe store offered to order them specially for me. But when the shoes arrived, I could see right away that something was wrong. The soles were an odd, pale colour and they looked really awful. They didn't fit properly, and to add insult to injury, they cost more than I had ever paid for a pair of Wallabees in the past. I looked inside under the tongue to check the size. The size was correct, but it also said: Made in China! There, in a nutshell, is the problem with free trade!

Briefly put, we have

> Claim: Free trade is a bad idea

> Evidence: The Chinese-made shoes had the wrong colour, the wrong fit, and were very expensive.

What, we may justifiably ask, does this disappointing shoe order have to do with free trade? Why is this evidence relevant to his claim? From his tone, it seemed so clear to him that this evidence was telling! If it is not so obvious to you, you are not alone. It requires some thought to make his underlying assumptions explicit. Here is an interpretation of what he *might* have said had he been pressed to explain the link between the evidence and his claim:

1. Free trade has opened the floodgates to products made in less-developed countries.

2. Because labour is cheap in less-developed countries like China, the cost of manufacturing products there is low.

3. The quality of these products is also very low; for example, many shoes made in the less-developed countries are of poor quality.

4. People in Canada are sensitive to price and like the opportunity to buy cheap shoes.

5. Traditional, high-quality shoe manufacturers cannot compete at these prices. They either go out of business or start making their shoes in the less-developed countries as well, in which case the shoes are lower in quality.

Therefore, the argument is

My new Wallabees are low-quality because of free trade.

Assumptions #1, 2, 4, and 5 seem necessary to explain why Wallabees are now made in China. Most economists would agree that these assumptions are reasonable. Assumption #3 seems necessary to explain why he does not like the quality of his new Wallabees. Note that complex arguments often conceal *multiple* underlying assumptions.

The next stage for the critical thinker is evaluating these underlying assumptions. Is #3 an accurate assumption? This is debatable. His performance could just be subjective, and other people might find the new shoes look and fit just fine. Moreover, assumptions #1, 2, 4, and 5 seem inconsistent with his statement that the shoes are expensive. How could the shoes from less-developed countries have undermined the market for high quality shoes if they were not cheaper? In his price comparison, has he taken inflation into account? Is he taking into account the fact that perhaps he is being charged more for this special order? In sum, we will need some more careful explanations before we accept the story of the shoes as relevant evidence for the undesirability of free trade.

Reconstructing and evaluating underlying assumptions sometimes requires that we *learn more* about issues and a variety of points of view. Knowledge of economics helps us to flesh out the assumptions being made about free trade. As you continue to take courses in business, your knowledge base will increase, which will allow you to detect underlying assumptions more easily, and to be able to judge their worth.

Reality assumptions

There are two major types of assumptions, *reality assumptions* and *value assumptions*. Reality assumptions are our beliefs about what events have taken place, what exists, or how things work in the world. In other words, they are our beliefs about reality, the way things really are. Our first-hand experiences, our conversations with others, the things we read or see on television — all these shape our beliefs. In particular, when we have considerable experience that is consistent with a given belief, the belief becomes *taken for granted*. The example given in the section above is based on reality assumptions about the economics of free trade. We can guess that the man on the radio talk show had developed these ideas about how international trade works through reading, conversation, and his experiences as a consumer over many years.

Another reality assumption was encountered in the previous chapter in the text that claimed that students are more knowledgeable now than they used to be. One piece of evidence offered was that teachers have more advanced degrees today than was the case in the past. The evidence is relevant only on condition that (a) People with advanced degrees have more and better quality knowledge; and (b) they can pass this better knowledge base on to students effectively. These two underlying assumptions describe the author's taken-for-granted beliefs

---

Box 4.1: Reality assumptions about employees

It's human nature for people to do as little work as they can get away with; the average employee is indolent, unambitious and dislikes responsibility. Employees must be supervised closely or they will not work to fulfill organizational goals. If, however, they are given enough money, they will generally accept direction and will be productive.

These assumptions about employees are the basis of the motivational policies, practices, and programs of many firms. Douglas McGregor, a management scholar, coined the term **Theory X** to label this set of beliefs. McGregor proposed that Theory X assumptions were an inadequate description of human motivation. He made an alternative set of propositions, which he called **Theory Y:** *People are not passive or lazy by nature. They only become so because that is how they are treated in organizations. The capacity for assuming responsibility and using creativity and imagination to further organizational goals does exist in employees. It is up to managers to create the organizational conditions that will release employees' potential.*[1]

McGregor first formulated Theory X and Theory Y over 40 years ago. In those days, Theory X, with its focus on external control of behaviour, was the conventional view. McGregor described Theory Y, which relied on self-control and self-direction, as a bold and innovative proposal.

Arguably, management today is still dominated by Theory X reality assumptions. For example, when managers install systems to monitor employees' use of the Internet during working hours, they are acting on Theory X assumptions. They may believe that without control employees will spend company time in frivolous surfing of the net. Firms that hire roving, "mystery" customers to check up on the service provided by their sales representatives are reflecting a Theory X assumption that, without this surveillance, employees would be lackadaisical or rude. It is true that we do hear a lot about empowerment and self-managing teams nowadays. These are practices that are consistent with a Theory Y framework. But we have to ask ourselves whether these terms represent a true change in management assumptions — one often has the impression that managers are just paying lip service to these ideas; all the while their actual behaviour is thoroughly "X".

McGregor anticipated that progress toward the goal of Theory Y would be slow and difficult. After generations of Theory X management, it was unlikely that employees or managers could shift to a Theory Y framework overnight. Clearly, many firms are taking steps in the direction of Theory Y, but it is equally clear that Theory X continues to be the predominant reality assumption among managers today.

Note

1. D. McGregor, "The Human Side of Enterprise", *Management Review*, November 1957, pp. 41–49.

---

about what makes a teacher effective. **Box 4.1** presents another example of reality assumptions in organizations.

Challenging reality assumptions

Once an author's reality assumptions are made explicit, the next step is to evaluate their accuracy. As mentioned above, this usually consists of critiquing the quality of the assumptions. In the free trade example, we could argue that the assumptions were logically inconsistent, and did not take into account important economic variables such as inflation. Another way of challenging reality assumptions is to provide data that would show that the assumption is incorrect. In the "knowledgeable students" example, we might show that people who have developed great expertise often find it *harder* to communicate their knowledge to lay people, since they have forgotten what it was like to be so naive. We might present data to show that only a small percentage of graduate programs offer serious training in how to teach. *In general, to challenge reality assumptions, we must present information showing that the author's notions of reality and how the world works are debatable or just plain wrong.*

Value assumptions

Values are our ideals, our standards of right and wrong, the way things ought to be. We can recognize them through the use of words like *ought, should, desirable, unacceptable,* and so on: "You should keep your promises," "Teachers ought to treat students fairly," or "Co-operative work is desirable." Often, values are learned early in childhood from our parents, teachers, classmates, or through religion; other values are adopted later on, in our adult lives. Some values are very commonly held: being honest, helping those less fortunate than ourselves, having the freedom to express our views as citizens are widely seen as good things. In the world of business, there are many specific values that embody our ideas of what is right and wrong. Bosses *ought* to be helpful and encouraging to their subordinates. They *ought not* to use their power to gain sexual favours. Large, successful companies *should* exhibit social responsibility by making donations to community, cultural, or sporting events, and by not polluting the environment. Businesses *should* adopt strategies that allow them to stay competitive. **Box 4.2** illustrates how "competitiveness" is part of our everyday life.

Although there is widespread agreement about some values in our society, *value conflicts* are also quite common. Because I value honesty, I might feel I should tell the boss about my co-worker who confessed to me that he'd lied about his qualifications for the job. You might disagree, feeling that I shouldn't tell the boss, since you value loyalty to one's peer group. Sometimes these value conflicts happen within the individual. When approached by a beggar, we may feel torn between compassion and the feeling that people ought to work for their living. Values may be *ranked* differently by different people. Some people feel much more strongly about corporate social responsibility or sexual harassment, for example, than others do.

Challenging value assumptions

Value conflicts and differential value rankings are reasons for disagreements about the relevance of the evidence presented for a claim. In the following example, three business students are discussing the term paper about a successful company which they must write for one of their courses.

Box 4.2: Competitiveness as a value

"Life has become for us an endless succession of contests." Thus begins a critique by author Alfie Kohn of the value our society places on competitiveness.[1] Throughout our school years, he notes, we are trained to compete, to think of our classmates as standing in the way of our own success. The entire economic system is based on competition: "It is not enough that we struggle against our colleagues at work to be more productive; we also must compete for the title of Friendliest Employee."[2] Even when we socialize with people from other departments of the organization or other companies, this often takes the form of competitive games, like softball or golf.

The examples of competitiveness in the world of business are countless. Margaret Wente, a journalist with *The Globe and Mail* newspaper, notes that "the prevailing metaphors of business are borrowed from the battlefield. Your competition is the enemy, and your job is to grind them to dust. Takeovers are battles. Marketing is warfare."[3] The legendary Ray Kroc, the founder of McDonald's restaurant chain, once said: "What do you do when your competitor is drowning? Get a live hose and stick it in his throat!" Ricardo Petrella works in forecasting in the European Community Commission and decries what he calls the "gospel of competitiveness". One negative outcome he describes is accelerating obsolescence — firms must constantly develop new products, not because there is anything wrong with the old ones, but just because of the pressure to stay ahead of the competition.

Even when individuals or groups are not directly competing with one another, we seem to have an urge to compile rankings of who is best and who is not. Business magazines regularly publish lists of the top 100 firms, cutting across diverse industries. News magazines report on the best universities in the country. In 2004, a ranking of the wealthiest Canadians was made public. The late Ken Thompson, chairman of the publishing company Thompson Corp., with a net worth of over $22 billion, was in the number one position at the time. One is tempted to wonder: What exactly is the point of this ranking? In 2001, the federal government reported with concern that Canada's ranking in the ability to innovate had slipped to 16th place internationally. They set a goal to bring Canada to 5th place in the rankings by 2010. What will this mean to us? To others?

For many people, competitiveness is seen not just as the best way of doing things, but as "a fact of life" that is, the *only* way of doing things. Are there viable alternatives? One such alternative is co-operation — working with others, says Alfie Kohn. Or independence — comparing oneself not to others, but to an objective or self-set standard.

Notes

1. A. Kohn, *No Contest*, Revised edition (Boston: Houghton Mifflin, 1992), p. 2.
2. M. Lamey, "Downside Seen to Competitiveness", *Montreal Gazette*, June 8, 1992.
3. M. Wente, "Why I'll Never Be CEO", *The Globe and Mail*, October 25, 1992, D7.

Rosa: We should do our paper on Hotshot Inc. It's a great company.

Katy: Why do you think Hotshot is so great?

Rosa: Its founder is fabulously wealthy. He's worth billions! And it's all from this one company.

Tom: Yes, she's right. I've read a lot about Mr. Hotshot and his company in the newspapers, and the company's share prices have been climbing steadily for years now.

Katy: Well I don't think that Hotshot's so wonderful. Sure, the top guys are making a lot of money, but the company is horribly exploitative. They treat their employees like dog turds, and they use strong-arm techniques to squeeze out their smaller competitors.

Rosa: But that's just business. You can't argue with success!

Rosa and Tom clearly value the *material success* of the entrepreneur and owners, whereas Katy places more importance on *corporate social responsibility* as a measure of what makes a firm successful. Katy does not deny the accuracy of the evidence provided about Mr. Hotshot's financial worth and the return on shareholders' investments. She just does not believe that profits are the most important aspect of what makes a great firm, so the financial information is dismissed as irrelevant. Rosa and Tom, with their focus on monetary worth, may also accept the characterization of Hotshot's business strategies, but they maintain that these practices are of little importance in evaluating the company. Each side could continue to add more evidence about financial success or about business strategies, but the additional evidence would not persuade the other side, since the disagreement about the underlying value assumptions remains. Can Katy persuade the other two that Hotshot's billions are not worthy of consideration? Can Rosa and Tom convince Katy that Hotshot's aggressive tactics are perfectly acceptable? It might be difficult in either case.

Values, as we have said, are often developed early in life and are quite resistant to change. It is not easy to make a profiteer out of someone who has been taught early in life that the love of money is the root of all evil. In the same way, it might take an extraordinary and jolting personal experience to create an iconoclast out of someone who has always believed in the value of obedience to authority. Not all values are so deep-seated, of course, but our value preferences form a significant part of our self-concept and are not relinquished lightly. In general, challenging value assumptions is a more difficult task than challenging descriptive assumptions. *The task of the critical thinker becomes one of demonstrating that the author's argument is rooted in a particular, idiosyncratic set of value assumptions. Since other people might have a different, but equally valid, set of values, the argument is therefore not universally acceptable.*

Effective writing

Critical thinking about underlying assumptions can help you to improve your own writing. A large quantity of evidence for your claims and ensuring that the evidence is of good quality are both necessary but not enough to be convincing. It is also important to make it clear that each piece of evidence is relevant. As you compose your text, articulate all your underlying assumptions and examine them with care. Keep asking yourself the following questions: Is this assumption *always* true? Are there circumstances in which the reality assumptions might not hold? Are there people whose value preferences might be different or in conflict with my own? Are all of the assumptions that underlie my argument logically consistent with one another? This self-questioning will allow you to understand the foundations of your own rea-

---

Box 4.3: Invented dialogues

A fruitful way of exploring underlying assumptions is by constructing an **invented dialogue**. You start by imagining a discussion between two people who hold reality or value assumptions that conflict. This exercise is easier if you can think of people you actually know who have opposing views. Write a brief dialogue, about five or six exchanges between the two participants. Try to make their comments persuasive, lively, and natural. It often helps to read your dialogue out loud.

Here is an example of an invented dialogue between a Human Resource manager [HR] and a Vice-President, Operations [VP].

HR: Well, we've boiled it down to two potential candidates for the position. Both candidates have the relevant work experience and education. They both have impeccable track records with rave reviews from previous employers.

VP: Great! I'm looking forward to interviewing them myself.

HR: The first candidate is a woman in her mid-thirties who's been working...

VP: Hold on, a woman?!? You know we've never had a woman in this position before. She would have to supervise over 50 men. I sure hope your other candidate is a man.

HR: Come on, Eric. You know we can't discriminate against anyone based solely on gender.

VP: Who's talking about discrimination? We're talking about a person who will fit the shop-floor culture. I'm not against hiring a woman for a middle-management position, but we're talking here about the guys on the floor! They've never had to report to a woman before. Her life will be hell!

HR: Well, things will have to change around here, unless you prefer to have the Human Rights Commission knocking on our door. And then there's the Employment Equity bill which says....

VP: What the devil does the government know about our shop floor? We at headquarters understand about cultural diversity, and how it makes good business sense in a global environment. But this is a particular case. We simply can't hire a woman to handle those boys in the shop. It's a pretty rough environment down there.

HR: Well, with your attitude, of course it will never work. If head office backs a woman, you'll send a clear message to everyone that we value people for their skills, not their sex or race.

VP: I can picture the guys' reaction already. I know it won't fly.

How would you characterize the conflicting assumptions of these speakers? Consider their reality and value assumptions about (a) the relative importance of education and experience; (b) compatibility with the company culture; (c) vigilance of government agencies; (d) gender roles; (e) impact of top management attitudes on workers; and so on.

Inventing dialogues of this sort can help you to clarify your own assumptions and train yourself to develop a richer understanding of alternative points of view.

---

soning, and to spot any weaknesses in your argument before your readers do. One method that aids self-questioning about conflicting assumptions is the development of *invented dialogues*, described in **Box 4.3**.

Next, you must decide which of the assumptions you should include explicitly in the text and which can be left unstated. You may find that the majority of the assumptions are so obvious that they may remain implicit. But take care! What seems obvious to you may not be obvious to all your readers. In particular, if you can think of any circumstances in which your reality assumptions might not be true, it is best to describe these scenarios explicitly and limit your argument accordingly. Think about who your audience is likely to be. If they do not share your values, your carefully compiled evidence will be seen as irrelevant or wrong-headed. Think about the type of evidence that would be convincing for your expected readers. State your value preferences explicitly and argue for them so that your audience can at least appreciate your viewpoint. In the final chapter of this handbook, we will discuss *techniques of persuasion*, developing the notion of how a focus on your audience can help you to make your writing more convincing, even when your audience initially disagrees with you.

Causal Claims

Many of the claims authors make can be classified as causal claims. They argue that certain events or factors *(causes)* are responsible for bringing about other events or situations *(effects)*. Cause-and-effect relationships are an essential aspect of understanding the business environment. In fact, most of our attempts to make sense of the world around us — whenever we pose the question: *Why?* — lead to cause-and-effect explanations. "Why are sales of our firm's frozen foods falling?" "Why are there so few women CEOs in large companies?" "Why is there currently a boom in the home renovation industry?" "Why is Professor Merton so well liked by his students?" When we provide answers for these questions, we are identifying causes for observed outcomes. For example, we may determine that sales of frozen foods are falling because consumers are increasingly concerned about high salt content in their foods. In this cases, concern for salt content would be the cause; falling sales would be the effect.

Sometimes we know the "cause" and we are trying to predict the "effect". "What will happen if we decrease our printing budget by 15%?" "If we allow commercial advertising on the walls of public institutions like hospitals and schools, what reactions can we anticipate?" "What would be the result of an increase in the per litre tax on gasoline?" When governments make decisions about taxes on gasoline *(cause)*, there is much discussion about possible outcomes, such as increased use of public transit, decreased urban pollution, or increased prices of products that need to be transported *(effects)*.

Causal reasoning is natural — and useful

Trying to identify connections between causes and effects is basically human nature — as natural as breathing. Very young children start asking *Why?* as they take the first steps towards developing their understanding of the world. Much of our thinking is devoted to figuring out why things occurred and predicting what is likely to happen next. Without causal links between situations, nothing would make sense. Every event would be random and disconnected. Life would simply be a "buzzing, blooming confusion". The identification of causal relationships gives meaning to the world that surrounds us.

Cause-and-effect relationships are also the basis for decision making and reasoned action. For example, the belief that consumers' concerns about nutrition are changing might lead the marketing department of our firm to develop new products, such as low-sodium frozen foods. It is also likely to change the way these products are advertized.

Reproduced with permission from Linda Dyer, *Critical Thinking for Business Students*, 2nd edition (Concord, ON: Captus Press Inc., 2011), Chapter 5.

Causal reasoning can be very difficult

Although we recognize the importance of establishing causal relationships, it is also true that doing so is very difficult. In the complex situations we encounter in the world of business, it is sometimes difficult to find reasonable and likely causes for certain outcomes. "Why is innovation lower in some countries than in others?" "Why is the presence of graffiti on the increase in our cities?" Causes can be elusive.

Even more frequently, the difficulty in determining cause-and-effect links arises from the fact that outcomes may have multiple causes. Let's say you notice that winter is over and you've managed to escape your usual winter cold. Well, you think, it must be because you've been drinking that special echinacea herbal tea your Aunt Minnie gave you, saying it is good for avoiding colds. You decide to call her and tell her it worked. But upon further thought, you realize there may have been other causes for your good health during the season. It was an unusually mild winter, with few dramatic swings of temperature. Also, since your new apartment is not far from downtown, you've been able to walk to school and your job instead of taking the bus, and so you have had less contact with other people. You've started exercising twice a week as well, and you recall reading somewhere that being in good physical shape helps to ward off colds. In short, there could have been many potential causes, so you are not sure any more that Aunt Minnie's herbal tea was really a cause of your cold-free winter. On their own, the other factors could well have caused your good health, quite independently of whether or not you drank the tea.

As critical thinkers, we must examine carefully the causal claims of authors. Are they describing genuine cause-effect relationships? Can we think of plausible *rival causal explanations* that would account for exactly the same events? If we can, then we do not really know whether it is the factor proposed by the author, the rival cause we came up with, or a combination of both causes that led to the observed effect. The author's claim becomes less convincing.

Let us now look at some examples of plausible rival causes. There are three types of rival causes that will concern us here: rival causes related to differences between groups; correlation between characteristics; and the *post hoc ergo propter hoc* fallacy. We will explain each of these in turn.

Differences between groups

An alumni survey produces evidence showing that graduates of Academy University are more successful on the job market than graduates of Ivory Tower University. The administrators at Academy claim that this success is caused by its superior programs — the up-to-date curriculum content, the talented teaching, and the advanced technological resources available at their institution. The top-notch facilities and programs cause its students to develop excellent, marketable skills, which impress company recruiters and lead to rapid and remunerative job offers. If you come to Academy University, their brochures claim, you'll do better than going to that other school.

Perhaps. But is the content of the academic programs the only difference between Academy and Ivory Tower graduates? It may turn out that Academy has more-rigorous admission requirements, so the students who *enter* their programs are smarter than the Ivory Tower students to start with. Even if Academy teachers had been dull as ditch water and used blackboard chalk instead of clickers, their smart students would still have excelled on the job market. Academy is claiming that their *programs* are the cause of their comparative success. Our rival cause is that their *selectivity in admissions* causes success. It is also possible that a combination of both factors is the true (multiple) cause. Another possibility is that Academy University is in an urban centre where many students have good part-time jobs, while Ivory Tower is in a rural setting and few students have part-time jobs of any consequence. It might be, then, that it is the *work experience* of the graduates that is causing the differences in success, and the academic programs are completely irrelevant.

In general, whenever an author says that an outcome is caused by a specific difference between groups, we must pause and think: *Are there any other differences between these groups that may be relevant?* If we can think of some other relevant factor that differs between the groups, we have a plausible rival cause.

Here's another example for you to think about. It has been noted that women who choose to have their babies at home have healthier babies than women whose babies are born in the hospital. One causal explanation that has been offered is that a hospital is an uncaring, unnatural environment and is no place for the natural function of bringing babies into the world. The heavy focus on medical technology in the hospital environment, and the stress this produces in pregnant women causes physical problems in newborn infants. People who believe this explanation often recommend that if a woman stays at home, and has her baby using the services of a midwife in familiar surroundings, there are psychological and physical benefits for both mother and child. Briefly put, the argument is that the hospital setting causes health problems in infants. Can you come up with plausible rival explanations of this relationship?

Correlation between characteristics

Here is an example of the type of writing often seen in the business press:

> It is important for all companies to have a strategic vision. What does your company stand for? What are your business values and mission? How do you see your future? Your firm's vision must be clearly communicated to employees at all levels of the organization. Business scholars have studied these "visionary" companies and found that they enjoy greater long-term success than other companies whose vision is less pervasive. The more careful you are to articulate a clear vision, the better the performance of your firm. Why? Because vision inspires employees and focuses their energies. Poor visioning leaves your resources scattered and your employees unmotivated. Start developing your vision now — don't get left behind!

The claim here is that a stronger company vision causes better performance. A weaker vision causes poorer performance. The authors have taken a *correlation* between these two factors and are claiming a *causal* link. Their explanation that a clearly communicated vision results in motivation and focus seems reasonable.

But is this the only explanation that will fit with the observations? Is it not possible that the link works in reverse? It may be that the better the performance of the firm, the more attention is paid to it in the media. Journalists visit the company, interview its managers, and write up their description of what it is that "makes the organization tick". The news reports are widely read, and the readers include the firm's own employees and managers, who end up with greater awareness and understanding of their company, its mission, and values. In this interpretation, it is the company's stellar performance that is causing the strong vision to develop. If this rival explanation turns out to be true, working on your company's vision is a dead-end strategy. Instead of vision causing performance, performance is actually causing vision. This is an example of *reverse causation*. In general, when two factors, A and B, are correlated, it may be that A is causing B, but it is also possible that B is causing A.

Yet another interpretation must be considered. Sometimes two factors may be strongly correlated, but there is no causal link at all between the two. It is well known, for instance, that when ice-cream consumption is high in a given year, the rate of heart attacks among the population is also very high. It would be absurd to suggest that eating ice cream brings on a heart attack within a year. It would be even more ridiculous to claim that when someone has a heart attack, this creates a craving for ice cream. Neither direct causation nor reverse causation is likely. The correlation is high because there is a *third factor* that is linked to both ice-cream consumption and heart attacks. This third factor, of course, is heat. The hotter the temperature, the more ice cream is eaten, and the hotter it gets, the greater the number of people who succumb to heart attacks. No matter how strong the correlation between two variables, we cannot automatically assume that there is a causal connection.

The ice-cream/heart-attack example is clear-cut, but in other cases it may be harder to see that causal links are not really there. Returning to the case of vision, it is possible that there is no causal relationship at all between the strength of strategic vision and firm performance. Perhaps there is a third factor linked to both vision and performance, say, the *use of information technology (IT)* in the company. Firms that embrace IT and other technological advances may be the better performers in their industries because they are the first to exploit the new technologies and cost efficiencies, or their employees may work longer hours because they can log in to the company site in order to work from home (that is, "use of IT" causes "performance"). As well, in technologically advanced companies, there may be much more communication among employees — using the company intranet, visiting the company website, and so on. The accessibility and sharing of information about the firm's strategies improves awareness and understanding of the vision among managers and employees (that is, "use of IT" causes "vision"). So there may be neither a direct causal link nor a reverse causal link between vision and performance, apart from the operation of this third factor, the use of IT.

Another third factor could be having an innovative and charismatic CEO. An innovative CEO makes decisions before the firm's competitors do, creating competitive advantage and better firm performance. An innovative CEO makes changes that catch the attention of employees, who talk about the new ideas throughout the company, creating a strong vision. Again, there may be no direct link between vision and performance.

In summary, a correlation between two factors might be explained by one of three causal links. There may be a direct causal relationship, a reverse causal relationship, or no relationship, except through the effect of a third factor. Whenever an author describes a correlation and proposes a causal explanation for this correlation, as critical thinkers we must ponder the likelihood of reverse causation as well as the third factor effect.

Now think about this case:

> Strong entrepreneurial ambition, that is, desire to start one's own business, has been found to be associated with lower interest in higher education. Several business thinkers have discussed this inverse correlation, arguing that people who have an entrepreneurial personality are "hands-on", creative, and risk-taking. Entrepreneurship is quite different from the world of higher learning, which tends to be structured, low-risk, and detached from the excitement of the real world of business. The stronger your entrepreneurial personality, the more likely you are to shun university, preferring to start your own company as early as possible.

Can you come up with other possible causal explanations of this link?

The *post hoc ergo propter hoc* fallacy

An opinion piece in a community newspaper reads:

> Community policing came to our neighbourhood last summer. The police officers are now much more accessible than they were before; they ride around the streets on bicycles instead of patrol cars, and they often wear shorts and look much more friendly than they used to. The new police station is much smaller than the old one and looks more inviting — you can see plants in the windows and there is occasionally an open-house where the neighbours can go in and meet the police officers. This new strategy is very effective. I read in the newspaper recently that acts of vandalism and theft have decreased in the neighbourhood over the past 12 months. I know I feel much more comfortable when I am walking home from work this summer.

The claim is that the community policing strategy has caused the decrease in crime. The reasoning appears to be that the police now have much more of a presence in the neighbourhood than used to be the case. Presumably, this increased visibility has discouraged would-be criminals, and so rates of criminal activity have gone down. But is this the only plausible explanation? It may be that the past 12 months have seen a high frequency of inclement weather — perhaps is has been colder, rainier, or snowier than usual — and this has kept people at home and off the streets, both the potential criminals and the potential victims. In other words, unusual weather would have led to a drop in the crime rate, whether or not the policing strategy had changed. Here's another possibility:

> Economic conditions in the city have been brighter over the past year than they had been for quite some time. There have been announcements in the newspaper that the unemployment rate is decreasing. The house construction and renovation markets are enjoying a surge of activity. If more people are finding jobs and are thus better able to make ends meet, this alone could have caused a drop in the crime rate, quite independently of the police officers' bicycles and open-house sessions.

Post hoc ergo propter hoc is a Latin phrase. Loosely translated it means: After this *(post hoc)* therefore *(ergo)* because of this *(propter hoc)*. *After* the new policing strategy was introduced, the crime rate decreased; *therefore*, we assume that the decrease in crime must have occurred *because of* the strategy. This is a fallacy, an error in our reasoning. Just because an event was followed by another event does not necessarily mean that the first event caused the second.

Superstitious behaviour often has its root in the *post hoc ergo propter* hoc fallacy. Some years ago, a student of mine came to an in-class test with a large key ring in the shape of a rubber animal, which he put on his desk. He had got the key ring from his girlfriend the previous term and happened to have it during a test he took. He did very well on the test, much better than he thought he would. Now the animal has become his test-taking mascot — always at his side to give him good luck. Having the animal and doing well on exams were associated, so he claims that the former caused the latter. I am certain that to a great extent, he was joking about this superstition, but it continues to affect his behaviour. Similarly, colleagues of mine have lucky ties, lucky pens, even a lucky restaurant in which to have lunch before a big presentation. All of these are claimed, tongue-in-cheek, to cause success at work. All started with events that were given a *post hoc ergo propter hoc* causal explanation.

A friend of mine was called Rita throughout her childhood and adolescence. When she started working and moved out on her own, she changed her name to Catherine. "Rita is an unlucky name," she maintains. "My life was miserable until I changed my name, so I don't want anybody calling me Rita again, and bringing problems into my life." If we apply our critical thinking skills to my friend's causal reasoning, can we come up with plausible alternatives as to what, apart from her new name, may be causing her presently happy life?

Can we ever be sure?

We have shown that there are often multiple causes for an outcome. Whenever an author makes a causal claim, it is generally not difficult for the astute reader to come up with a rival cause that provides an equally good explanation for the outcome. It may be that the author's proposed cause is indeed the correct explanation. Any one of the plausible rival causes that occur to the critical reader may be the true interpretation.

What is more, there may be *multiple causes*, that is, the correct explanation may involve more than one of these causal factors.

How, then, can we ever be sure about causal relationships? Can we ever rule out alternative causes and be confident that it is indeed one particular cause that leads to a given effect? Often, it is important that we be sure of what is causing what. What would be the point of long hours spent working on our company's vision statement if it is not the true cause of business success? Why invest in all the changes necessary for community policing if we are not sure that our investments will really pay off in a low crime rate? In the applied, practical world of business, we have to be confident about causal relationships if we are to avoid wasting money and human effort.

Experimental research

Testing causal claims is the raison-d'être of *experimental designs in business research*. The primary aim of an *experiment* is to rule out rival causal explanations. Experimental research designs increase our confidence in causal explanations. Here is an example of the simple experiment in business. Let's say that we want to determine the best schedule of rest breaks for call centre agents. Do they work most productively if they are given one hour for lunch, a 15-minute break in the morning, and a 15-minute break in the afternoon? Would it be better to allow agents to vary the length and timing of the breaks however they please, as long as the total is 90 minutes? We call these two scenarios the 15-60-15 schedule and the 90-variable schedule. The next step is to separate the agents into two groups, each of which works to one of the two schedules. After a few work days, we compare the productivity of the two groups and find that the productivity of the 90-variable schedule agents is higher than that of the 15–60–15 agents. We conclude that having flexibility in rest breaks causes higher productivity.

You can see that it would be important to ensure that there are no differences between the two groups *other than* the different schedules. If, for example, all the native English-speaking agents were put in one group and all the non-native speakers in the other, we would not know whether the productivity difference was due to language, schedule, or to both factors. Language would be a plausible alternative causal explanation. If one group had brand new equipment and the other group had older equipment, or if one group worked in a noisier environment than the other, differences in equipment or noise levels would be plausible alternative explanations.

Researchers use a technique called *random assignment* to ensure that the characteristics of the people in different experimental groups are identical. With random assignment, every call centre agent, whatever his/her language, gender, skill level, job tenure, etc, has an equal chance of being in either group. Researchers would also control variables such as noise levels, pay rates, etc., keeping them as similar as possible across groups so that they can rule out alternative causal explanations. Random assignment and control of extraneous variables help researchers to establish causal relationships with confidence. **Box 5.1** presents another example of an experiment in business.

This is just a very brief introduction to experimental research. Close study of how to conduct valid experiments is beyond the purview of this handbook, but it is important to note that experimental research in business has become an essential tool in improving our understanding of business practice. In **Box 5.2**, you will find a description of a classic set of experiments in organizational research.

Formal experimentation can be costly and is not a tool that can be applied to every question. Intelligent, critical thinking, however, can be. As readers and managers, it is always important to be able to discern when an author has a strong, well-supported causal claim, and when the causal claims are contestable and open to many interpretations. In the latter case, when we recognize the existence of alternative causal explanations, we must use our logic to assess the *likelihood* of each possible cause. The most likely cause (or causes) will shape our overall evaluation of the author's claims and the seriousness with which we will take her argument.

Box 5.1: Charismatic leadership and task performance

What is the best kind of boss to have? One who inspires and excites you, one who helps you understand the details of the tasks to be done, or one who is friendly and concerned about your personal welfare? Business researchers label these three types of bosses as *charismatic* leaders, *structuring* leaders, and *considerate* leaders, respectively. Which of these three different leadership styles is best at motivating subordinates to work hard and effectively? Researchers Jane Howell, a professor at the University of Western Ontario, and Peter Frost, a professor at the University of British Columbia, conducted an **experiment** to examine this causal relationship between *leadership style* and *task performance*.[1]

The research participants were 144 undergraduate business students at the University of British Columbia who were each asked to play the role of a general manager dealing with a pile of items in his or her in-basket. The in-basket contained letters, reports, and memos, and the participants had to exercise their managerial judgment about how to handle each item — making decisions, delegating tasks, requesting further information, and so on.

The task was presented to each student by a leader who used one of the three leadership styles. Although the participants did not realize it, the leader was actually an actor who had been carefully trained by the researchers to direct the work of the students using the three styles. As a *charismatic leader*, she presented an exciting goal, explaining how the task could foster links between the university and downtown businesses and would have a long-term effect on the future commerce programs at UBC. Her tone was engaging, her body language was dynamic, and she expressed confidence that the participant would perform very well at the task. As a *considerate leader*, she was friendly and approachable, showing concern for the comfort and satisfaction of the participant. Her tone was warm; she leaned towards the participant, smiling and keeping eye contact. As a *structuring leader*, she went through the directions point by point, explaining in detail how the task should be done and emphasized the standards of work performance. Her facial expressions and body language were neutral and business-like.

The participants were *randomly assigned* to one of the three experimental conditions. Apart from these differences in leadership style, however, they all worked in the same workroom, had the same in-basket exercise, and were given the same length of time to work on the task. The leader always followed the same scripts and wore identical clothes — a dark, conservative business suit. By *controlling* these extraneous variables, the researchers were ensuring that the only difference between the three groups of participants was the leadership style they encountered. They can have confidence, therefore, that the level of performance achieved by the students can be attributed to the type of leadership style and nothing else.

So how did it turn out? You may be interested to know that the researchers found that charismatic leadership caused the best task performance. Participants who had the charismatic leader had the highest quality of work and suggested the most courses of action in the in-basket task. The other two styles caused similar, lower levels of performance. The researchers concluded that training leaders to be charismatic is not only possible, but desirable. The study needs to be repeated in a "real-life" work place, but on the basis of this experiment, it would appear that the boss's charisma causes high task performance in subordinates.

Note

1. This research study was published in J. Howell and P. Frost, "A Laboratory Study of Charismatic leadership", *Organizational Behaviour and Human Decision Processes*, 43 (1989), 243–69.

Box 5.2: The Hawthorne experiments

The Hawthorne experiments were a series of large-scale experimental studies that formed an early milestone in the understanding of behaviour in organizations. Between 1924 and 1933, a group of investigators from the Harvard Business School conducted research studies at the Hawthorne plant of the Western Electric Company. The research was funded in part by manufacturers of electricity, who wanted to show that higher levels of electrical lighting would cause improvements in industrial efficiency.

One of the studies employed two groups of workers whose average skill and productivity was the same. The first group worked under a constant illumination of 11 foot-candles. (A foot-candle is equal to the amount of light thrown by one candle on a square foot of a surface which is one foot away.) The second group, the test group, were asked to work under progressively lower levels of light, going down to less than two foot-candles. The experimenters expected that the productivity of the test-group workers would decline as illumination got poorer. Instead, production increased in *both* groups. This increase in productivity was also found when the researchers changed other working conditions, such as the length and frequency of rest periods and the length of the work day. When improvements in working conditions were taken away after several months, production continued to rise.

It appeared that whether lighting, work schedules, and other working conditions were improved or made poorer, the productivity of the workers increased. In other words, any manipulation of working conditions, either for better or worse, improved productivity. The researchers concluded that variations in working conditions could *not* therefore be the *cause* of improved production. The cause seemed to lie in the fact that the workers who participated in the research were given *special attention* by the researchers and the plant managers. Getting special attention had been a much more powerful impetus to perform than any of the experimental conditions. This phenomenon has since been observed in innumerable experiments and has become known as the "Hawthorne effect".

Note: For more about the Hawthorne experiments, see F. Roethlisberger, and W. Dickson, *Management and the Worker* (Boston: Harvard University Press, 1966 [c. 1939]).

Techniques of Persuasion

What makes an argument persuasive? How do authors convince readers to agree with their point of view? A variety of factors, several of which we have encountered in the earlier chapters, affect the persuasiveness of a text. Certainly the *quality of the evidence* presented for the claims is one such factor; we are persuaded when the evidence is accurate, precise, sufficient, representative, authoritative, and clear. But just as it is essential to evaluate the evidence that is *presented*, it is equally important to think about the evidence that is *omitted*. Think, for example, of the possible reaction of an author who encounters a piece of evidence that contradicts his claim. In composing his text, he decides to omit several bits of data that are inconsistent with the conclusion that he wants to draw. As critical thinkers, we must ask ourselves: What evidence is left out because it is incompatible with the argument?

The *soundness of the causal argument* also makes a text persuasive. Yet it often happens that evidence presented may be compatible with more than one causal interpretation. When alternative causal explanations exist, this undermines confidence in the author's conclusion. For example, having found evidence of a strong relationship between A and B, the author might believe strongly that A caused B, but knows that another interpretation is that B caused A, a reverse causal explanation. How do writers deal most effectively with this problem of *rival explanations*?

Finally, we have seen that the extent to which readers *agree with the underlying assumptions* of a writer plays an important role in their decision to accept or challenge the author's claims. *Conflicts in value preferences or reality assumptions* are common. How can an author be persuasive when her audience may not share her underlying beliefs or values?

The foregoing issues are related to the basic structure of an argument — claims, evidence, and assumptions. A further aspect to be considered is the language and writing style used in the text. How does an author present her case most effectively, bringing her readers to appreciate fully the significance of her evidence? Do her words capture our attention and imagination, bringing her claims into clear (and persuasive) focus? In this chapter, we shall also introduce *rhetoric*, which is the use of language to convince.

A "how-to" approach

The approach taken in this chapter is to describe *how to* build a persuasive argument; we shall then use this information to understand why certain authors are convincing, while others are not. We answer the questions posed above, deciding how to deal with contradictory evidence, alternative causal explanations, and value conflicts, in a way that will be most persuasive to an audience. We take a brief look at effective use of words and other rhetorical devices that help us to present our claims most convincingly. Again, it must be stressed that

Reproduced with permission from Linda Dyer, *Critical Thinking for Business Students*, 2nd edition (Concord, ON: Captus Press Inc., 2011), Chapter 6.

we are *not* recommending that words be used as a smokescreen to conceal weak reasoning. As critical thinkers, we must always analyze the structure of the argument (claim, evidence, and assumptions), however well or poorly the argument is worded. What we *are* advocating is clear and vivid writing that puts the reader in the author's shoes and allows him to live the experiences of the author or her sources.

The following sections discuss general strategies for building a persuasive argument. First, we look at how to deal with objections to the structure of your argument. Next, we focus on how to use language persuasively.

A theme that will come up repeatedly is the important requirement that you *think about your audience*. How much do your readers already know about the issue under discussion? How familiar might they be with the evidence you are about to present? Have they already formed their own ideas about the issue, and are they likely to agree or disagree with your claim? What might be the values that underlie their beliefs? Granted, you rarely will know all these details about the beliefs and values of everyone who is likely to read your work. Further, you may have to write for a very diverse audience, making it more complicated to tailor your argument to a particular group. As we shall see, however, the more you think about your potential readers, the stronger the argument you can build. Forewarned is forearmed.

Anticipate and counter readers' objections

The first step in writing persuasively is a brainstorming, troubleshooting process in which you should put yourself in the shoes of your audience and perform "destructive testing" on your ideas. What objections could possibly be made to your argument? If your readers are fully engaged critical thinkers, they will continually be consulting their own knowledge and beliefs, and will undoubtedly raise questions as they watch your reasoning develop. Recall that most interesting claims in the study of business tend to be *contestable* claims, so it is small wonder that they will be contested! If readers' objections are unaddressed in your writing, your claim will be dismissed out of hand. It follows that if you want to be persuasive, your job is to answer these expected questions as they arise. To do this, you have to present the question or objection explicitly, then provide a convincing answer or rebuttal in your text. By mentioning and refuting objections, you will show your readers that you have considered the issue fully. If you *don't* address their concerns, they will simply think that it was your ignorance or naivete that led you to such a wrong-headed conclusion!

Some common types of objections that you can anticipate occur when (i) readers are aware of negative evidence that refutes your claim; (ii) readers can come up with alternative causal explanations that are consistent with your evidence; and (iii) readers disagree with your value preferences or reality assumptions.

Negative evidence

The world is a complex and contradictory place, and it is rare that every piece of evidence that bears on an issue will lead irrevocably to a clear and unassailable conclusion. In fact, when they are doing research to support a claim, writers often have the experience of finding data and descriptions of events that run counter to the claim. So it should not be surprising

147

that some readers are bound to think of contrary evidence that would undermine your argument. If you are aware of negative evidence, the sensible response is to present such evidence in order to show that you have given it due consideration. Thus, you will show that, properly interpreted, it is not negative, that it actually is not reliable, or that its importance is overstated. Consider how you might deal with very salient — and widely believed — evidence that contradicts your thesis about crime:

> In summary, the crime rate is definitely on the decrease. Statistics from major cities across North America show this. However, when we read newspapers, watch television, or go to the movies, it would appear that crime and violence are rampant. These reports cannot be disregarded. Crime news, both on TV and in newspapers, is much more explicit than it used to be; things that used to be passed over are now shown and described in full graphic detail. Movies that horrified people 20 years ago are just commonplace now. "Gangsta rap" is chic. Crime has become entertainment. But depictions of violence must not be mistaken for the phenomenon itself. Although it *seems* as though we are inundated with crime, this is quite misleading. The crime rate is indeed falling.

Or, perhaps, your claim is that successful entrepreneurs are very independent, but you know that there is a lot of focus on business networks as sources of advice for the entrepreneur. Again, you would mention the negative evidence and then show why it is misleading:

> Many research surveys conclude that successful entrepreneurs have large networks of business colleagues and advisers. That, at least, is what the entrepreneurs say on paper-and-pencil questionnaires. But when we use a less-superficial research technique, the in-depth interview, entrepreneurs go on to admit that they rarely use these networks for advice about business problems, and when they do, they find the advice they get is not particularly helpful. The networks may be there, but when it comes to advice about running the business, successful entrepreneurs make their own decisions and are fiercely independent.

Rival causes

If the claim you are proposing is a causal claim, it is likely that there are rival causal explanations of your evidence. Recall that plausible rival causes may be located in differences among groups, reverse causation, the effect of a third variable, or the *post hoc* fallacy (see Chapter 5). Certainly, if you can think of a possible rival cause, it makes no sense to just keep quiet about the problem and hope that readers will not see the hole in your argument. It is guaranteed that some careful reader will catch the problem, especially if he or she disagrees with your claim. So, as part of the brainstorming process, you must discipline yourself to find and propose alternative causes, then rebut them, showing the reader why they are unlikely to be the real explanation. For example:

> All the firms we studied devoted a great deal of time and resources in managing relationships with their clientele. This relationship marketing was pivotal in ensuring their profitability. We considered the possibility that only profitable firms could afford to spend time focusing on relationship marketing.

148

Could success have preceded their use of this marketing approach? A careful review of the history of each firm showed that the focus on client relationships generally came before they were successful. From the very beginning, the entrepreneurs emphasized the importance of getting to know the needs and personalities of their clients. It was not success, then, that caused this strategic approach. Rather, the strategy led to the ultimate success of the enterprise.

As another example, consider how the systematic consideration and rejection of other explanations, anticipates the reader's questions about the causes of good course evaluations:

> The students who were in small classes gave the course much higher ratings than the students in the large classes. Note that the time of day the course was held, the proportion of full-time and part-time students, and the average GPA of the students were all uncorrelated with the ratings. Moreover, most of the instructors taught both large and small sections, so it was not the skill of the instructors that made the difference. We can conclude, therefore, that it was the small class size that caused students to be more enthusiastic about their courses.

Debatable assumptions

In Chapter 5, we discussed how critical thinkers can challenge underlying reality assumptions and values: first, they make the author's assumptions explicit, then they present counter-arguments to show that the assumptions are incorrect. To write persuasively, then, you must anticipate these challenges to your assumptions. If you know that there are reality assumptions that your audience might feel are debatable or wrong, you must provide explicit data to back up your assumptions. Here is an example:

> The series of workshops on stress relief for executives, organized by the Employee Assistance Program, has been a great success. A survey conducted by the HR department showed that workshop participants were enthusiastic about the sessions and reported that the stress-reduction techniques had a substantial positive impact on their performance on the job. Management should move quickly to make the program available to all employees. *Of course, this assumes that lower-level employees could benefit from stress reduction just as much as those at the executive level can. And there is no question that this assumption is warranted.* Studies show that first-line supervisors, sales representatives, secretaries — people in a variety of jobs — experience stress in this complex world of rapid change and uncertainty.

Since stress, in the popular imagination, is often associated with high-powered, high-responsibility executive jobs, you have to anticipate that this reality assumption will lead some readers to disagree with your claim. So you deal with it explicitly, refuting the erroneous assumption with data.

When your readers' values differ from your own, again, your job is to show them that your values are worth serious consideration. Some values may be just based on unthinking tradition and a feeling that "... well, doesn't everybody think the way I do?" In this case, people have not actively questioned some of their values. If your writing poses a strong and logical challenge to their value assumptions, they may discover that they are not all that strongly committed to certain values. In cases like this, you have a chance of persuading them to reflect on, and perhaps accept, your viewpoint. Let's say, for example, that a reader believes an individual's right to privacy is important, but has not really thought carefully about what that might mean in a business context. You will need to anticipate this value conflict, and your counterargument will show the reader that the case for individual privacy is not clear-cut. Perhaps seeing your rationale might actually sway the reader to agree with your position.

> Pzasz Executive Search has thorough and reliable head-hunting procedures. They are the consultants of choice for recruiting a senior administrator for our university. Their investigators research the accuracy of all resumé items, follow up on all references, and check with a variety of past co-workers about the candidate's credentials, character, and integrity. They have even been known to question neighbours about the good citizenship of prospective administrators. Now, some may feel that this close investigation invades the privacy of the individual. But let us balance the value of individual privacy against our responsibility to our institution. We need ethical leadership. Good moral character is demanded of teachers, police chiefs, and heads of state. So, too, in university administrators. This person will represent our institution to the world, and must serve as a role model for hundreds of academics and tens of thousands of students. Let us ensure that our choice is a good one.

Limit your claims when you have no rebuttal

What of the objections that you can anticipate, but for which you cannot find a plausible rebuttal? It happens, even to the most practised researchers and writers. You must concede points that you cannot refute. This concession may take various forms.

1. Limits to your generalizations: *All our evidence is drawn from large, high-tech corporations. Further research is necessary before we can confidently extend the claim to smaller firms, or those in other, more mature, industries.*

2. An assessment that the level of probability of your claim is less than 100%: *Although the evidence for my conclusion is mixed, it still is very probable that when firms embrace environmental sustainability goals, profitability increases; the few contradictory cases are far outweighed by the evidence that is consistent with my claim.*

3. A refinement or re-defining of your terms: *I've been arguing that entrepreneurs born outside of Canada are more dedicated to growing their firms and going global than entrepreneurs who are native Canadians. Admittedly, Guy Laliberté of the Cirque du Soleil and Alain Bouchard of the Couche-Tard convenience-store chain are counter-examples. However, both these businessmen are from Quebec and it can be argued that Quebec is different from the rest of Canada. The key success factor, then, may be one's status as an outsider — a businessperson who is outside the Canadian business establishment.* (This paraphrases an argument made by Andrea Mandel-Campbell in her 2007 book, *Why Mexicans Don't Drink Molson*.)

It may seem to you that making these concessions and describing limitations to the truth of your claims weakens your argument. Actually, it does just the opposite. It is paradoxical, but true, that *acknowledging limitations makes your writing more persuasive.* By considering the full complexity and nuance of the claim, you show yourself to be thoughtful and judicious. Readers can see that you have weighed pros and cons and used your critical powers of judgment to reach a conclusion. If an author just presents a "bare-bones" claim-and-evidence text, her argument often seems naive, if not downright simple-minded.

Rhetoric

In this section, we consider how the use of language affects the credibility and persuasiveness of your argument. Language is the primary tool to communicate thinking. One of the attributes that sets human beings apart from other animals is our ability to convey complex, abstract, or personal experiences to other human beings through speech, reading, and writing. Some writers know how to use language well; others are sloppy, imprecise, and therefore unconvincing. Some people are good at conveying emotions with their words — they create in their readers and listeners feelings of anger, pride, indignation, fear, etc. The art of using language to persuade is known as *rhetoric.* We study rhetoric to understand the techniques used by authors and speakers to convince an audience of the rightness of their views. **Box 6.1** provides an analysis of the rhetoric commonly used by textbook writers.

Box 6.1: The rhetoric of textbooks

The world of business organizations is an unpredictable place. When we read the business news, work as employees in organizations, observe managers at work (see **Box 2.1**), or make decisions about our stock market investments, our impression of the business environment is characterized by ambiguity and uncertainty. Firms can be so fragile — here today and gone tomorrow. Managers may be "downsized" without warning. Technological advances, cultural diversity, and globalization create constant change, unpredictability, even chaos in the world of business.

Yet, how are business organizations portrayed in introductory business textbooks? Stephen Fineman and Yiannis Gabriel have pointed to an interesting gap between the unpredictability of today's organizations and the way in which these organizations are portrayed in introductory textbooks. The researchers studied textbooks on organizational behaviour, but their conclusions are probably applicable to textbooks in other disciplines of business. The standard textbook, Fineman and Gabriel argue, does not reflect our current understanding of business but portrays organizations as structured, solid, and stable. Their contention is that the *rhetoric of the textbook* makes this portrayal inevitable. The rhetorical devices commonly used in textbooks — definitions, case studies, and lists — all make it appear that the information presented is factual, not contestable.

> *Definitions* are usually highlighted or placed in boxes or margins for emphasis. Definitions convey the idea of science, precision, and rigour. They represent a conveniently sized piece of information that can be memorized and reproduced in examinations and reports. By their very nature, definitions encourage students to accept the information presented as indisputable facts.

151

Box 6.1 continued

Case studies are often used in textbooks to illustrate concepts. It might seem that case studies can demonstrate the chaos and unpredictability of "real life". Typically, they do not. The "characters, plots, and narrative are condensed, reduced to a minimalist state ... [which serves to] reinforce the image of organizations as orderly and impersonal" (pp. 382–83).

Lists aid memorization but eliminate argument. Authors rarely present their arguments for the inclusion or exclusion of elements on the list. Too often, learning comes to mean associating a list of authors' names with theories, and each theorist with a list of key terms.

In general, then, the definitions, case studies, and lists that are characteristic of textbooks leave the reader with the impression that the facts are clear. The effect of these devices is practically to eliminate critical thought, argument, and debate.

Buying an introductory textbook is a part of "rite of passage" into a discipline that is new to the student. Since it is establishing the discipline in the student's mind, the emphasis is on what is known, on the power of the discipline. Everything seems clear-cut and well understood. "The textbook is a ticket to a club, a fount of knowledge and a guarantee of safe passage" (p. 379). Issues that raise too many questions are necessarily excluded as inviting unwanted ambiguities. As a result, the turbulence that characterizes the real world of organizations vanishes, and the reader is left with an inaccurate picture of organizational stability and orderliness.

Note: For Stephen Fineman and Yiannis Gabriel's complete argument, see "Paradigms of Organizations: An Exploration in Textbook Rhetorics", *Organization*, 1, 2 (1994): 375–99.

You may have heard people speak disparagingly of rhetoric, often when using the phrase, "empty rhetoric". In this construction, rhetoric means the use of language that is artificial, elaborate, and showy, with little real substance to support the arguments. Rhetoric in this sense usually involves a deliberate intent to mislead. There is a vast public relations industry whose major task is to ensure that the information that people get about the corporate world is presented in the best possible light (see **Box 6.2**). It is unfortunate that language can be used to manipulate readers and conceal insincerity, but it should be equally obvious that not all people who use words effectively are hypocrites. People also use language to convey sincerely held opinions, to inform, enlighten, and share their human experiences. The existence of spin doctors should not lead to a cynical rejection of rhetoric. Most students of rhetoric are people who want to convey their ideas as clearly and accurately as possible.

Here follows a brief overview of some of the rules of rhetoric.

Be complete

The first rule is that you must present your reasoning in full and clear detail, since much of the evidence you present will be new to the reader. The world of business is vast, and a multitude of issues and events are subsumed under the heading of business studies. Even experi-

---

Box 6.2: Press releases and the business news

Where do newspaper reporters get information for their articles? A substantial portion of the business information we read in newspapers comes from **press releases** written by the firms themselves and transported, holus-bolus, into the news articles. **Press conferences** are often called when major firms are changing their leadership or introducing new products. As we might expect, the information presented to the news media in press releases and at press conferences is carefully worded by skilled public relations professionals to make the firm look efficient, progressive and successful. They are written to produce what PR specialists have termed "good ink". So to the extent that rushed and harried reporters rely on the information and even the wording of press releases (conveniently crafted for this purpose), it may be unwise to expect that articles reported in newspapers are unbiased facts. There's another factor that creates bias in business reporting. Too much bad press might lead companies to withdraw their advertisements, and corporate advertisements are an important source of revenue for newspapers. For most newspapers, advertisements typically bring in much more revenue than individual and subscription sales of the newspaper to readers. It is little wonder that the news is full of flattering stories and glowing reports about business.

---

enced managers and business scholars cannot keep track of it all. It is important to present your writing with sufficient points to allow potential readers to make the connection to their own experience. Moreover, you will have spent a lot more time thinking about your particular argument than most of your readers. You have worked hard to collect evidence and to organize it into a coherent position. Use your evidence thoroughly — to its maximal potential. This does not mean a painstaking reconstruction of all your initial mistaken thoughts, your difficulties in finding reliable evidence, or all the blind alleys you ran into as you developed your ideas. But do give enough detail (within your space or time restrictions) to allow your audience to appreciate fully the import of your data and logic. Undeveloped ideas and an assumption that your audience will "fill in the blanks", are not persuasive.

Use an appropriate tone

When you write, you create a relationship between yourself and your audience. This relationship may be quite formal and distant, or it may have a more informal and personal quality. The quality of the writer/reader relationship that is inherent in your writing is known as *tone*. By thinking of your future readers, you can decide whether a formal, *scholarly* tone or a less formal, *narrative* tone would be more appropriate.

The scholarly tone is characterized by rational exposition of the structure of your argument. Logic is highly prized. The scholarly tone uses formal, technical language or abstract analysis, and makes frequent reference to the ideas of academic experts and researchers in the field. Academic journals and most textbooks are written in this way. Citations, footnotes, and reference lists are standard. In some areas of business, scholarly writing is very mathematical. Essentially, the scholarly tone is an *appeal to authority*.

The narrative tone is characterized by stories and anecdotes. Vividness is emphasized. The writer uses many descriptions and examples, sometimes including actual quotations from managers, customers, consultants, etc., where they are relevant to the argument. Striking personal experiences, first-hand observations, and dramatic case studies are frequent when writers use a narrative tone. Business newspapers and magazines, as well as popular business trade books, tend to use this tone (see **Box 6.3**). The narrative tone often entails an *appeal to emotion*.

Determining your tone means thinking about your audience. Publishers usually know who their main audience is, and business authors choose their tone depending on where their work will be published. As a business student, you should probably aim for a middle ground in your writing. You will want to demonstrate to your teachers that you are becoming increasingly familiar with the work of scholars in your field of study. At the same time, business studies is an *applied* field, and it is equally important that you learn to write for an audience of business practitioners who might be suspicious of, or bored by, a strictly academic style. As will be argued in the next section, even the most analytical, matter-of-fact texts can profit from vividness and detail, if the author wants to be convincing.

Be vivid

By using vivid language, you bring your evidence to life, attracting attention to your points and making them memorable for your readers. In this section, we shall mention a few techniques that are commonly used to make writing more vivid, and therefore more persuasive. These brief pointers, however, are no substitute for a good guidebook on writing style. Countless style guides exist that are invaluable aids for the beginning, as well as the experienced writer. Find one you like and use it regularly.

As you read the following report from an employee newsletter, ask yourself whether vivid images of the event and its impact on the employees' morale spring to mind.

> The meeting was well attended and pretty interesting. The division manager said that profits were low last quarter, and people were not too happy, but a new supplier has made a good offer to provide raw material at a more reasonable cost, and there is a window of opportunity to bring in some high-tech equipment soon. This means that by next year things should be better in the division, especially if there is belt-tightening in other areas, so by the end of the meeting people felt pretty good about that.

Why is this piece not vivid? First, there are many **vague words**, words that are imprecise and do not stimulate readers' imaginations. "Interesting", "low", "reasonable", and "pretty good" are vague. In the paragraph, few **concrete details** are provided to make the incident memorable. Metaphorical phrases like "window of opportunity" and "belt-tightening", which may once have been vivid, have been so over-used in business writing that they are now listless **clichés**. Now we rewrite the text, replacing vague words more precise ones, providing concrete details of the setting of the meeting and the actual words of the participants, all of which are designed to bring the event to life for the readers. Fresher, more vigorous phrases take the place of the cliches.

> Practically the entire department attended the open meeting, which was originally scheduled to meet in the departmental training room. Because of the unprecedented numbers, the meeting had to be moved to the board room. The extraordinary interest was a result of last month's financial results: profits

Box 6.3: Marketing myopia and the power of rhetoric

Theodore Levitt, a professor of marketing, wrote an extremely popular article in a 1960 issue of the *Harvard Business Review*.[1] Levitt's major claim was that firms should think of themselves, not in terms of the particular product or service they offer, but in terms of the broad industry within which the product or service is located. Railways, for example, should define themselves as operating in the transportation industry; oil companies are in the energy business. This broader focus will ensure companies' continued growth, even in the face of technological change. Why? Because transportation will always be necessary, even if rail travel is eroded by growing use of cars, airplanes, and trucks. Since all particular products (and services) are bound to be obsolete eventually, a *product* orientation is therefore myopic. A *customer* orientation, on the other hand, offers more growth opportunity in an environment of technological change. Firms that focus heavily on production methods, and on product research and development, but ignore customers and markets are said to be suffering from **marketing myopia** and are destined for obsolescence.

Levitt's article was enormously influential. His ideas were put into practice by airlines, publishing houses, car companies, oil companies, shoe stores, and cosmetic firms, among others. In the first fifteen years after its publication, *Harvard Business Review* sold over a quarter of a million reprints of the article. The results of implementing these ideas have been mixed. Some firms benefited greatly from this heightened awareness of the market in which they operated, but some others ended up defining themselves so broadly that they lost focus and diversified into inappropriate areas. In the words of one of Levitt's critics, "Why should a few clever words on a piece of paper enable a railroad company to fly airplanes, or for that matter, run taxicabs?"[2]

In a retrospective commentary, Levitt pondered the astounding impact of his article: "Why its appeal throughout the world of resolutely restrained scholars, implacably temperate managers and high government officials, all accustomed to balanced and thoughtful calculation? Is it that concrete examples, joined to illustrate a simple idea and presented with some attention to literacy, communicate better than massive analytical reasoning that reads as though it were translated from the German? Is it that provocative assertions are more memorable and persuasive than restrained and balanced explanations, no matter who the audience?"[3]

Levitt is suggesting that it was primarily the **rhetorical quality** of his article that accounted for its success, in particular, his use of a strong **narrative tone**. The article is full of vivid, colourful examples of Hollywood movie producers, the first supermarkets, oil companies, and car manufacturers. He makes dramatic over-statements of his case, suggesting, for example, that product-oriented engineers in R&D see customers as "unpredictable, varied, fickle, stupid, shortsighted, stubborn, and generally bothersome". He describes a Boston millionaire who declared that his entire estate should be invested solely and forever in streetcars because of his myopic belief that this product would always be in demand. He mentions John Rockefeller creating a market by sending free kerosene lamps to China. These and other examples combine to grab the readers' attention and make his article very convincing.

Notes

1. T. Levitt, "Marketing Myopia", *Harvard Business Review*, Sept./Oct. (1975). Reprint of 1960 article.
2. H. Mintzberg, *The Rise and Fall of Strategic Planning* (New York: Free Press, 1994), p. 280.
3. T. Levitt, *Marketing Imagination* (New York: Free Press, 1986), p. 14.

had plummeted from $460,000 a month to just over $135,000. What had gone wrong? Who was to blame? Anxiety levels were high.

The fundamental problem according to Bert Sheldon, the manager, was skyrocketing raw material costs. Lupu Inc., the regular supplier, had changed its pricing policy with scarcely any notice. That, together with a tightening supply market, caused raw material costs to go up 22%, all but wiping out profit. He had remonstrated with Lupu at the highest level, but to no avail. So two decades of working with Lupu ended in a call for bids. A new arrangement now exists with Playfair & Long who, in exchange for an exclusive contract, will supply us at 5% less than the spot rate on the London Metal Exchange. Moreover, P & L can supply and install high tech sealant machines which, in the long run, should reduce operating costs by 2 to 3 percent. Initial financing costs are hurting, but with a sharp eye kept on other costs, strong performance is expected within a year.

The meeting left employees with a clear signal that head office has the situation firmly in hand. The initial glum atmosphere was entirely dispelled, and optimism reigned.

Rewritten, the text is considerably longer, but much easier to visualize. The use of precise, vivid language convinces the reader of the importance of the meeting and conveys clearly the shift in morale among the employees. Again, it cannot be emphasized enough that almost all writers rely on dictionaries, thesauruses, and style guides to help them seek appropriate words and phrases, to ensure correct usage, and to rise above vagueness and cliche.

Effective reading

The intelligent use of rhetoric, then, goes hand-in-hand with the development of a sound, logical argument. Neither aspect is sufficient by itself. By analogy, when you have cooked a delicious meal, you want to be sure to serve it on a clean plate with an attractive table setting. It detracts greatly from good food if it is served on dirty dishes or in unappetizing surroundings. Everyone appreciates a skilful wordsmith, but if your argument is not sound and you try to cover up its deficiencies with emotional or authoritative language, then you are encouraging fallacious thinking. As a writer, you must make every effort to ensure that there is substance underlying your well-crafted prose.

You cannot assume, however, that all writers marry a sound argument with persuasive writing. It sometimes happens that an author's excellent command of rhetoric is accompanied by a weak argument structure. As a critical reader, your first task is to expose and criticize the bare bones of the argument — the claims, evidence, and assumptions, independently of the rhetorical devices that the author added for impact and readability.

And consider the other possibility. Occasionally, you will encounter a writer who has a poor command of language and style. Try not to be distracted; invaluable ideas may often be found in unappealing packages. Again, by focusing on claims, evidence, and assumptions, you may find that the awkward prose conceals a treasure trove of intellectually stimulating information.

Public Speaking: A Quick and Easy Way

Dale Carnegie

PART ONE: PUBLIC SPEAKING – A QUICK AND EASY WAY

You may be saying to yourself: "Is there really a quick and easy way to learn to speak in public—or is that merely an intriguing title that promises more than it delivers?"

No, I am not exaggerating. I am really going to let you in on a vital secret—a secret that will make it easier for you to speak in public immediately. Where did I discover this? In some book? No. In some college course in public speaking? No. I never even heard it mentioned there. I had to discover it the hard way— gradually, slowly, painfully.

If, back in my college days, someone had given me this password to effective speaking and writing,

I could have saved myself years and years of wasted, heartbreaking effort. For example, I once wrote a book about Lincoln; and while writing it, I threw into the wastebasket at least a year of wasted effort that might have been saved had I known the great secrets that I am going to divulge to you.

The same thing happened when I spent two years trying to write a novel.

It happened again while writing a book on public speaking—another year of wasted effort thrown into the wastebasket because I didn't know the secrets of successful writing and speaking.

2

From *Speak More Effectively*, Part One (Washington, DC: Dale Carnegie Training, 2008). Reproduced with permission.

IF POSSIBLE, SPEND YEARS IN PREPARATION

What are these priceless secrets that I have been dangling before your eyes? Just this: talk about something that you have earned the right to talk about through long study or experience. Talk about something that you know and know that you know. Don't spend ten minutes or ten hours preparing a talk: spend ten weeks or ten months. Better still, spend ten years.

Talk about something that has aroused your interest. Talk about something that you have a deep desire to communicate to your listeners.

To illustrate what I mean, let's take the case of Gay Kellogg, a housewife from Roselle, New Jersey. Gay Kellogg had never made a speech in public before she joined one of our classes in New York. She was terrified. She feared that public speaking might be an obscure art far beyond her abilities. Yet at the fourth session of the course, as she made an impromptu talk, she held the audience spellbound. I asked her to speak on "The Biggest Regret of My Life." Gay Kellogg then made a talk that was deeply moving. The listeners could hardly keep the tears back. I know. I could hardly keep the tears from welling up in my own eyes. Her talk went like this:

"The biggest regret of my life is that I never knew a mother's love. My mother died when I was only a year old. I was brought up by a succession of aunts and other relatives who were so absorbed in their own children that they had no time for me. I never stayed with any of them very long. They were always sorry to see me come and glad to see me go.

They never took any interest in me or gave me any affection. I knew I wasn't wanted. Even as a little child I could feel it. I often cried myself to sleep because of loneliness. The deepest desire of my heart was to have someone ask to see my report card from school. But no one ever did. No one cared. All I craved as a little child was love—and no one ever gave it to me."

Had Gay Kellogg spent ten years preparing that talk? No. She had spent twenty years. She had been preparing herself to make that talk when she cried herself to sleep as a little child. She had been preparing herself to make that talk when her heart ached because no one asked to see her report card from school. No wonder she could talk about that subject. She could not have erased those early memories from her mind. Gay Kellogg had rediscovered a storehouse of tragic memories and feelings away deep down inside her. She didn't have to pump them up. She didn't have to work at making that talk. All she had to do was to let her pent-up feelings and memories rush up to the surface like oil from a well.

Jesus said: "My yoke is easy, my burden is light." So is the yoke and burden of good speaking. Ineffective talks are usually the ones that are written and memorized and sweated over and made artificial. Good talks are the ones that well up within you as a fountain. Many people talk the way I swim. I struggle and fight the water and wear myself out and go one-tenth as fast as the experts. Poor speakers, like poor swimmers, get taut and tense and twist themselves up into knots—and defeat their own purpose.

3

BECOME EXCITED ABOUT YOUR SUBJECT

Even people with only mediocre speaking ability may make superb talks if they will speak about something that has deeply stirred them. I saw a striking illustration of that years ago when I was conducting courses for the Brooklyn Chamber of Commerce. It was an example that I shall remember for a lifetime. It happened like this:

We were having a session devoted to impromptu talks. After the class assembled, I asked them to speak on "What, If Anything, Is Wrong with Religion?"

One member (a man, by the way, who had never finished high school) did something to that audience that I have never seen any other speaker do in the years I have been training people to speak in public. His talk was so moving that when he finished, every person in the room stood up in silent tribute.

This man told about the greatest tragedy of his life: the death of his mother. He was so devastated, so grief-stricken, that he no longer wanted to live. He said that when he went out of doors, even on a sunny day, it seemed as if he were wandering in a fog. He longed to die. In desperation, he went to his church and knelt and wept and said the rosary, and a great peace came over him—a divine peace of resignation: "Not my will, but Thine be done."

As he finished his talk to the class, he said, in the voice of one who has had a revelation: "There is nothing wrong with religion! There is nothing wrong with God's love."

I'll never forget that talk because of its emotional impact. When I congratulated the speaker on his deeply moving talk, he replied: "Yes, and I made it without any preparation."

Preparation? Well, if he hadn't prepared that talk, I don't know what preparation is. He meant, of course, that he had had no advance notice that he would have to talk on that subject. I am glad he didn't, because if he had had advance notice, his talk might have been far less effective. He might have labored over it and tried to make a speech and been artificial. Instead, he did just what Gay Kellogg did years later—he stood up and opened his heart and talked like one human being conversing with another.

The truth of the matter is that he was preparing to make that talk when he knelt and wept and said the rosary. Living, feeling, thinking, enduring "the slings and arrows of outrageous fortune"—that is the finest preparation ever yet devised for either speaking or writing.

4

LOOK INSIDE YOURSELF FOR TOPICS TO TALK ABOUT

Do beginners know the necessity of looking inside themselves for topics? Know it? They never even heard of it! They are more likely to look inside a magazine for topics. For example, I remember meeting in the subway one day one of our students—a woman who was discouraged because she was making so little progress in this course. I asked her what she had talked about the previous week. I discovered that she had talked about whether Mussolini should be permitted to invade Ethiopia. She had gotten her information out of an article in Time. She had read the article twice. I asked her if she was interested in the subject, and she said, "No." I then asked her why she had talked about it. "Well," she replied. "I had to talk about something so I chose that."

Think of it: here was a woman who had tried to speak about Mussolini's Ethiopian war, yet she admitted she had little knowledge and no interest in the subject. She had neglected to speak on a subject she had earned the right to talk about.

After a discussion, I said to her: "I would listen with respect and interest if you spoke about something you have experienced and know about, but neither I nor anyone else would be interested in a subject which you yourself are not interested in, such as Mussolini's invasion of Ethiopia. You don't know enough about it to merit our attention or respect."

TALK FROM YOUR HEART—NOT FROM A BOOK

Many students of public speaking are like that woman. They want to get their subjects out of a book or a magazine instead of from their own knowledge and convictions. For example, a few years ago, I was one of the three judges in an intercollegiate speaking contest over the NBC network. The judges never saw the speakers. We listened to them from Studio 8G in Radio City. I wish, oh, how I wish that every student and teacher of public speaking could have witnessed what went on in that studio. The first speaker spoke on "Democracy at the Crossroads." The next one spoke about "How to Prevent War." It was painfully evident that they were merely repeating carefully rehearsed and memorized words. So neither the guest in the studio nor the judges paid much attention to them. One of the judges was Willem Hendrik Van Loon. When he began drawing a cartoon of one of the contestants, everyone stood and watched him and ignored the amateurish "orations," the memorized words, which were coming over the air.

However, the next speaker caught my attention immediately. A senior at Yale, he spoke about what was wrong with the colleges. He had earned the right to talk about that. We listened to him with respect. But the speaker who got the first prize began something like this:

"I have just come from a hospital where a friend of mine is near death because of an automobile accident. Most automobile accidents are caused by the younger generation. I am a member of that generation and I want to speak to you about the causes of these accidents."

Everyone in the studio was quiet as he spoke. He was talking about realities, not trying to make a speech. He was speaking about something that he had earned the right to talk about. He was talking from the inside out.

5

HAVE AN EAGER DESIRE TO COMMUNICATE

However, let me warn you that merely earning the right to talk about a subject will not always produce a superb talk. Another element must be added—an element that is vital in speaking. Briefly, it is this: in addition to earning the right to speak, we must have a deep and abiding desire to communicate our convictions and transfer our feelings to our listeners.

To illustrate: suppose I were asked to talk about raising corn and hogs. I spent twenty years on a corn and hog farm in Missouri, so surely I have earned the right to talk on that subject. But I don't have any special desire to talk on that subject. But suppose I were asked to speak on what was wrong with the kind of education I got in college. I could hardly fail if I talked on that subject, because I would have the three basic requirements for a good talk. First, I would be talking about something that I had earned the right to talk about. Second, I would have deep feelings and convictions that I longed to convey to you. Third, I would have clear and convincing illustrations out of my own experience.

When Gay Kellogg spoke on the biggest regret of her life—never knowing a mother's love—she had not only earned the right through suffering to talk on that subject, but she also had a deep emotional desire to tell us about it. So did the class member who spoke in the Brooklyn Chamber of Commerce class about the death of his mother—"Not my will, but Thine be done."

History has repeatedly been changed by people who had the desire and the ability to transfer their convictions and emotions to their listeners. If John Wesley had not had that desire and ability, he could never have founded a religious sect that has girdled the globe. If Peter the Hermit had not had that desire and ability, he could never have stirred the imagination of the world and plunged Europe into the futile and bloody Crusades for possession of the Holy Land. If Hitler had not had the innate ability to transfer his hate and bitterness to his listeners, he could not have seized power in Germany and plunged the world into war.

TALK ABOUT YOUR EXPERIENCES

You are prepared right now to make at least a dozen good talks—talks that no one else on earth could make except you, because no one else has ever had precisely the same experience that you have had. What are these subjects? I don't know. But you do. So carry a sheet of paper with you for a few weeks and write down, as you think of them, all the subjects that you are prepared to talk about through experience—subjects such as "The Biggest Regret of My Life," "My Biggest Ambition," and "Why I Liked (Disliked) School." Do that and you will be surprised how quickly your list of topics will grow.

Here is good news for you: your progress as a speaker will depend far more on your choosing the right topic to talk about than upon your native ability as a speaker. You can feel at ease and make a fine talk immediately if you will only do what Gay Kellogg did: talk about some experience that has affected you deeply, some experience you have been thinking about for twenty years. But you may never feel completely at ease if you try to make speeches about "Mussolini's Invasion of Ethiopia" or "Democracy at the Crossroads."

6

TALK ABOUT THINGS YOU HAVE STUDIED

Talking about your own experiences is obviously the quickest way to develop courage and self-confidence. But after you have gained a bit of experience, you will want to talk about other subjects. What subjects? And where can you find them? Everywhere. For example, I once asked a class of executives of the New York Telephone Company to jot down every idea for a speech that occurred to them during the week. It was November. One person saw Thanksgiving Day printed in red on the calendar, and spoke about the many things for which to be thankful. Another person saw some pigeons on the street. That inspired an idea. The person gave a talk about pigeons that I shall never forget. But the prize winner that night was a class member who had seen a bedbug crawling up a man's collar in the subway. The class member gave us a talk that I still remember after twenty years.

CARRY A SCRIBBLING BOOK

Why don't you do what Voltaire did? Voltaire, one of the most powerful writers of the eighteenth century, carried in his pocket what he called a "scribbling book"—a book in which he jotted down his fleeting thoughts and ideas. Why don't you carry a "scribbling book?" Then, if you are irritated by a discourteous clerk, for example, jot down the word "Discourtesy" in your scribbling book.

Then try to recall two or three other striking incidents of discourtesy. Select the best one and tell us what we ought to do about it. Presto! You have a two-minute talk on Discourtesy.

As soon as you begin to look for topics for talks, you will find them everywhere: in the home, the office, the street.

"SING SOMETHING SIMPLE"

Don't attempt to speak on some worldshaking problem such as "The Atomic Bomb." Take something simple—almost anything will do, provided the idea gets you, instead of your getting the idea. For example, I recently heard a student of this course, Mary A. Leer, of Chicago, talk on "Back Doors." You may find her talk dull as you read it; but if you had only listened to it, as I did, you would have loved it because she herself was positively excited about her back door. In fact, I never before heard anyone speak with such glowing enthusiasm about painting the back door! The point I am trying to make is this: almost any subject will do for a talk provided you yourself have earned the right to talk about it through study or experience, and are excited about it and eager to tell us about it.

7

THIS IS THE FAMOUS TALK ABOUT BACK DOORS!

"Four years ago, when I moved into my present apartment, the back door was painted a drab shade of gray. It was terrible. Every time I opened the back door it gave me a depressed feeling. So I bought a can of beautiful blue paint and painted the outside of the back door, the jambs and the inside of the screen door. That paint was the most exquisite shade of blue that I had ever seen; and every time I opened the back door after that, it seemed as though I was looking upon a bit of heaven.

"I was never more angry in my life than when I came home one evening not long ago and found that the house painter had pried open my screen door and painted my beautiful blue door a most hideous shade of putty gray. I could have cheerfully choked that painter.

"You can tell a lot more about people from their back doors than you can from their front doors. Front doors are often prettied up just to impress you. But back doors tell tales. A slovenly back door tattles on slovenly housekeeping. But a back door that is painted a cheerful color and has pots of blooming plants sitting around and garbage cans that are painted and orderly, that kind of back door tells you that there is an interesting person with a lively imagination living behind it. I have already bought a can of beautiful blue paint; and next Saturday, I am going to have a gorgeous time. I am again going to make my back door cheerful and inspiring."

And so it goes. A volume could be filled with examples to show the power of speakers who:

(a) Have earned the right, by study and experience, to talk about their subject;

(b) Are excited about it themselves; and

(c) Are eager to communicate their ideas and feelings to their listeners.

8

163

HOW TO PREPARE AND DELIVER YOUR TALKS

HERE ARE EIGHT PRINCIPLES THAT WILL HELP IMMENSELY IN PREPARING YOUR TALKS:

I.   Make brief notes of the interesting things you want to mention.

II. Don't write out your talks.

Why? Because if you do, you will use written language instead of easy, conversational language; and when you stand up to talk, you will probably find yourself trying to remember what you wrote. That will keep you from speaking naturally and with sparkle.

III. Never, never, never memorize a talk word for word.

If you memorize your talk, you are almost sure to forget it; and the audience will probably be glad, for nobody wants to listen to a canned speech. Even if you don't forget it, it will sound memorized. You will have a faraway look in your eyes and a faraway ring in your voice. You won't sound like a human being trying to tell us something.

If, in a longer talk, you are afraid you will forget what you want to say, then make some brief notes and hold them in your hand and glance at them occasionally. That is what I usually do.

IV. Fill your talk with illustrations and examples.

By far the easiest way to make a talk interesting is to fill it with examples. To illustrate what I mean, let's take this booklet you are reading now. Approximately half of those pages are devoted to illustration. First, there is the illustration of Gay Kellogg's talk about the suffering she endured as a child. Next, the illustration of the speaker on "What, If Anything, Is Wrong with Religion?" Next, the example of the woman who tried to talk on Mussolini's invasion of Ethiopia. That is followed by the story of the four college students in a speaking contest over the radio—and so on. My biggest problem in writing a book or preparing a speech is not to get ideas, but to get illustrations to make those ideas clear, vivid, and unforgettable. The old Roman philosophers used to say, "Exemplum docet" (the example teaches). And how right they were!

For example, let me show you the value of an illustration. Years ago, a congressman made a stormy speech accusing the government of wasting our money by printing useless pamphlets. He illustrated what he meant by saying the government had printed a pamphlet on "The Love Life of the Bullfrog." I would have forgotten that speech years ago if it hadn't been for that one specific illustration, "The Love Life of the Bullfrog." I may forget a million other facts as the decades pass, but I'll never forget his charge that the government wastes our money by printing and giving away pamphlets such as "The Love Life of the Bullfrog!"

Exemplum docet. Not only does the example teach, but it is about the only thing that does teach. I have heard brilliant speeches which I promptly forgot because there were no examples to make them stick in my memory.

V.   Know far more about your subject that you can use.

Ida Tarbell, one of America's most distinguished writers, told me that years ago, while in London, she received a cable from S.S. McClure, the founder of McClure's Magazine, asking her to write a two-page article on the Atlantic Cable. Miss Tarbell interviewed the London manager of the Atlantic Cable and got all the information necessary to write her five-hundred word article. But she didn't stop there. She went to the British Museum library and read magazine articles and books about the Atlantic Cable, and the biography of Cyrus West Field, the man who laid the Atlantic Cable. She studied cross sections of cables on display in the British Museum, and then visited a factory on the outskirts of London and saw cables being manufactured. "When I finally wrote those two typewritten pages on the Atlantic Cable," Miss Tarbell said, as she told me the story, "I had enough material to write a small book about it. But that vast amount of material which I had and did not use enabled me to write what I did write with confidence and clarity and interest. It gave me reserve power."

9

Ida Tarbell had learned through years of experience that she had to earn the right to write over five hundred words about the Atlantic Cable. The same principle goes for speaking. Make yourself something of an authority on your subject. Develop that priceless asset known as reserve power.

VI. Rehearse your talk by conversing with your friends.

Will Rogers prepared his famous Sunday night radio talks by trying them out as conversation on the people he met during the week. If, for example, he wanted to speak on the gold standard, he would wisecrack about it in conversation during the week. He would then discover which of his jokes went over, which remarks elicited people's interest. That is an infinitely better way to rehearse a talk than to try it out with gestures in front of a mirror.

VII. Instead of worrying about your delivery, find ways of improving it.

Much harmful, misleading nonsense has been written about delivery of a speech. The truth is that when you face an audience, you should forget all about voice, breathing, gestures, posture, emphasis. Forget everything except what you are saying. What listeners want, as Hamlet's mother said, is "more matter, with less art." Do what a cat does when trying to catch a mouse. It doesn't look around and say: "I wonder how my tail looks, and I wonder if I am standing right, and how is my facial expression?" Oh, no. That cat is so intent on catching a mouse for dinner that it couldn't stand wrong or look wrong if it tried—and neither can you if you are so vitally interested in your audience and in what you are saying that you forget yourself.

Don't imagine that expressing your ideas and emotions before an audience is something that requires years of technical training such as you have to devote to mastering music or painting. Anybody can make a splendid talk at home when angry. For example, if somebody hauled off and knocked you down this instant, you would get up and make a superb talk. Your gestures, your posture, your facial expression would be perfect because they would be the expressions of genuine anger. And remember, you don't have to learn to express your emotions. You could express your emotions superbly when you were six months old. Ask any mother.

Watch a group of children at play. What fine expression! What perfect emphasis, gestures, posture, communication! Jesus said: "Except ye become as little children, ye cannot enter the kingdom of heaven." Yes, and unless you become as natural and spontaneous and free as little children at play, you cannot enter the realm of good expression.

10

IF YOUR ATTITUDE IS GOOD—YOUR TALK WILL BE

Your problem isn't to try to learn how to speak with emphasis, or how to gesture or how to stand. Those are merely effects. Your problem is to deal with the cause that produces those effects. That cause is deep down inside you; it is your own mental and emotional attitude. If you get yourself in the right mental and emotional condition, you will speak superbly. You won't have to make any effort to do it. You will do it as naturally as you breathe.

To illustrate, a rear admiral of the United States Navy once took this course. He had commanded a squadron of the United States Fleet during World War I. He wasn't afraid to fight a naval battle, but he was so afraid to face an audience that he made weekly trips from his home in New Haven, Connecticut, to New York City to attend this course.

Half a dozen sessions went by, and he was still terrified. So one of our instructors, Professor Elmer Nyberg, had an idea that might make the admiral come out of his shell. There was a radical in this class. Professor Nyberg took him to one side and said: "I wonder if you will be good enough to make a strong talk to support your philosophy of government? Obviously, you will make the admiral angry, which is exactly what I want. He will forget himself and in his eagerness to refute your position, he probably will make a good talk." The radical said,"Sure, I'll be glad to." He had not gone far in this talk, when the rear admiral leaped to his feet and shouted: "Stop! Stop! That's sedition!" Then he gave a fiery talk on how much each of us owes to our country and its freedom.

Professor Nyberg turned to the naval officer and said, "Congratulations, Admiral! A magnificent talk!" The rear admiral snapped back: "I'm not making a talk, but I am telling that little whippersnapper a thing or two." Then Professor Nyberg explained that it had all been a put-up job to get the admiral out of his shell, and make him forget himself.

This rear admiral discovered just what you will discover when you get stirred up about a cause bigger than yourself. You will discover that all fears of speaking will vanish and that you don't have to give a thought to delivery, since the causes that produce good delivery are working for you irresistibly.

Let me repeat: *Your delivery is merely the effect of a cause that preceded and produced it. So if you don't like your delivery, don't muddle around trying to change it. Get back to fundamentals and change the causes that produced it. Change your mental and emotional attitude.*

VIII. Don't imitate others; be yourself.

I first came to New York to study at the American Academy of Dramatic Arts. I aspired to be an actor. I had what I thought was a brilliant idea, a shortcut to success. My campaign to achieve excellence was so simple, so foolproof, that I was unable to comprehend why thousands of ambitious people hadn't already discovered it. It was this: I would study the famous actors of that day—John Drew, E. H. Sothern, Walter Hampden and Otis Skinner. Then I would imitate the best points of each one of them and make myself into a shining, triumphant combination of all of them. How silly! How tragic! I had to waste years of my life imitating other people before it penetrated my thick Missouri skull that I had to be myself, and that I couldn't possibly be anyone else.

To illustrate what I mean: A number of years ago, I set out to write the best book on public speaking for business people that had ever been written. I had the same foolish idea about writing this book that I had formerly had about acting: I was going to borrow the ideas of many other writers and put them all in one book—a book that would have everything. So I got scores of books on public speaking and spent a year incorporating their ideas in my manuscript. But it finally dawned on me once again that I was playing the fool. This hodgepodge of other people's ideas that I had written was so synthetic, so dull that no business people would ever stumble through it. So I tossed a year's work into the wastebasket, and started all over again. This time I said to myself: "You've got to be Dale Carnegie, with all his faults and limitations. You can't possibly be anybody else." So I quit trying to be a combination of other people, and rolled up my sleeves and did what I should have done in the first place: I wrote a textbook on public speaking out of my own experiences and observations and convictions.

Why don't you profit by my stupid waste of time? Don't try to imitate others.

11

DON'T BE AFRAID OF BEING YOURSELF

Be yourself. Act on the sage advice that Irving Berlin gave to the late George Gershwin. When Berlin and Gershwin first met, Berlin was famous—but Gershwin was a struggling young composer working for thirty-five dollars a week in Tin Pan Alley. Berlin, impressed by Gershwin's ability, offered Gershwin a job as his musical secretary at almost three times the salary he was then getting. "But don't take the job," Berlin advised. "If you do, you may develop into a second-rate Berlin. But if you insist on being yourself, some day you'll become a first-rate Gershwin." Gershwin heeded that warning and slowly transformed himself into one of the significant American composers of his generation.

"Be yourself! Don't imitate others!" That is sound advice in music, writing, and speaking. You are an original. Be glad of it. Never before, since the dawn of time, has anybody been exactly like you; and never again, throughout all the ages to come, will there be anybody exactly like you. So make the most of your individuality. Your speech should be a part of you, the very living tissue of you. It should grow out of your experiences, your convictions, your personality, your way of life.

In the last analysis, all art is autobiographical. You can sing only what you are. You can paint only what you are. You can write only what you are. You can speak only what you are. You must be what your experiences, your environment, and your heredity have made you. For better or for worse, you must cultivate your own garden. For better or for worse, you must play your own instrument in life's orchestra. As Emerson said in his essay, "Self-reliance":

> There is a time in every man's education when he arrives at the conviction that envy is ignorance; that imitation is suicide; that he must take himself for better, for worse, as his portion; that although the wide universe is full of good, no kernel of nourishing corn can come to him but through his toil on that plot of ground which is given him to till. The power which resides in him is new in nature, and none but he knows what that is which he can do, nor does he know until he has tried.

IN A NUTSHELL

HOW TO MAKE RAPID AND EASY PROGRESS IN LEARNING TO SPEAK IN PUBLIC

Speak about something that:

    (a) **You have earned the right to talk about through study and experience;**

    (b) **You are excited about; and**

    (c) **You are eager to tell your listeners about.**

I. Make brief notes of the interesting things you want to mention.

II. Don't write out your talks.

III. Never, never, never memorize a talk word for word.

IV. Fill your talk with illustrations and examples.

V. Know far more about your subject than you can use.

VI. Rehearse your talk by conversing with your friends.

VII. Instead of worrying about your delivery, find ways of improving it.

VIII. Don't imitate others; be yourself.

INDIVIDUAL PITCH PRESENTATION RUBRIC
Expectations and Marking Guide

	4 Exceeded expectations	3 Meet expectations	2 Below expectations	1-0 Failed to meet expectations	Grade
STRUCTURE	• very clearly and effectively used elements of a pitch in structuring presentation • clarity and conciseness demonstrated very thorough thought and planning	• clearly used elements of a pitch in structuring presentation • clarity and conciseness demonstrated adequate thought and planning	• some elements of a pitch were unclear or not used effectively • clarity and conciseness demonstrated less than adequate thought and planning	• pitch elements unclear and/or missing • clarity and conciseness demonstrated very little or poor thought and planning	
OPEN & CLOSE	• very effective and engaging opening and closing	• effective opening and closing	• opening and/or closing not as effective and/or engaging as could be	• opening and/or closing weak and ineffective	
DELIVERY	• delivery of pitch demonstrated very strong conviction, passion and enthusiasm • pitcher was very natural, poised and confident • thorough practice was very clearly evident	• delivery of pitch showed conviction, passion and enthusiasm • pitcher was reasonably natural, poised and confident • practice was clearly evident	• delivery of pitch showed less than adequate conviction, passion and enthusiasm • pitcher was less than natural, stiff, and/or lacking confidence • practice was not clearly evident	• delivery of pitch showed little conviction, passion and/or enthusiasm • pitcher was unnatural, stiff and/or lacking confidence • more practice was needed	
CONNECTION WITH AUDIENCE	• pitch clearly considered and incorporated audience's point of view • strong eye contact • effectively grabbed and kept audience's attention throughout • audience very engaged throughout pitch	• pitch considered audience's point of view • good eye contact • grabbed and kept audience's attention throughout • audience reasonably engaged throughout	• pitch didn't appear to consider audience's point of view • weak eye contact • didn't effectively grab and/or keep audience's attention • audience not engaged throughout pitch	• pitch didn't consider audience's point of view • little to no eye contact and/or reading pitch • lost audience's attention	

/16

= /5

Week #4 / Lab #3

Lab #3 – Critical Thinking & Case Analysis Tools

In preparation for this lab:

- Review the following readings (also found in the BU111 Lab Manual):
    - o What is a Case?: An Introduction to the Case Method
    - o Case Analysis & Write-up: Summary Checklist

- Read "Case Analysis: Tips & Tools"

- Prepare *The Entrepreneur's Marketing Source, Inc.* case for discussion, using the *What is a Case?* approach, and considering the analytical tools presented in the readings and that you have learned in BU111, that might be appropriate to use in working through this case.

What Is a Case? An Introduction to the Case Method

A case is a description of a "real life" business situation that commonly results in an issue that requires a decision. The decision-maker in the case must determine the problems or opportunities (issues) that exist, analyze the situation, generate and compare alternative courses of action, and recommend both a solution and plan of implementation or course of action.

In case discussions you will assume the role of the decision-maker in the case, and will be expected to go through the same process, and face the same constraints, as the "real life" decision-maker.

Why Cases?

Management is not an exact science. Managers learn what works best through experience — through repeated exposure to decision-making situations. The ability to analyze a situation, determine what needs to be done, and follow through with an appropriate course of action is critical to your success in business. Cases allow you to develop and practice these skills in a low-risk situation where a bad solution will not result in damage to a real company.

Cases also bridge the gap between theory and practice. Students must learn which theories are relevant to understanding and resolving the issue and apply them appropriately. Furthermore, theories that appear to be simple and straightforward in the classroom must be adapted based on the situation at hand. There is no universal right or wrong way to solve a problem. The correct approach is contingent upon the situation at hand. Decision-makers must learn to modify and apply the theory on the basis of their experience, and use what fits. Cases give you the opportunity to gain that experience.

Finally, when you write up a case for hand-in, you will also develop proper business writing skills to use in the "real world".

Case Frustrations

Any "real life" decision-maker will tell you that he/she must often make decisions without perfect or complete information and within tight time constraints. You will experience the same frustrations. You may also feel overwhelmed by the amount of information in the case and confused about what is relevant and what can be ignored. This is necessary in order to truly experience realistic decision-making scenarios. You will also find that often there aren't clear cut, right or wrong answers. Although there are poor solutions and approaches, there is often more than one way to address the case issue well. The best solution is often the one that maximizes the positives while minimizing the effects of the negatives. This can be very frustrating if you prefer the "black and white" associated with subjects such as mathematics. Usually trade-offs must be made.

What Is Expected?

Thoughtful and thorough analysis

You must demonstrate that you can logically think through a situation and make an appropriate decision. The following is a checklist that will give you some guidance and structure in handling cases:

✓ Do I have a good handle on the situation — have I assessed all the relevant information, do I understand the implications of the situation on all the parties involved, and have I separated fact from opinion?

✓ Have I identified, prioritized and dealt with all the issues?

✓ Are my assumptions reasonable given the situation?

✓ Have I determined and ranked the appropriate criteria for making the best decisions to resolve the situation in this case?

✓ Have I considered and appropriately evaluated all the feasible alternative courses of action?

✓ Have I made a decision that meets the criteria, and have I defended it with a persuasive, convincing argument that considers the possible drawbacks?

✓ Have I suggested a thorough action plan that attempts to deal with the potential problems with implementing my solutions?

✓ Have I considered a contingency plan to deal with any potential events that could occur, or assumptions that might prove incorrect, that would render my solution inappropriate?

If your analysis is thorough and your suggested solution(s) logically flow(s) from the analysis, your solution may be very different than your classmates and still receive a reasonable grade if the above expectations are met.

Effective communication

You must also effectively communicate your ideas. Discussing cases in your lab provides an excellent opportunity to practice both speaking and listening. Sharing your ideas and actively listening to and building upon your peers' insights are skills that are essential for successful case discussion. Furthermore, effective speaking and listening are also important for success in your professional career. Even though you may find it difficult or intimidating to speak up in your lab, it is essential that you do so in order to develop these important skills. The best way to begin is to prepare your case analysis in advance and share your insights and listen to and build on your classmates' during the lab. Don't worry about making mistakes — remember that your fellow classmates are in the same boat, and the more you practice with cases in university the less mistakes you will likely make in the business world where the "cost" of making a mistake is much larger.

When a case is assigned for hand-in, you also have an opportunity to practice your written communication skills. Whether in case reports or business reports, if you have not effectively and persuasively communicated your recommendations in writing, then the value of your work will be lost. In the business world, if your team does not understand what you want them to do to implement your solution, it is not likely to succeed. In university, if we can't understand what you are trying to say then you are not likely to be given the marks for your thinking and analysis.

171

Finally, format is also important. The case should be in the form of a business report that you would be comfortable handing to your superior. It should be carefully prepared using the suggestions provided in the link to the writing materials provided on the course website. It should be thorough and organized but at the same time concise and to the point.

Case Analysis — How to Analyze the Case

Where do you start? How do you think through the case? The following format provides a structured, logical process to guide your analysis. A note of caution is necessary, however, this is only the process for thinking through the case; it is not the process for writing up the case.

Step 1 — Skim the Case

Most students begin their case analysis by reading the case from start to finish. This often results in frustration and feeling lost and overwhelmed by the amount of information in the case. To avoid this and improve your case analysis, you should first "skim" the case to get a rough idea of what it is about. This will ensure that a closer reading will be more focused, organized, and productive. Read the opening and closing paragraphs (two to four paragraphs in total) of the case. Then familiarize yourself with the headings of the case so you know what information to expect and where you might find it. Finally, spend a few minutes looking at the exhibits and considering the information they present. If there are financial statements, take a moment to consider the financial health and situation of the organization.

The objective of skimming is to answer the following questions:

- Who are you, i.e., who is the decision-maker and what position does he/she hold?
- What is/are the issue(s)/problem(s)? What decision must you make?
- Why has this issue appeared/why is a decision needed?
- When does the problem/issue occur (time context — year, season, date) and what is the deadline by which it must be resolved?
- Where is the case taking place — the setting, i.e., company name, country, department of the company?

Now you are ready to go through a detailed reading and analysis of the case in order to generate the elements of case analysis identified below. Make notes in the margin, highlight as you read and record your ideas and reactions to what you are reading. Note what is fact and what is opinion in the case information.

Step 2 — Read Thoroughly and Prepare an Analysis of the Case

✓ THE ISSUES

Identify the issues and/or decisions the decision-maker must make.

This can be one of the most difficult and crucial parts of case analysis. You are unlikely to come up with a good solution if you do not correctly identify the problem and its implications. Often you will be confronted with a series of problems, some of which appear to be interrelated, and others that may be totally separate and unrelated issues (secondary problems). What appears to be the problem may only be an effect or symptom (immediate problem) of a deeper underlying issue/problem (primary problem). You must take care to separate immediate problems, symptoms, underlying causes, and secondary problems. The following breakdown may help in distinguishing the issues in a case:

Immediate Problem	—	This is the specific decision/issue/opportunity faced by the decision-maker and it must be resolved in your recommendation.
Primary Problem	—	This is often the root cause of the immediate problem or a more generic issue that is ever-present or common that has led to the immediate problem. For example, if the immediate problem is what to do about an employee who drinks during his lunch break, the primary problem may be that there is no company policy on drinking during business hours or that employee orientation did not make clear company expectations regarding drinking. If the primary problem is solved, the immediate problem is less likely to occur again in the future. You also need to address the primary problem in your solution.
Secondary Problem	—	This is not necessarily solved when the immediate and primary problems are solved. Secondary problems should be acknowledged but are not always necessary to solve immediately.

You must identify all problems/issues as specifically as possible. A good case analysis and solution will identify and recognize the relationship between the immediate and primary problems/issues. The immediate problem will be resolved by the recommended solution, but the primary problem should also be dealt with either in the recommendation and/or during the implementation to ensure that the primary problem does not occur again in the future.

Remember ... the case may not involve a problem per se. Often the case involves an opportunity or an issue that needs to be dealt with. Whatever it is, always finish off by knowing the decision(s) that need to be made.

✓ ANALYSIS OF THE SITUATION

Discuss causes, effects, and relationships between the issues. Identify constraints and opportunities that will affect your recommendations.

In order to solve the problem you must understand both its causes and effects. You must identify what is *really* happening, what is relevant, and what implications exist for the people involved as well as the organization.

o Don't summarize or repeat the facts in the case — go beyond that; you can assume that the people you will ultimately be communicating with are already familiar with the situation.

o Look at the exhibits and information and generate your own observations, but anchor your views with evidence from the case.

o Identify constraints and opportunities that will impact your recommendations; consider the key resources of the company.

o Pay attention to both qualitative and quantitative information.

o Don't be afraid of numbers — analyze those that have been provided and generate your own, but know why you are doing a calculation before you start it — what are you trying to prove or uncover?

o Apply relevant theory to understanding the issues and solving them. The theory you use should convince the decision-maker of the validity of your analysis. This is where you back up your identification of the issues and create support for your recommended solution.

✓ DECISION CRITERIA

Identify the objectives that a good solution must satisfy.

Decision criteria are goals or objectives that the decision or solution must meet in order to be effective. They reflect the top priorities of the organization and/or decision-maker in the case. To determine these criteria you must understand what is important to both the individuals and organization in the case, and as such this should flow from your analysis of the situation. Criteria can be quantitative such as, "the solution must restore the company to a more viable cash position" or "the solution must increase profitability", or they can be qualitative such as "the decision must minimize the potential loss of valuable employees" or "the solution must create a competitive advantage".

✓ IDENTIFICATION AND EVALUATION OF ALTERNATIVES

Identify your options for solving the problem and compare them using the decision criteria.

You must identify and analyze all possible alternatives to all of the issues in the case according to your decision criteria. Be sure to consider all alternatives presented in the case, as you shouldn't ignore what options the people in the case are considering. However, you may also come up with your own alternatives, which could be quite superior.

Your alternatives should be complete solutions to the issues you have identified in the case. In other words, each alternative should be a different approach you can take to solving all the issues in the case. In this way when you choose an alternative to recommend as a solution it will solve all the issues you have identified without having to be combined with other alternatives to form a complete solution.

Don't waste your time and the reader's by suggesting and evaluating the pros and cons of alternatives that are highly improbable or unrealistic.

Be sure to consider both the short- and long-term effects of each alternative and predict their outcomes. If there are quantitative effects of your alternatives these should be shown in detail in exhibits and referenced and discussed in the comparison of alternatives. Lastly you must make a decision on each, and justify this decision.

✓ DECISIONS/RECOMMENDATIONS/SOLUTIONS

What should we do to solve the problem and what outcome should we expect?

The key to case learning is that you are put in the position of the decision-maker. Don't fall into the trap of recommending deferring the decision to someone else or to further research and analysis. You must make a decision(s) with respect to each of the issues in the case, and justify this decision(s). This of course will be one of the alternatives you have evaluated.

✓ IMPLEMENTATION/COURSE OF ACTION

What should be done in the immediate, short, and long-term to execute the solution?

This final step ultimately determines the success or failure of your solution(s). Even the best solution will fail if you don't have an effective plan to follow through and implement it. You must therefore specify *what* should be done *when* (immediate, short and long term) and *where*, by *whom*, for what reason — *why*, and exactly *how*. This necessitates that you understand the elements that determine success in this situation (your decision criteria) and that you deal with the implications that the situation has for the people and organization involved. In other words, in order to be successful, your implementation must be thorough and must take into consideration your analysis of the situation and its effects on everyone involved. Your implementation should address both the immediate and basic problem.

✓ CONTINGENCY PLAN

What problems might arise as you try to implement your solution and what should you do?

It is always critical to plan for an alternative course of action that you can take if your intended plan of action is unexpectedly disrupted or rendered inappropriate by a contingency event. Often students think that a contingency plan is simply a Plan B if your recommended solution is unsuccessful. Thus they suggest choosing one of the rejected alternatives as a contingency plan. This is tantamount to suggesting you have no confidence in your recommended solution and think that one of your other options might be better! This is never a good idea. Instead think through what "contingency events" could occur — for example the economy being weaker than you had anticipated — that would make your solution less appropriate than it otherwise would be. Then you can suggest, for example, slowing your suggested rate of expansion down and outline specifically which stores you would hold off opening until the economy picks up. This is a true contingency plan. Don't underestimate its importance.

✓ ASSUMPTIONS AND MISSING INFORMATION

What assumptions have you made in order to deal with missing information?

As stated earlier in this reading, a frustration with cases and real-life decisions is that you often don't have all of the information you want. In case analysis you must often deal with this by making assumptions. You should recognize when you are making an assumption, state it explicitly, and be able to justify it. Be sure that your assumptions are reasonable and realistic. It is reasonable to assume that the data presented in the case is accurate unless there are also hints within the case itself that indicate otherwise.

Case Write-Up — Communicating Your Thinking

It would be a lot easier to just hand in your analysis notes using the format stated above. Although we may ask for these notes on a supplied worksheet, this is not the way it works in the "real" business world. Unless this is a decision you will simply be making and implementing yourself, you will normally be asked for a report outlining your recommendations. This is the assumption that we make in this course — you have been asked by your superior to provide a report.

We have provided guidelines for business communication on the course website. These guidelines provide information on writing more informal memo reports suitable for cases, and more formal reports suitable for research projects. Guidelines are also provided for presentations. Read through all of the materials provided.

✓ USE THE DIRECT ORDER

Writing for business is very different from writing for an English class. One of the most distinct differences between them is that in business we normally use the direct order. The direct order places the key points (conclusion) before the explanation of how we arrived at that conclusion, as opposed to building up to the conclusion as in a typical English essay. In other words, in business writing we usually make our point — the decision that we are recommending, for example — up front in the first couple of paragraphs, and follow this with our supporting analysis, rather than building the reader up with our arguments and then stating the decision. The direct order is typical when we assume that the reader has asked for this information and is looking forward to our suggestions. An indirect order with the conclusion at the end would only be used if the reader would be displeased or skeptical.

The direct approach to writing an informal memo report, therefore, does not look the same as the way you thought through the case. Once you have analyzed the case you must now think through how to communicate your recommendations and convince the reader to follow them.

✓ ORGANIZE YOUR THOUGHTS LOGICALLY

Start by trying the *elevator test* ... You have been asked to prepare a report recommending what you feel should be done to boost productivity in your department. You have analyzed the situation and come up with recommendations that meet what you feel are the key factors to the success of your solution (your decision criteria), and thought through the steps that need to be taken to implement your recommendations effectively. You're about to write your report when you get on the elevator to go to your office and the boss steps in with you. She asks you what your thoughts are on the situation. Beads of sweat start to pour down your back as you realize you only have ten floors to impress your boss with an intelligent synopsis of the situation as you see it. Do you start with a statement of the problem, and then discuss your analysis and the alternatives you considered? You'd probably still be on the analysis as your boss steps out of the elevator shaking her head and thinking she may have asked the wrong person. The same goes for the actual report. This is a busy person. She wants to know what you recommend first, and why second.

Very often the whole report is not even read in its entirety. You must get the key points out upfront — what is the issue(s) and what do you suggest doing about it. Then organize your justification for your suggestion(s) in such a way that your boss can see at a glance what you are saying. Your information must therefore be well-organized and easy to locate.

One of the most effective ways to write for business is to write as you would speak. For example, if you were trying to decide what movie to see with your friends for example, and you wanted to go to a particular film, how would you justify your choice? You might say that Movie A is the best movie to see because it is at a cheaper theatre than Movie B, the popcorn is better than at Movie Theatre B, and the movie is a more action-packed one than Movie B. Notice that you didn't discuss the decision criteria you are using (cost of ticket, popcorn quality, type of movie) and then examine each alternative discussing the pros and cons. You simply focused your argument on your recommendation, justifying it based on the decision criteria and how it meets the criteria better than the other option.

Of course, you would say this clearly and concisely or the other person would stop listening! The same goes for business writing — or maybe even more so because the reader is not faced with the social dilemma of walking away while you're talking, whereas they can definitely stop reading your report!

✓ FORMAT YOUR WRITING FOR BUSINESS

Remember to use space creatively in your report by dividing it into sections and subsections — the more you break up the body of the report and the more white space you have, the more inviting it is to read. It should not look like an essay.

Another way to make the report easier to read is to use bulleted lists with parallel phrasing (similar grammatical structure) that's easy to follow. Just make sure the group of bullets all relate to the same point.

You should also use short descriptive headings that indicate the main point of the information beneath it. For example, instead of using the title, "Recommendation" you should state the actual recommendation, i.e., "Expand operations into Europe". These are referred to as high information headings. Ideally the reader should be able to quickly understand what you are saying by reading the headings and looking at the bulleted lists, and only reading the report if he/she wants more detail.

All of these ideas and many others are included in your readings, and the style expectations from the rubrics will serve as another reference as well.

Even though the write-up of the report will not look the same as the way you thought through the case, it does have the same elements. To get you started, once you've read the writing materials that have been provided, refer to the following checklist to make sure that you are following the guidelines properly and including all of your content in the right place and in the right way ...

☐ Do I have a memo heading directed to the appropriate party(ies)?

☐ Have I first given a clear, concise synopsis of the *situation* and *issues* that need to be resolved without restating the facts but discussing instead what they imply, showing insight and understanding into the situation and issues it presents?

☐ Have I then immediately stated my *decision(s)* with respect to resolving the current issues as outlined?

☐ Next have I outlined what *criteria* I used to make the decision(s)? In other words, what my decision(s) does that will result in successful resolution of the issues.

☐ Have I justified why my decision(s) more effectively meet(s) the criteria than the other alternatives I have examined? You can certainly point out those alternatives, but should not discuss them each separately; only in comparison to your chosen decision(s). This is where your *analysis of the alternatives* will show through. Just remember that you are justifying why your solution is better than the alternatives on the basis of the decision criteria, not walking your reader through a boring pros and cons analysis of each of your alternatives.

☐ Have I outlined how the decision(s)/solution(s) needs to be *implemented* in order to ensure success?

☐ Have I suggested a *contingency plan* should something happen that would render my decision(s) inappropriate?

☐ And lastly, have I checked back over my content worksheet to ensure that all the key points I want to make have been communicated effectively through the informal report?

CASE ANALYSIS & WRITE-UP: Summary Checklist

Section of Case	Thinking	Communicating
IDENTIFICATION OF ISSUE(S)	• What is the problem/opportunity? Immediate, primary and secondary.	*First* — Outlined immediately after memo heading to tell reader what memo is about.
ANALYSIS OF SITUATION	• What are the causes and effects of the problem and the relationship between problems? • What evidence do you have to support the points in your analysis? What are the constraints and opportunities you face in coming up with a solution? • What analysis did you do to develop your recommendation(s)? • Is there any theory that you apply to analyze the situation or develop a solution?	This section is not placed directly in your write-up but is used to aid in your thought process and *Fifth* — to support your recommendations & arguments.
DECISION CRITERIA	• What are the objectives that the solution must satisfy?	*Third* — Discussed after your recommendation(s) to explain what was considered in arriving at that solution — why it was chosen.
ALTERNATIVES AND ANALYSIS	• What are your options for dealing with the issue(s)? • Each alternative should be an alternate approach to solving all the issues. • Alternatives given in the case should be considered in addition to any others you have developed.	*Fourth* — Alternatives are stated to present options that were considered, and then — *Fifth* — they are incorporated into the justification of why your recommendation is best. Ex: We recommend (solution) because it will (meet the criteria better — for ex. create greater cash flow) than (alternative).
DECISION(S)	• What is your recommended solution? What are its expected outcomes?	*Seconds* — Stated up front immediately after the issue(s) to indicate what you suggest be done to deal with them.

CASE ANALYSIS & WRITE-UP: Summary Checklist (continued)

Section of Case	Thinking	Communicating
IMPLEMENTATION	• What are the specific short, medium, and long-term steps that must be taken to make the solution successful?	*Sixth* — Discussed after the justification of your recommendation to demonstrate what must be done and how it must be done to ensure success.
CONTINGENCY PLAN	• What might go wrong and how will you deal with it?	*Last* — Discussed last to show that you have thought through what could go wrong in your implementation and that you have a plan to deal with these risks.
ASSUMPTIONS	• What assumptions have you made and how are they justified?	These should be specified where they are applied/ appear in the case analysis. They can be communicated in footnotes or within the text.

Case Analysis: Tips & Tools

PART 1 — CASE ANALYSIS TIPS

You should now know what a 'case' is and understand the process for 'solving' a case, and you have even experienced case discussions and handed in a case 'write-up' using the informal report format if you took BU111. As you move on in your courses however, you will need to build on that process to tackle more complex cases. The purpose of this reading is to give you some tips to do just that. We'll take a look at:

- How to 'read' a case
- How to prepare for a case discussion
- How to improve your participation
- Strategies for tackling a case exam
- Strategies for writing a solid case report
- Case ethics

How to Read a Case

As Terrance Power states in "Power's Case Study Analysis and Writer's Handbook" (2009):

> Your responsibilities (in a case discussion) are the 4 Ps: preparation, promptness, presence, and participation ... Generally, case study courses assume that both you and the instructor will accept responsibility for learning, and that the flow of information, knowledge, and ideas will be two-way. Your duty is to accept responsibility for your own learning by being prepared to contribute and to take the opportunity to express your ideas frequently ... The goal is that, by the end, you will be competent and confident in critical thinking and in the skills of argument persuasion. (p. 17)

Well that is not going to happen until and unless you have at least 'read' the case appropriately to get a good start on your preparation. Obviously I know you can read; what I am talking about is reading the case in a way that will help you to "comprehend its contents as efficiently as possible." (Ronstadt, 1988, p.11)

The key is to read the case in the shortest amount of time and get the most out of it, so that you can focus your time on the analysis and have something of value to contribute to the case discussion. Also, having a proper approach to reading the case will prevent the common problem that a lot of students have — that is, starting to analyze as you're reading, only to discover that your analysis makes no sense or is unnecessary as you get further into the case

---

Many of the ideas for this reading have been inspired by and adapted from Ronald Ronstadt, *The Art of Case Analysis*, 2nd edition (Natick, MA: Lord Publishing Inc., 1988), and Terrance P. Power, *Power's Case Study Analysis and Writer's Handbook* (Toronto, ON: Nelson Education Ltd., 2009).

— therefore completely wasting your time. 'Read' the case as suggested below, digest the case — give yourself time to really think about it and look at it in a 'big picture' way, asking yourself 'so what?' questions, and *then* start to analyze and solve it using whatever tools from your toolkit that are appropriate.

Some tips for 'reading' a case:

1. Most cases should be read at least twice

2. Read the case well ahead of time
   - To allow you more time to digest it and really understand the issues and the appropriate analytical tools to use, as well as giving you time to discuss it with others vs a rushed reading just before class

3. Start by reading the first page or so to understand the situational context
   - This is very critical to your understanding of the case and will prevent you from going off on a tangent that might prove to be completely wrong

4. Quickly skim the rest of the case, noting headings and the first few sentences of the lead paragraphs
   - To give you an overall sense for the direction of the case

5. Quickly leaf through the exhibits
   - Look to see if there is anything unusual about the typical exhibits (financial statements and organizational charts) or anything revealing about the exhibits unique to the case

6. Once you've done this, then you can actually read the case normally
   - But don't underline or highlight; instead jot notes in the margins regarding your observations and the concepts that you are learning that you think might be relevant (remember there is likely a reason your Professor has assigned this particular case)

7. As you are doing a thorough read, look at the exhibits as they are referred to in the case so you understand their context

8. Be careful to separate fact from opinion, and what people are saying from what they are doing, and dig deep into the information
   - This is what 'critical thinking' is all about. Power (2009) suggests that you " 'peel the onion' by asking yourself a series of 'So what?' questions to analyze the data and look beyond the surface level meaning. For example: Our competitor is opening a factory in China. So what? Well, labour in China is less expensive than our labour. So what? Well, our competitor's cost base will go down. So what? Our competitor will be able to make its product for less than we can (and therefore price it lower). Ah-ha!" This way you can "uncover deeper meaning from the facts". (p. 3)

9. Then reread the case — your Professor or Teaching Assistant certainly has and they'll be able to tell if you haven't!

How to Prepare for a Case Discussion

A good case 'reading' will prepare you for a case discussion in which you will be able to participate, learn, and be rewarded for both! The aspects of the case that you want to focus on to be truly prepared for the discussion are:

- the key issues in the case and why it is being discussed now in the course — therefore what concepts you could apply
    - o but don't get misled thinking that just because you've learned something it necessarily will or should apply!

- the analytical tools you can use in the case — that are actually relevant and needed to support your ideas

- how you will focus your analysis — the facts you'll need to support your ideas, and the assumptions you may have to make to get that information

Ask yourself what kinds of questions will be raised in the discussion so you can be ready for them. Undoubtedly, if you are ready with some numbers you have crunched to support your position you will make a better impression. In the 'real world', you'll find that you won't just make a better impression, it will be expected, and you'll be embarrassed if you don't have that information when asked. This is a good habit to get into!

A very insightful and important point about case discussion was made by Robert Ronstadt in *The Art of Case Analysis* (1988): "Remember, people do not do poorly in case courses for being honestly wrong. They do poorly for not doing." (p. 36) You may be prepared at this point, but you have to participate. DO NOT wait until you are completely confident about what you can add to the discussion. If you have prepared, enter the discussion when you are *reasonably* confident. That is how you learn, by taking risks and trying.

How to Improve your Participation

Much of what has been said in the earlier section on preparing for a case discussion will help you to improve your participation in class. Obviously if you aren't prepared you can't participate! (at least not very well) But here's some really practical advice for improving your participation — pick a good seat. Yes, I'm serious! Products are placed strategically on supermarket shelves to be at eye level and where the consumer is most likely to look and see them. And marketers fight tooth and nail to get those positions for a reason. So you need to be just as strategic in picking your seat if you want to be noticed for participating. In our u-shaped and banked case rooms, there are seats where you will be noticed and seats where you will be more hidden, so choose wisely. Also, the more visible you are, the more likely you will be to engage. If you're less likely to engage, get out of your comfort zone and choose a visible seat. But if you're likely to talk too much, you might want to pick a less visible seat! And if you're shy and don't want everyone to turn around and look at you when you're talking, sit at the front vs. the back, or you may be less likely to participate.

When you aren't talking, you should be actively listening and making notes that might be relevant to future cases. This is critical. The point of using cases is not to solve just that situation, but to learn how to apply what happened in one situation to other situations. A good suggestion from Ronstadt (2009) is to develop a 'FIG' list. (p. 37) Don't write down everything that is being said. Listen, participate, and write down important notes that you take from the discussion, grouped under these 3 headings:

> Facts

> Ideas/insights

> Generalizations

At the end of the class, summarize what you've learned that you may be able to apply to other situations. If you put if off until another time you'll forget to do it and the knowledge gained will be lost. It's as simple as that.

Strategies for Tackling a Case Exam

Don't panic... You won't have a 'case exam' per se in this course. You will be tested on cases and the case process though, as well as the analytical tools you can use to tackle a case (in Part 2 of this reading). But in more senior courses you can and will have exams that are comprised entirely of one case, and you will be expected to demonstrate what you have learned and your ability to apply that knowledge. My hope and intent in providing this information to you is that you will keep and refer to this reading to help you throughout the program, adding to it as you are learning in order to build your toolbox. So here's some advice.

The good news is that preparation for a case exam will be fairly light. You have already done most of the work, hopefully, if you have prepared for your cases through the term. According to Ronstadt (1988), "a history of strong efforts at case analysis throughout the course pays rich dividends" (p. 77).

The best preparation would include:

- Reviewing the cases you had throughout the term and the key findings you recorded — your FIG lists
- Preparing a list of the skills and concepts you've learned that your Professor might expect you to apply
- Reviewing your process for reading and analyzing a case
- Sleeping! (Yes, I'm serious!)
    - o Do not underestimate the power of this one simple habit. Don't stay up late and cram; an alert, rested mind will help you to think more logically and clearly.
        - • According to Ronstadt: "Sitting down already mentally fatigued for a ... case exam qualifies you for observation for suicidal tendencies" (Ibid, p. 78),
- If you are allowed to bring in case notes, make sure they are well organized so it is easy to find information
    - o but don't rely on them, as experience suggests that you won't likely use them or being able to find what you need if you try

During the exam, rely on the process for analyzing cases that you've developed and practised during the term. It will pay off here. Don't panic and start analyzing using all the tools in your toolkit. Give yourself time to 'read' the case, decide what are the appropriate analytical tools, perform your analysis in a neat and organized way on scrap paper, and don't write anything until you have thought through how to clearly and persuasively present your case.

I completely agree with Ronstadt when he says "you are better off writing a few pages that are right on target, rather than pages of comment and analysis that just do not hang together." (Ibid, p. 79) In fact, in my final case exam in my final strategic policy course at this very university I wrote 3 pages. I'm not suggesting that you do that, and I can tell you that I was pretty nervous when I looked around and saw my fellow students asking for their 2nd and 3rd booklets! But then I'm teaching this course, so it must have been a pretty decent 3 pages! ☺

Quality content and simple presentation should be your goal. A few key observations that are defended well and supported by your analysis are worth more than a lot of words that don't zero in on anything of value and are presented haphazardly.

Strategies for Writing a Solid Case Report

Just as you won't have an exam in this course that is comprised of a single case, you also will not hand in a written case report. However you will prepare many written hand-in cases in senior courses. We've spent time in BU111, and will again in BU121, working on writing skills. There is no substitute for this in the business world. Good writing skills are necessary for success — period. But, again, a few words of advice:

- It's easy to spend too little or too much time on doing a written case. The key is to spend an *appropriate* amount of time on the different tasks involved and then you'll be spending your time more wisely. Particularly if you are doing a group case, as many of yours will be, Ronstadt suggests the following breakdown (Ibid, p. 70):
  - o Initial reading of the case and individual analysis (4–5 hours)
  - o Initial group meeting to analyze the facts and situational context, identify problems and assign tasks (2–3 hours max)
  - o Re-read case and perform analysis assigned (4–5 hours)
  - o Second group meeting (2–3 hours max)
  - o Organize report — determine key messages and prepare first draft (5–7 hours)
  - o Rewrite paper and do final proofread (2–3 hours) — I would suggest reading the final draft out loud. If it's difficult or uncomfortable to speak and doesn't sound like how you'd present it verbally — rewrite it until it flows better!

The time guidelines may or may not be applicable depending on the case assigned, however what I feel is important to note are 3 things:

- Set a max time for meetings and make them shorter than your individual prep outside of meeting

- You should do your own analysis prior to the first meeting and come prepared with your assigned tasks to the second meeting — or you may be meeting way more times than necessary!

- The writing of the report should be given a sufficient allotment of time. Most students do not spend sufficient time on the writing *and re-writing* of the report and marks suffer as a result. The more time that you spend in the other steps means the less time you will have to put together a coherent report — don't fall into that trap! More analysis poorly presented typically means a lower, not a higher grade.

When writing the report keep this in mind... your Professor or TA will likely spend only about 20 minutes to a half hour reading and marking your case. He or she is reading a large number of cases and will not spend time trying to figure out what you are saying, nor will anyone in the 'real world'. You generally have only one chance to say what you mean clearly and succinctly — don't waste it. Your main points and supporting analysis must be easy to spot and follow.

I can't help but also remind you to follow a bottom–up approach to writing your case report. In other words, start with the end — with the recommendation. And develop an outline for the report, with a defined message for each paragraph that supports the main points you are trying to make. Structure is everything. And nothing annoys Professors more, except for lack of structure and clarity, than exhibits that aren't relevant or tied in to what you are trying to say. Make sure that each of your exhibits provides further detail for a point that you are making in the report and they are fully integrated and referenced in the body of the report. No floating exhibits! — there must be a point to each of them that is clear and connected to what you're saying in the body of the report. They also should stand on their own, in that the reader shouldn't have to keep referring back to understand the nature and context of your exhibits.

Case Ethics

I know we've talked about business ethics and you have signed a Statement of Academic Integrity. But I do feel a few words specifically about the ethics of doing cases is warranted... Here are some of the ethical dilemmas that arise with using cases, and which should be avoided:

- using/sharing old case notes or reports
- using/sharing case notes with someone who has the class at a later time
- trying to find out "what really happened"
- contacting the actual company without permission
- and of course, not doing your fair share of the work on a group case

Bottom line, all of these actions result in you not learning. You only learn when you do the work. And if you help others by passing on information, you are robbing them of the learning experience. If this doesn't seem important to you, all I can suggest is that you reflect on why you are at university. Enough said.

PART 2 — CASE ANALYSIS TOOLS

The question now is... how to actually tackle a case that is more complex and which requires that you apply knowledge that you have learned. Isn't that really the whole reason for using cases? — to apply knowledge and skills to a simulated real life business situation so that you can transfer that knowledge and skill-set when you are working in the 'real world'.

If you're anything like me when I was a business student, you will read the case you are assigned and then stare blankly at the pages wondering "What next?" The process of applying knowledge and skills to business cases sounds good in theory, but without some solid tools to draw upon, it is difficult to know how to get started.

This is the purpose of this part of the reading — to help you develop a 'toolkit' to draw upon when faced with a business situation that you need to analyze in order to determine the issues, assess alternatives, and decide on and justify appropriate solutions.

Some of these tools you will have already discussed in classes and will now see how they can be applied (hopefully), and others will be discussed later in the course. The tools can be used in this course and any other business courses you take, and your toolkit will continue to grow as you take other more senior business courses.

So let's get started...

Here is a list of tools that will be covered in this reading, and which will be discussed in more depth in your lab:

- Key analytical tools:
    - Financial analysis
    - Cost/benefit analysis
    - Situational analysis
    - Alternative analysis

Key Analytical Tools

Now to the part you've been waiting for... If you're like I was as a student, you are looking for a 'template' — something you can use with each case as if it were a mathematical problem you can apply a formula to. Unfortunately it's not that easy. If you've learned anything about cases by now it is that they are not black and white — they are grey — ill-defined and with information missing. Remember, cases are simulated real-life situations designed to help you learn to apply your skills and knowledge to make a decision. Seldom is real life ever packaged up nice and neat. Every situation is different, requiring different tools from your toolkit. Do you approach every teacher you have the same way, every person you ask out, or each time you ask your parents for money? If you answered yes — ask yourself: did it always work out the same way?

So I'm going to give you some tools you can use, but here's the guidelines for using them:

- As long as the list may seem to you; it is not an exhaustive list. You will need to add to it as you continue through the program, learning new tools to apply to new situations, and expanding on your understanding of the tools presented. The tools presented are general tools that can be used in many different courses. You will undoubtedly learn more specific tools in some of your courses that you can add to this list.

- Not all the tools presented here necessarily can or will be used by you in the cases we do for this course. They are presented here to give you a basic toolkit to start with and build. The tools you apply to any given case depend on the case.

- Like carpentry tools, each one has a purpose and needs to be used to suit the situation. Just as there is no sense using a hammer to tighten a screw just because you have one, don't try to use all the tools to show you can! More is not better — appropriate and effective should always your goal. Using the wrong tool and wasting your time is not impressive and will not get you more marks, nor more importantly will it help you achieve greater success in your career. In fact, applying the wrong tool in real life can be very expensive, so focus on learning what is appropriate vs. just applying a tool because you can. Each tool needs to give meaning — to help uncover the issues/analyze the current situation, and/or compare alternatives according to the decision criteria to help arrive at a solution, and hence to justify your solution.

- You will also find, as happens with cases, that often you might want to use a tool but don't have enough information. Sometimes you can make reasonable assumptions, but other times there just isn't enough information even to make reasonable assumptions. Don't push it. Do what you can.

- I'll try to give you some clues as to when a tool might be appropriate, but you need to use your common sense and build your understanding of how to use your toolkit as you experience different cases. Also different Professors may have their own biases as to what they want to see in your cases. This is again a working document.

Financial Analysis

> Ratio Analysis

> Time Value of Money

> Projected Statements

I've presented the financial analytical tools first, because in my experience most of you will shy away from using them. This way hopefully they'll be top of your mind. Not all cases will present you with numbers (yes, you can breathe now!), but most of them will. If there are numbers in a case, as much as you'd like to, don't ignore them. Instead, explore them.

One of the first things you should do is to assess the organization's financial health. This can be very revealing. It can pinpoint issues that are not eluded to in the text, help you determine your decision criteria and hence analyze your alternatives and make an appropriate decision, and help you determine some key issues to watch for in your implementation.

Ratio Analysis

One of the most obvious financial tools to use first is ratio analysis. We will be covering ratio analysis is Week #6 of the course. Here are some tips:

- Your first clue as to whether or not this tool applies is that there are financial statements included in the case. It's that simple. If they are included, you need to look at them with an eye to what they are telling you about the company. So pay attention when we cover this in class and labs, as to how this tool can be used; don't just memorize the formulas.

- Ratios can help answer many questions such as:
  o Does the company have sufficient cash and is it managing its cash flows appropriately; can it pay its debts? (*liquidity ratios*)
  o How has it been funded and what are the implications of this? (*stability ratios*)

- Ratios can also be used analyze the impact of alternatives on profitability:
  o What is the return we can expect on this investment? (*ROI*)
  o How long will it take to recoup our investment? (*Payback*)
    - Net Investment ÷ Net Annual Return
      = number of years to recover the initial investment

Time Value of Money

In BU111 you learned about time value of money. This introduction will set you up to learn more about and apply the tool in 3rd year finance courses. This tool will let you compare alternatives to determine which will give you the best *Net Present Value* (the difference between the discounted cash inflows and outflows, or the return in today's dollars — remember that?) or just to look at one alternative to make sure its NPV is positive (greater than zero).

You can apply the same thinking to get the *Internal Rate of Return* — the discounted rate of return you will earn on the investment. It will allow you to compare alternatives without needing to have a specific rate of return for the calculation (also called the interest rate/alternative investment rate/hurdle rate/cost of capital) as you need to have to calculate NPV. It is essentially the same formula you would use for NPV, but NPV is set to zero and you are solving for the rate of return.

Financial Statements

If one of your decision criteria is to increase profitability, or some other financial result for example, then to analyze your alternatives and justify your solution you will want to create projected or 'pro forma' financial statements. We will not be learning how to create financial statements in this course; that is something you will be doing in 2nd year. However, all you really need is a current set of financial statements, an estimate of future sales, and an estimate of costs related to your alternative(s).

- You can create a *Pro Forma Income Statement* by determining past expenses as a percentage of sales and then project them forward based on your sales projections, adjusting for any increases/decreases based on the cost of your alternative(s).

- You can create a *Pro Forma Balance Sheet* by applying existing ratio levels from the current statements. It's more complicated so make sure it is needed to make a point. The Income Statement would be more applicable for demonstrating profitability.

- You can also create a *Pro Forma Cash Flow Statement*. Cash, as we will discuss in class, is always critical for a business. You can show profitability and still go bankrupt because there is essentially no cash to pay the bills. If improving the cash position for the company is part of your decision criteria, you will want to do a projected cash flow to justify your solution.

What you need to do is calculate the cash inflows from your recommendation for the relevant period of time and add them to the existing cash balance. Then subtract all cash outflows for the same period to get the net cash flow. This may sound simple but the key is in knowing what is actually cash vs. what the Income Statement is showing you. We'll discuss this in class, but a simple way to understand this concept is to relate it to your own experience. When you buy something you don't always pay in cash; you may use a credit card, for example. Businesses therefore don't always collect the cash from a sale when the sale is made. They have to wait to collect. So the cash inflow is the 'accounts receivable'/monies owed to you from your sales that you expect to collect in the period, not the sales revenue reported on the Income Statement. The same goes for outflows.

Another way to use cash flow is to consider the company's internally generated cash flow to see if it can fund your recommendations from operations rather than from external borrowing or additional investments from its owners. This will be a consideration in any decision — where will the money come from? Looking at the company's Income Statement or your Pro Forma Statement, you would need to add back any non-cash items, such as amortization of assets, to its Net Profit after dividends (not shown on the statement), and subtract the cash items that don't show on the Income Statement, such as loan payments. How does this compare to what you are proposing? Will the company need to generate more capital? And how capable is it of carrying more debt (this would come from your ratio analysis) or selling more equity (again from your ratio analysis)?

Cost/Benefit Analysis

> Cost–Volume–Profit Analysis — Breakeven and Contribution

> Operating Leverage

> Relevant Cost/Benefit Analysis

The basis concept underlying a cost/benefit analysis is to compare the costs and benefits of a particular alternative using a common metric (unit of measurement) such as money; often taking into account the time value of money as discussed earlier. The costs in a case are generally tangible — such as land, labour, machinery, etc., however benefits can be both tangible

— such as revenue, and intangible — such as customer and employee satisfaction, brand awareness, etc. These intangibles are obviously more difficult to value.

Cost–Volume–Profit Analysis

In this course we will be discussing CVP or cost–volume–profit analysis in some depth. In so doing, we will be learning about *Breakeven* and *Contribution*. They are concepts that will come in very handy in a number of situations, as any time you plan to do anything that will affect costs and/or will result in a change in the volume sold, you will need to determine the impact this action will have on profits — a classic cost/benefit analysis.

In order to do this type of analysis you will need to be able to determine the breakdown of the company's costs into *fixed* (those that do not change regardless of sales volume, given a normal range of activity) and *variable* (those that fluctuate in total depending on the volume of sales). If you have access to this kind of information — and it will not always be labeled as such in the case (however given a cost breakdown you should be able to divide the costs into the two categories) — a CVP analysis is helpful to analyze and justify alternatives as most decisions do impact costs and/or volume.

If you are recommending doing anything that is 'new' and/or risky, doing a **breakeven** is a necessity. You always want to know if you will be able to make money — so what will you need to sell to get past the breakeven level (0 profit/loss) and start making money. This can also be done on a purely cash basis (removing non-cash items as discussed earlier) to see when you will start generating cash flow vs. just profit.

The key to this type of analysis is interpreting what it is telling you. Once you have calculated the breakeven level of sales, you need to compare it to your forecasted sales. This is fairly obvious, but you should also look at what that forecast represents as a share of the market — is that realistic for the company to attain? And you should compare it to the company's capacity — can they realistically produce and sell that volume? You can also play with the formula (solving for x — remember learning that? — there was a reason) to determine any variable that might be useful. For example you could calculate the breakeven selling price; the lowest price the company can sell at before losing money, using the company's volume capacity for the breakeven figure. This would be useful if you are recommending dropping the price, or if there is a lot of price competition. Or you could substitute in the new fixed cost figure that will have after your recommended improvements to machinery and equipment are implemented to see the impact on breakeven — can they afford your recommendation? There are a lot of options; the key is to know what you are looking to determine to make the calculation relevant and useful.

The real beauty in this type of analysis, I believe, is in the concept of **contribution**. Contribution cuts to the heart of what is going on and allows you to go further than a strict breakeven analysis. We'll be learning this in Week #7 but for now, contribution is what is left over once variable costs are covered from each sale that goes toward/contributes to covering fixed costs. That may not mean much to you now, but it is very powerful. It is used to calculate breakeven, but it also allows you to test out the implications of your recommended changes in costs and the potential resulting changes in profit, to see if they make any sense. These two concepts together will tell you a lot about what is going on in the company, and will help you to decide on and justify your recommendations. If you *can* calculate it with the available information in a case, not knowing the company's contribution and how it will be affected by your recommendations is a serious flaw.

Operating Leverage

Both these concepts (breakeven and contribution) involve a concept called operating leverage. This is similar, but not the same, as financial leverage that you discussed in BU111. They both describe situations in which a company has "used the idea of levering or increasing resources to better accomplish some purpose" (Ibid, p. 103) or to essentially magnify the results. But for financial leverage it is debt that is levered, whereas for operating leverage it is fixed costs. We will also be discussing this in class, however what is important to remember is that all other things being equal, for a company with high operating leverage the risk is higher in that more sales have to be made to cover fixed costs, but past the breakeven point total profit/return will increase at a faster rate.

To fully understand a company's situation and the resulting implications of your recommendations, it is therefore necessary for you to understand the degree of operating leverage in the company, or more simply the cost structure — essentially, it is a high fixed or high variable cost business? Therefore to what degree will your recommendations impact the bottom line? This explains why some businesses will put more emphasis on marketing and sales activities, whereas others will put more emphasis on reducing raw material and direct labour costs — because the impact is different depending on the cost structure. Thus it is important that you understand what the company's priorities likely are and don't make a recommendation that shows a lack of understanding for the very nature of the business the company is in.

Relevant Cost/Benefit Analysis

A final related tool is relevant cost/benefit analysis. Not to say that what we've been discussing is irrelevant! ☺ The point in this type of analysis is to focus on what is different vs. everything. This will save you time and effort and get right to the heart of the issue. That's got to sound good to you right about now, am I right? It will also make your marker happier (which is always a good thing), because he or she won't have to wade through a lot of irrelevant detail. It is analogous to you suggesting a reduction in labour costs of $10,000 and showing an entire Income Statement to demonstrate the impact. Would it be safe to say that profit will increase by $10,000, all things being equal, or do you need to do the entire statement to see that?

The key to this type of analysis is identifying costs and benefits that change or differ as a result of your alternatives — the *incremental* or *marginal* costs and benefits. Costs and benefits that stay the same, in this case, are considered irrelevant and would not be included in the analysis. You can use this type of analysis to focus in on the real benefit the company would gain from each alternative — the net incremental benefit = incremental revenue — incremental costs. Don't forget that there may be qualitative factors to consider as well, so once you've done this kind of analysis you should also consider the qualitative factors that might override the best quantitative alternative.

This type of analysis works very well when you have information on the company's cost structure. This allows you to analyze the incremental contribution compared to the incremental fixed costs associated with your alternatives to compare the net incremental benefits. Using this same line of thinking you can also determine the level of sales at which the incremental increase in fixed costs associated with an alternative is covered by the incremental contribution. This provides more information to help justify your recommendations.

Situational Analysis

> PEST

> Porter's Five Forces Model

> Stakeholder Analysis

> Diamond E

> SWOT Analysis

> Porter's Generic Competitive Strategies

There are many tools you can use to analyze the current situation a company is in to better understand its issues and also to justify your recommendations in the context of the situation. This includes the tools we have already discussed. The specific tools listed above could also be listed under industry and market analysis, however I have chosen the term situational analysis for a reason — it is critical that whatever analysis you do on the industry and market is relevant to the company and its issues in the current situation it is facing. There is no sense doing an extensive analysis that isn't relevant and useful. Therefore the key is to understand the factors related to the industry and market environment that impact specifically on the organization in the case.

The first 4 tools listed — **PEST, Diamond E, Porter's Five Forces Model, and Stakeholder Analysis** — have all been covered in BU111 and will continue to be useful throughout a wide range of cases. Using these tools will undoubtedly allow you to get a solid picture of the overall environment facing the company in a case.

According to Ronstadt (1988, pp. 115–120) there are some key questions that you want to answer to understand the company's current situation. Some of these questions can be answered with the help of these tools, but other questions need to be answered in order to properly use these tools. For example:

• What is the relevant *definition of the industry* the company is in?

'Relevant' is the key word as changing environmental circumstances can change the relevant definition of an industry for a company. Ronstadt (Ibid, p. 115) defines relevant as the "direct competitors or potentially direct competitors within a product-market-technology grouping that serves a basic function (e.g., transportation)". You need to make sure you are not defining it too narrowly or too broadly for the analysis. Another key question to consider is if the company is defining its industry appropriately.

• What is the size of the *market*, what is its past growth rate, and what is expected for the future?

Looking at this will give you an idea of the potential growth prospects for the company. Your answer to this question will depend on your answer to the first question — how you have defined the industry — as a more narrow definition can lead to growth being limited. Is the company in a growing market where more competition is likely to be entering and companies will be vying for market share, or in a declining market at the end of a product/ industry's lifecycle where competition is leaving and the market it shrinking? The options are numerous and they each have implications that may be important for understanding the issues and the context in which your decisions are made. The product life cycle material covered in Week #5 will help you to start building the tools for understanding and applying this knowledge.

If you look at our Integrative Model of a Successful Business that we use as our course model for BU111 and 121, you should notice 2 things:

- the first 4 tools are implicit in the model — PEST (the external environment) is one of the building blocks, Porter's is used to analyze the industry forces in the business environment (an extended PEST analysis), Stakeholders are another building block, and all the elements of the Diamond E can be overlaid on the model

- strategy is another building block of our model, and is shown to be impacted by the environment, as is also demonstrated in the Diamond E model ...

SWOT Analysis

...But what is the company's strategy? That is a key question to answer and one for which we also have tools in our toolkit. One of the key strategic analysis tools is the SWOT. Along with financial analysis, it is one of the tools you will use most often in a case. A SWOT analysis helps you to assess both the internal/micro and external/macro environments of a company. SWOT stands for strengths, weaknesses, opportunities and threats. Essentially a SWOT analysis assesses the internal strengths and weaknesses of a company (in its marketing, finances, operations and/or human resources) and compares that to the external opportunities and threats that exist in its environment (typically using the PEST model). It is similar to the Diamond E — that provides a framework for analyzing the alignment and consistency between a company's strategy, its environment and its resources — but in a more detailed and explicit way.

The combination of these factors should lead to the most appropriate strategy for the company to undertake to succeed in that environment. What you are looking for is a better understanding of why a company might have pursued a particular strategy and/or possibly uncovering a hole you have recognized in its strategy that can form part of your recommendations — such as missing an opportunity or recognizing an area of weakness that needs to be strengthened. Some of the combinations include:

- taking advantage of an opportunity that lies within the company's strengths
- turning what could be a threat into an opportunity by capitalizing on its strengths
- defending itself from a threat in an area of weakness
- minimizing weaknesses to take advantage of an opportunity

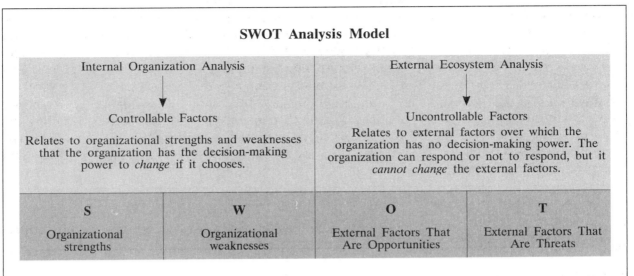

SWOT Analysis Model

Internal Organization Analysis		External Ecosystem Analysis	
↓		↓	
Controllable Factors		Uncontrollable Factors	
Relates to organizational strengths and weaknesses that the organization has the decision-making power to *change* if it chooses.		Relates to external factors over which the organization has no decision-making power. The organization can respond or not to respond, but it *cannot change* the external factors.	
S	**W**	**O**	**T**
Organizational strengths	Organizational weaknesses	External Factors That Are Opportunities	External Factors That Are Threats

Source: From T.P. Power, International Business: A Canadian Perspective, 1st ed. © 2008 Nelson Education Ltd. Reproduced with permission.

As you can see in our course model, the SW and OT are on opposite sides of the model but are connected to strategy because they influence strategy. What you should also see is that before strategy is decided upon the company determines its vision, which takes into account its critical success factors and stakeholders, as well as the internal and external environments. This is then articulated in the company's mission, which leads to the strategy that will implement the vision and mission. So an understanding of the company's vision and mission are also helpful in understanding its strategy and therefore cannot be ignored in determining the appropriateness of your strategic recommendations.

Porter's Generic Competitive Strategies

Porter's generic competitive strategies is another tool you can use to analyze a company's strategy. This model is a natural extension from what we have discussed so far, and will help you to understand the company's strategy on a more competitive level — how has it chosen to position itself to compete against other firms in its industry? If you are recommending a change in the strategy, using this model will be helpful to determine and justify your recommendation(s).

Michael Porter suggests that a firm's competitive advantage fits into one of two categories — low cost or differentiation (product uniqueness), and by applying this to either a broad or narrow market scope three generic competitive strategies emerge — cost leadership, differentiation, and focus. What actually emerges are really four strategies, as a company focusing on a narrow market segment can compete on either cost and hence price, or the uniqueness of its product. A fifth strategy emerges when a company attempts to compete on all fronts, which causes it to be "stuck in the middle" where it really has no competitive advantage. Porter argues that to be successful a firm must select one of the generic strategies. The strategies are

Porter's Generic Competitive Strategies		
	Low Cost	**Uniqueness**
Broad Scope (Industry wide)	Cost Leadership Strategy	Differentiation Strategy
Narrow Scope (Market segment)	Focus Strategy	
	Low Cost Focus	Differentiation Focus

called generic because they are not specific to a company or industry, but can be applied to all.

For a more in-depth analysis you could combine Porter's Generic Competitive Strategies with his Five Forces Model to determine the ability of a firm to deal with the forces in the industry given its competitive strategy. For example, a company using a cost leadership strategy could use a low price to defend against substitutes, and customer loyalty resulting from the use of a successful differentiation strategy could discourage potential entrants. For more information on Porter's models see Porter, Michael. (1980). *Competitive Strategy: Techniques for Analyzing Industries and Competitors*. New York, NY: The Free Press.

A Final Note

The purpose of a situational analysis is to get a big-picture view of the company, and its market and industry, in order to understand the context in which you will be making your recommendations. A question that you should be able to answer once you've done your analysis is what are the *key success factors* for this industry and this company? There is no sense making recommendations that don't demonstrate an understanding of what it takes for the company to succeed.

Alternative Analysis

> Mind Mapping

> Decision Trees

> Alternative Matrix

Mind Mapping

Mind mapping (also called concept mapping — see Box 2.2 in the "Claims" reading from Week #3) is a technique that we will be using extensively in this course. It is a tool that will help you structure information in a visual way that more closely resembles the way your brain

Mind Mapping

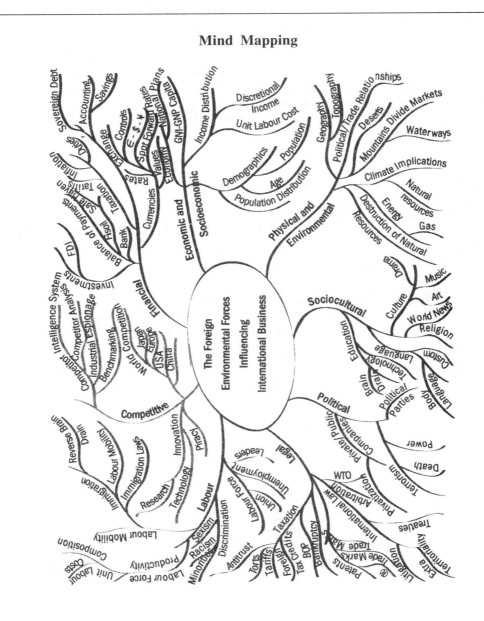

Source: Reproduced from Terrence P. Powers, *Power's Case Study Analysis and Writer's Handbook* (Toronto: Nelson Education, 2009) p. 20.

works than does typical note-taking. It can help you to better analyze, understand, integrate/consolidate, and remember information, as well as brainstorm new ideas.

It is a simple tool, which is a large part of its appeal, but it is also much more fun than taking regular notes. My interest in mind mapping comes from a long history of watching students struggle to see the connections between concepts and simply memorizing detached chunks of information without truly understanding them in context. This approach seldom leads to solid learning or solid marks.

By taking a central idea and drawing branches and twigs to represent related information, using images and colours to give visual clarity as well as arrows to connect information on different branches, you can literally 'map out' your thinking on a subject. That subject, of course, can be the case that you are solving. The act of mind mapping can therefore help you to both better understand the case and to think through the alternative solutions to the issues presented. In the process of doing so, the logical 'best' alternative may become evident, as well as the arguments you need to present to justify your recommendation.

Decision Trees

When you have to decide between different courses of action, particularly when those different paths lead to other decisions or when different circumstances can lead to different conclusions, a decision tree is helpful. It will force you to order your thoughts and provide a clear visual of what is involved in the decision.

A decision tree allows you to "diagram these decision alternatives and the events that make up each alternative." (Ronstadt, 1988, p. 111) It also allows you to adjust outcomes for each branch of the tree according to the probability of the events occurring, so that you can literally "calculate the net marginal or incremental benefits associated with each decision branch and, in a sense, "discount" these net benefits by the probability of occurrence." (Ibid., pp. 111–112) This approach is demonstrated in the diagram below:

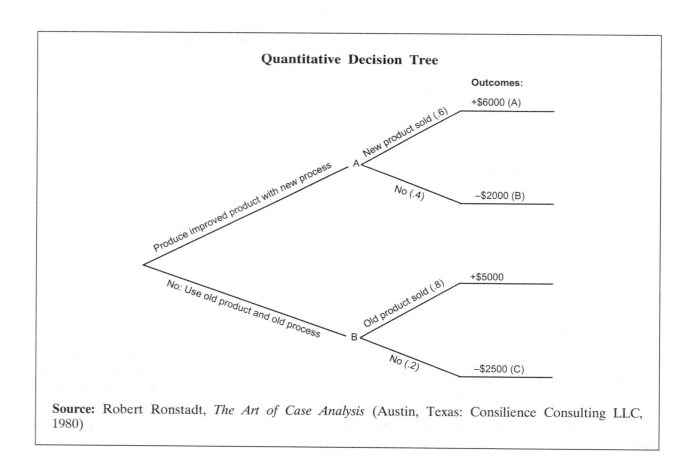

Quantitative Decision Tree

Outcomes:

Produce improved product with new process — A — New product sold (.6) — +$6000 (A)

No (.4) — –$2000 (B)

No: Use old product and old process — B — Old product sold (.8) — +$5000

No (.2) — –$2500 (C)

Source: Robert Ronstadt, *The Art of Case Analysis* (Austin, Texas: Consilience Consulting LLC, 1980)

It is not necessary to assign probabilities and/or $ values to make a decision tree useful, but with that added information it adds one more layer of value. You do this of course you have to be able to assign probabilities on some reasonable basis. However, if you are able to at least determine the probability of one event occurring to be .7 for example, that would mean the alternative event would necessarily have a probability of .3. Also if you can calculate the net benefit of one branch, then you could work backwards to determine the required probability to make an alternative branch have the same net benefit. Then you can assess if that probability is reasonable.

An example decision tree using only qualitative information is provided below:

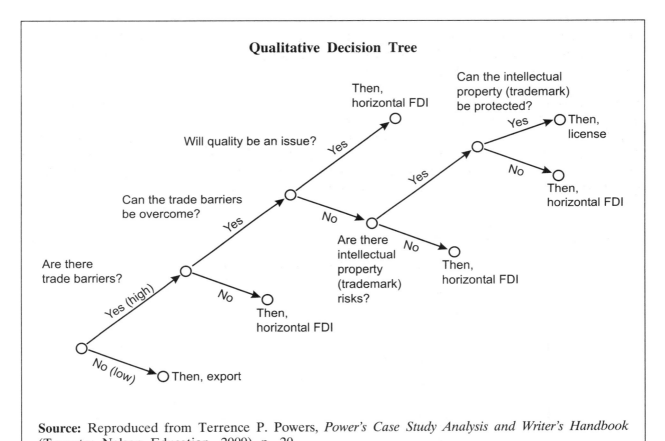

Qualitative Decision Tree

Source: Reproduced from Terrence P. Powers, *Power's Case Study Analysis and Writer's Handbook* (Toronto: Nelson Education, 2009) p. 20.

Alternative Matrix

When analyzing your alternatives you have been taught to analyze them according to the decision criteria. In other words, what does your solution need to do for it to be successful? These are the criteria you will use to make your decision. The alternatives therefore obviously need to be compared to the criteria. A popular way for students to do this is to construct a matrix that compares each alternative according to the decision criteria using an appropriate scale.

Alternative Matrix

Alternatives*	Decision Criteria								
	Increased Profits	Inventory Turnover	Reduced Costs	Time Needed	Growth Rate	Ease of Implementing	Customer Satisfaction	Competitive Advantage	Total
The status quo	2	3	1	5	2	5	1	2	21
Expand target market	4	5	2	1	5	1	4	3	25
Outsource production	3	1	4	4	3	4	3	4	26
Diversify products	5	4	3	2	4	3	5	5	31
Sell the business	1	2	5	3	1	2	2	1	17

* Ranking of alternatives: 1 = Worst possible outcome; 5 = Best possible outcome.

Source: Reproduced from Terrence P. Powers, *Power's Case Study Analysis and Writer's Handbook* (Toronto: Nelson Education, 2009) p. 50.

The example on page 200 uses a ranking for the alternatives — from 1 to 5 — on how well each alternative meets each decision criteria — 1 being the "worst possible outcome" and 5 being the "best possible outcome". However you set up your scale to judge how well the alternatives meet the criteria, you can see that it is possible using this system to get a numerical value for each alternative, thus implying that the alternative with the highest total would be the 'best' alternative. Exercise caution. It is never a good idea to simply pick the alternative with the highest value from the matrix and justify your decision on that basis. This is simply a tool to help you make your decision in an organized fashion. Take a step back from the matrix and prepare a thorough justification using the decision criteria.

GOOD LUCK and enjoy learning how to master cases. Remember that you will some day be in 'real life' cases and the more you learn and practice now, the more successful you will be!

The Entrepreneur's Marketing Source Inc.

After only nine months in business, Brent Banda, founder and owner of The Entrepreneur's Marketing Source Inc. (EMS), felt like he was facing the biggest challenge of his career. His business cards promised to provide "ideas, advice, and solutions" to other companies in Saskatoon, yet Brent wasn't sure what advice to give himself regarding the future of his company.

The City: Saskatoon

Saskatoon is the largest city in Saskatchewan with a population of 219,000. Situated along the banks of the South Saskatchewan River, the city prides itself on developing riverside parks and recreational facilities. Saskatchewan traditionally has relied on the agriculture industry and one-third of Canada's agricultural biotechnology companies are located in Saskatoon. Recently, Saskatoon has steered its growth toward becoming a transportation and supply centre for the mining industry. It is home to mining head offices for potash, uranium, gold, and diamonds.

The Company: EMS

Brent started EMS in Saskatoon just months after he graduated from the University of Saskatchewan with his Commerce degree in Marketing. Although EMS is incorporated, Brent owns 100% of the shares and is its only employee. He has operated EMS out of his home for the past nine months and aims to break even by the end of the year.

The mission statement of EMS is to "establish the company name as a reliable source of practical marketing information to North American small and medium-sized businesses." The idea for EMS was generated while Brent was working on projects for his university classes. He noticed many small businesses had little knowledge about, or expertise in, marketing. However, marketing was a crucial element in their continued success.

Brent created EMS to develop and sell a practical marketing workbook that could be used by small businesses in Canada and the United States. The workbook was envisioned as a general guide to help small business owners with no marketing experience create strategies tailored to their unique business situations. Brent was confident that, in the future, he could branch out and create a series of workbooks that focused on specific marketing problems, such as advertising or new product development.

The first set-back occurred when Brent approached his banker for a $7,000 business loan to start EMS. The banker demurred that a workbook would take some time to develop and suggested that EMS offer personalized, marketing consulting services to small business clients in Saskatoon. The consulting would furnish real-life examples that Brent could incorporate into the book and would provide EMS with steady income during the workbook's creation. Brent knew that EMS could not survive without the bank loan, so he agreed to become a consultant in the short-term while developing his long-term plans. He was worried, however, that his consulting projects would slow the progress of the workbook.

That worry turned out to be correct. Nine months after EMS was created, its consulting business is flourishing. However, Brent finds himself working 50 to 60 hours per week on personalized consulting and the workbook still is not completed. He also attends many meetings and community events in order to develop a referral network of small business consumers for his consulting activities.

The Entrepreneur: Brent Banda

Brent was raised in a working-class family, and worked as a waiter and in other service jobs to put himself through university. As a waiter, Brent had to talk to up to 25 strangers a day and he credits this training with giving him the confidence to approach new people when the opportunity arises. Brent does not consider himself to be a "thrill-seeking" risk taker, but feels that starting his own business is a risk that he can afford because he has nothing to lose. He is single with few assets and is just starting out in life, so even if EMS does not become successful, he can always start over working for another company.

Brent credits his education at the University of Saskatchewan for gaining business knowledge, project experience, and writing skills. The most difficult part of starting EMS for Brent was feeling confident in his ability to apply his education to practical problems. However after a short time at EMS, Brent realized that other small business owners did not possess extraordinary business skills either and Brent learned to be confident in his strengths.

Brent is constantly involved in business planning for EMS, both for the short-term and the long-term. Early on, Brent realized that he could achieve business success by either creating an image for EMS or creating an image for himself. Because he did not have the money to launch an image campaign for EMS, Brent chose to create an image for himself as a successful entrepreneur and small business owner. He was head of the committee for North Saskatoon Business Associates where he produced their awards banquet for two years. Recently, he has been named to the board of directors for the Provincial Exporters Association. Brent is described by others as outgoing, motivated, and hard-working.

The Consumer: Small-business Owners

EMS targets small and medium sized businesses in North America that do not have full-time marketing staff. These companies are usually managed by one owner. Industry Canada estimates that 60% of all Canadian businesses are run by one self-employed owner. An additional 30% of businesses have fewer than 5 employees and this number has grown by 30% in the

Table 1
Number of Small Businesses by Province

Province	Total Businesses	Self-Employment	Total Employers	Small Businesses
Canada	2,324,518	1,393,000	931,518	707,886
Newfoundland	44,274	22,000	22,274	17,854
P.E.I.	15,732	8,000	7,732	5,684
Nova Scotia	73,678	41,000	32,678	23,689
New Brunswick	56,852	29,000	27,852	20.488
Quebec	493,680	266,000	227,680	169,812
Ontario	826,733	518,000	308,733	225,655
Manitoba	100,135	64,000	36,135	24,495
Saskatchewan	127,899	87,000	40,899	30,617
Alberta	278,771	167,000	111,771	82,162
B.C.	340,323	191,000	149,323	109,170
Yukon	4,247	2,700	1,547	1,011
N.W.T.	9,154	4,000	5,154	3,455

Note:

• Provinces do not sum to the total for Canada because the same companies may be counted in more than one province.
• This table excludes the public sector.
• *Self-employment* is unincorporated self-employment only.
• *Small businesses* are employers with less than 5 employees.

Source: Entrepreneurship and Small Business Office, Industry Canada, 1994.

last 10 years. The number of small businesses by province is provided in Table 1. In addition, over 13 million home-based businesses exist in the United States.

Compared to larger companies, small businesses often lack depth and expertise in many business functions, including marketing. While larger companies have marketing departments and operate with a marketing plan in place, many small businesses have no formal marketing plan, strategy, or objectives. In fact, many small business owners are unclear what exactly marketing is and how to apply it to their situations. Consequently, they are unlikely to seek marketing help.

To understand the small business owner better, Brent conducted a focus group interview in Saskatoon. The informants agreed that they had a poor understanding of marketing concepts and felt that a marketing plan was too theoretical and difficult to use. They were interested in learning more about how to advertise their products, however. They indicated that they were too busy to read long books about marketing, but were enthusiastic when Brent introduced a prototype of his workbook and led the group in a strategic planning seminar. Brent felt that the positive response to this workshop indicated that his marketing workbook could be a success.

Table 2
Income Statement for the Nine Month Period Ended September 30, Year 1

Consulting revenue	$30,425.88	
Cost of services	9,824.04	
Gross margin		$20,601.84
Operating expenses		
Accounting	$850.00	
Marketing	850.73	
Memberships	250.00	
Interest and bank charges	804.44	
Office supplies	1,665.95	
Phone	2,266.26	
Business meetings	588.48	
Wages	16,350.00	
Total operating expenses		23,625.86
Net operating income (loss)		($3,024.02)

EMS Consulting Service

EMS is likely to meet its first-year objectives of breaking even and developing a consulting practice that provides a steady income to sustain the business. Table 2 provides EMS's financial results for the first nine months of operations. Examples of EMS's first-year clients include a husband and wife team who wanted to make their photography hobby into a full-time career, an architect who was losing clients to his competition, a real estate firm trying to attract developers, and a glass company that didn't know how to advertise. Customers like these contract with EMS to provide marketing research, create a marketing plan, and/or develop promotional strategies. Beyond marketing advice, an important part of EMS's service is the education Brent provides to small business owners. Instead of handing over a report, Brent explains the basis for his decisions and provides EMS's clients with long-range perspectives on their marketing situations.

Before any consulting work is started, EMS provides a written quote. Currently, EMS charges $75 per hour for consulting services, but Brent plans to increase this fee to $85 next year and to $100 after that. Billable hours are recorded as the work is completed and used as a guide when quoting future projects. However, if billable hours exceed the original estimate, EMS only charges the amount of the original quote. In the first year, Brent often has underestimated the amount of time a project would require, but he expects to improve this variance with experience. All clients provide a 25% deposit and are invoiced after the work is completed with 15 days to make payment. EMS has had no trouble collecting receivables from clients.

The Competition

Many other companies offer marketing services in Saskatoon. Large consulting and research firms and advertising agencies provide specific services to larger clients with marketing depart-

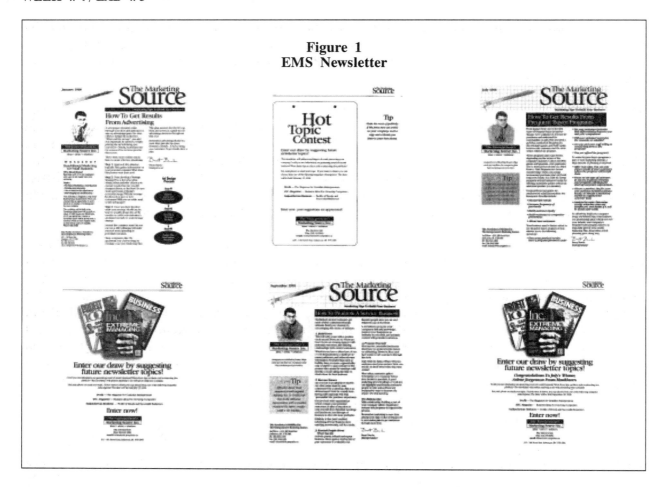

Figure 1
EMS Newsletter

ments. These consultants do not actively solicit small business clients given that small businesses lack marketing and promotional plans, require extra time and effort, and may not be able to afford their consulting fees. In addition to large consultants, sixteen small marketing consulting firms are listed in the Saskatoon Yellow Pages. Finally, many small businesses rely on media agents to help them with their marketing plans; for example, a local paper or radio station may design ads or help with strategic planning if a small business owner buys advertising space or time. Media agents provide this service free of charge.

To attract clients to EMS in this competitive environment, Brent has established a network of business contacts in the local community. A free newsletter offering practical marketing tips is mailed to these contacts each month. The newsletter is intended to build the awareness and credibility of EMS's service as well as prompting referrals and repeat business. The newsletter has a professional appearance and has been well-received by its recipients. A sample newsletter is provided in Figure 1.

The Offer

Although EMS creates promotional strategies and develops advertising plans, Brent is not a graphic designer; he relies on other local companies to create finished ads, artwork, and web pages. One design firm he has worked with is called Imagine and is owned and operated by two young designers who quit their jobs with a large local advertising agency less than a year ago when they became "fed up" with their boss. Many of the agency's clients transferred to Imagine shortly after the split.

Brent was surprised when the partners at Imagine approached him with a business offer. They wanted to create a strategic alliance with EMS; EMS would refer all of its clients' design work to Imagine, and Imagine would send its clients in need of marketing help to EMS. In addition, EMS would share office space with Imagine; the design firm is housed on the top floor of a building in the trendy Broadway district of Saskatoon. Although rent in this district can be pricy, Imagine was willing to let EMS share the space for only $185 per month. EMS would receive one office and share the reception area and meeting room.

Brent could see the benefits of aligning EMS with Imagine. He would have access to Imagine's clients, many of whom were much larger than those he currently had. Although the partners of Imagine would not allow him to see their financial statements or discuss their operating income because Imagine would remain a separate company from EMS, Brent had a good working relationship with Imagine's partners. In addition, the partners valued Brent because he wrote clear marketing strategies that allowed them to "concentrate on the fun part of the business-making ads." However, if EMS enters into the proposed strategic alliance and receives new clients from Imagine, Brent can see that all of his time will continue to be eaten up by consulting. Publication of the workbook would be delayed for at least another year.

The Workbook

If EMS does not enter into the strategic alliance with Imagine, Brent feels that he can reduce his consulting time by taking fewer clients and finish writing the workbook in the fall. He would like to begin marketing the workbook in Canada in January of Year 2 and enter the U.S. market in Year 3. Brent is encouraged by the fact that consumers purchased over $3 billion of products through direct sales in Canada in 1994, with books, newspapers, and magazines accounting for $1 billion of these sales.

Many marketing reference books, video and audio tapes, and seminars already exist and can be found in bookstores, public libraries, and economic-development facilities like Industry Canada. However, many of these materials require a significant amount of time to read, understand, and apply. The strength of the planned EMS workbook is that it will be a practical, hands-on workbook that is concisely written for the small business entrepreneur. Brent plans to conduct focus group interviews to further refine the workbook. In addition, focus group interviews can help in the creation of a direct response campaign where small business owners can buy the workbooks by phone after reading a print ad.

The workbooks will be sold through a two-part direct response campaign. First, direct response ads will be placed in magazines that the small business owner is likely to read such as *Home Business Report* or *Income Opportunities*. The average Canadian magazine is published quarterly, reaches 50,000 individuals, and charges $2,500 per ad. The average U.S. magazine is published monthly, reaches 300,000 individuals, and charges $5,000 per ad. The planned EMS ads will be one-half page size and in colour. On average, 0.2% of magazine readers order products from direct-response ads in the first month that the ad appears and 0.15% of readers order after that.

Table 3
Workbook Cost Information (in Canadian Dollars)

Cost	Canada	United States
Printing of workbook	2.37	2.37
Printing of survey	0.10	0.10
Postage	0.90	1.17
Envelope	0.15	0.15
1-800 number and answering service	2.00	2.00
Credit card fee	0.60	0.60
Total	6.12	6.39

Direct mail will also be used to generate orders. The mail piece will contain a magazine-style article on a small-business topic and a description of the workbook. Several companies sell lists of businesses that employ five or fewer employees for $.15 to $.45 per business name depending on the number of names purchased. In the future, when more than one type of workbook is available from EMS, past workbook customers will receive updated product lists through direct mail as well. On average, 3% of individuals who receive a direct mail solicitation respond; the response rate increases to 15% for individuals who have ordered from the company in the past.

Customers responding to the ads will order through a toll-free number. All orders will require payment in advance, which is standard with low-cost, direct-response products. A message service will take the order, including shipping information and credit card number. This information will be faxed daily to EMS and the order will be mailed through Canada Post the next day. EMS is able to take both Visa and MasterCard orders. EMS will include a postage-paid survey with all orders to gather information on its customers.

Brent estimates that the workbooks will cost between $6.12 and $6.39 to produce and mail, depending on whether they are sent to Canada or the U.S. Table 3 provides workbook cost information. EMS will sell each workbook for $29.95 (Canadian) which includes shipping, but does not include taxes. The type of marketing activity planned and the estimated number of workbooks sold in Year 2 and Year 3 are presented in Table 4. Brent also has estimated the amount of income he expects in Years 2 and 3 from workbook sales, given the above assumptions, which is shown in Table 5.

The Dilemma

Brent likes consulting and working with Imagine. The offer to form a strategic alliance with Imagine is tempting, given their larger client base. However, Brent's true dream is to complete and market the workbook. He is worried that another company may publish a similar product aimed at the same market. A tremendous amount of potential profit would be lost. Given the time that consulting currently takes, Brent is sure that he will only have time to pursue one option: the strategic alliance with Imagine or completion of the workbook.

Table 4
Marketing Activities and Estimated Workbooks Sold — Years 2 and 3

	Year 2	Year 3
Marketing activities in Canada		
Direct mail to list	3,000 pieces	—
Direct mail to previous customers	615 pieces	1,050 pieces
Magazine ads	3 ads	6 ads
Marketing activities in the U.S.		
Direct mail to list	—	—
Direct mail to previous customers	—	8,400 pieces
Magazine ads	—	8 ads
Number of workbooks sold in Canada		
From direct mail to list	90	—
From direct mail to previous customers	92	157
From magazine ads	525	1,050
Number of workbooks sold in the U.S.		
From direct mail to list	—	—
From direct mail to previous customers	—	1,260
From magazine ads	—	8,400

Note:

- *Direct mail to list* is sent to the names purchased from list providers.
- *Direct mail to previous customers* is sent to individuals who have purchased the workbook in previous months either from the direct mail to list or through the direct response ads.

Table 5
Estimated Income from Workbook ? Years 2 and 3

	Year 2		Year 3	
Sales (Workbook)	$21,174.65		$325,466.65	
COGS (Workbook)	4,326.84		69,114.24	
Gross margin		$16,847.81		$256,352.41
Marketing expenses				
Ad design	1,000.00		1,000.00	
Ad placement (Canada)	7,500.00		15,000.00	
Ad placement (U.S.)	0.00		40,000.00	
Direct mail design	2,000.00		2,000.00	
Mailing list	450.00		0.00	
Printing of mailer	723.00		1,890.00	
Postage of mailer	1,265.25		4,147.50	
Total marketing expenses		12,938.25		64,037.50
Operating income		$ 3,909.56		$192,314.91

Week #5 / Lab #4

Lab #4 — Pitches!

This week in labs you will be presenting your "elevator pitch". Pay close attention to the marking rubric on page 168 and posted on the course website, as this is worth 5% toward your final grade. More importantly, this is a critical skill that you will use everyday in the business world. Mastering it will increase your odds of success.

Your preparation for this lab will require that you rewrite and practice your pitch <u>many times</u>.

Don't be misled by the short time frame for presenting your pitch. Shorter is not easier. It is tough to get your point across effectively in a short time frame, and you must also get and keep the attention of your audience. <u>Practice, practice, practice</u>.

Week #6 / Lab #5

Class — Accounting

The following reading is included in this week's section of the Lab Manual as it is required for class this week and will form the basis for part of next week's lab:

- *Accounting for Non-financial Managers* by John Parkinson
  - o Financial Statement Analysis

Lab #5 — Writing Skills & the Business Model Canvas

In preparation for this week's lab, review the readings you did in Week #2 from:

- *Business Model Generation* by Alexander Osterwalder & Yves Pigneur
  - o Definition of a Business Model
  - o The 9 Building Blocks
  - o The Business Model Canvas

You will be applying the Business Model Canvas approach to a business you are familiar with.

Also review the text readings on business writing and <u>bring a sample of your writing</u> — approximately 500 words. The object of this exercise is to learn to write more clearly for business. Do not try to impress. Bring a sample that represents how you normally write. A good sample of your writing would be your individual writing assignment from BU111 (if you took the course).

Financial Statement Analysis

15.1 Introduction

Accounting ratios are used to better understand the numbers in financial statements. When an accounting number is compared to another accounting number, the ratio is sometimes very informative: more informative than the numbers would be by themselves. Thus, the dollar value of inventory from the balance sheet, by itself, tells us little. The value of inventory compared to the sales revenue gives us a valuable clue to assess the efficiency of the company's inventory control; it expresses the information as the number of times per year the inventory is turned over. The value of the inventory turnover ratio for one year when compared with the same ratio for a subsequent year tells us whether inventory management is improving or getting worse.

Within the various chapters of this text we have introduced a number of financial accounting ratios. In order to understand these ratios better and understand their interrelationships, in this chapter we carry out a financial ratio analysis on the results of Leon's Furniture Ltd.

We start off with the financial statements themselves. To make the task more straightforward, the financial statements have been summarized to some extent. (See Exhibit 15.1.) Their principal characteristics, however, remain intact.

The analysis will concentrate on the following:

- *Liquidity:* Whether or not the company is likely to run out of cash.
- *Profitability:* How well the company has performed.
- *Debt:* The extent to which debt increases company risk.
- *Efficiency:* How well the company used its assets.
- *Market-related measures:* Information about share values.

This is not an exhaustive list of financial ratios, but it is sufficient to give a reasonable assessment of the company's performance and prospects.

Reproduced with permission from John Parksion with Charles Draimin, *Accounting for Non-financial Managers*, 3rd ed. (Concord, ON: Captus Press Inc., 2011), Chapter 15 (pp. 416–428).

Exhibit 15.1: Summarized Financial Statements

Note that the following financial statements of Leon's Furniture Ltd. have been somewhat simplified for the purposes of illustrating the concepts covered in this textbook.

Leon's Furniture Ltd.
Balance Sheet
($ '000s)

	As at December 31		
	2007	2008	2009
ASSETS			
Current assets			
Cash and marketable securities	$142,279	$139,275	$170,726
Accounts receivable, etc.	34,966	34,507	32,634
Inventory	75,640	92,904	83,957
Total current assets	$252,885	$266,686	$287,317
Long-term assets (net)	222,341	246,722	241,839
Total assets	$475,226	$513,408	$529,156
LIABILITIES & EQUITY			
Current liabilities	$126,837	$129,585	$122,558
Long-term liabilities	26,384	30,465	31,460
Total liabilities	$153,221	$160,050	$154,018
Common shares	$ 14,020	$ 16,493	$ 17,704
Retained earnings	307,985	336,865	357,434
Shareholders' equity	$322,005	$353,358	$375,138
Total liabilities and equity	$475,226	$513,408	$529,156

Leon's Furniture Ltd.
Income Statement
($ '000s)

	For the Years Ended December 31		
	2007	2008	2009
Sales revenue	$637,456	$740,376	$703,180
Cost of sales	363,261	440,360	419,819
Gross profit	$274,195	$300,016	$283,361
Operating expenses:			
Salaries, etc.	$103,661	$116,591	$103,977
Advertising	32,008	33,752	34,732
Rent & property taxes	10,486	11,268	12,165
Other expense (net of other income)	22,983	28,016	33,391
Total cash expenses	$169,138	$189,627	$184,265
Amortization	14,034	16,253	16,562
Total operating expenses	$183,172	$205,880	$200,827
Operating income	$ 91,023	$ 94,136	$ 82,534
Income tax	32,529	30,746	25,670
Net income	$ 58,494	$ 63,390	$ 56,864

Exhibit 15.1 continued

Leon's Furniture Ltd.
Statement of Retained Earnings
($ '000s)

	For the Years Ended December 31		
	2007	**2008**	**2009**
Retained earnings brought forward	$ 276,037	$ 307,068	$ 338,960
Add: Net income for the year	58,494	63,390	56,864
Deduct: Cost of share purchases	(7,635)	(4,625)	(4,297)
Deduct: Dividend paid	(19,828)	(26,873)	(33,951)
Retained earnings carried forward	$ 307,068	$ 338,960	$ 357,576

Leon's Furniture Ltd.
Statement of Cash Flows
($ '000s)

	For the Years Ended December 31		
	2007	**2008**	**2009**
Operating Activities:			
Net income	$ 58,494	$ 63,390	$ 56,864
Add: Non-cash expenses (including amortization)	17,151	18,820	16,616
Deduct: Net increase in non-cash working capital	(7,112)	(12,482)	4,035
Cash from operations	$ 68,533	$ 69,728	$ 77,515
Investing Activities:			
Net cash used as investment in long-term asset	$ (43,629)	$ (24,402)	$ (20,215)
Financing Activities:			
Dividends paid	$ (19,671)	$ (26,870)	$ (33,965)
Repurchase of shares	(7,706)	(4,672)	(4,517)
Cash used in financing	$ (27,377)	$ (31,542)	$ (38,482)
Net increase (decrease) in cash	$ (2,473)	$ 13,784	$ 18,818
Cash brought forward	28,172	25,699	39,483
Cash carried forward	$ 25,699	$ 39,483	$ 58,301

Additional Information
1. Number of common shares in issue: 2007, 70,777,000; 2008, 70,729,000; 2009, 70,714,000.
2. Average share prices for 2007 to 2009 were $14.90, $8.30, and $11.80, respectively.

15.2 Liquidity

A major concern to any organization is its ability to survive. Short-term survival is critically dependent on the relationship between immediate obligations and the liquid assets that are available to pay them. Cash will be needed to pay these short-term debts, but cash is not the only available resource: other short-term assets may also be turned into cash and used to pay liabilities. Thus, liquidity analysis is concerned primarily with the current assets and the current liabilities. The greater the ratio of current assets to current liabilities, the more liquid the company is, and the lower the threat of running out of cash. Two ratios are used for liquidity analysis: the current ratio and the quick ratio.

15.2.1 Current Ratio

Definition: current assets ÷ current liabilities

2007	2008	2009
$\dfrac{\$252,885}{\$126,837}$	$\dfrac{\$266,686}{\$129,585}$	$\dfrac{\$287,317}{\$122,558}$
= 1.99 : 1	= 2.06 : 1	= 2.34 : 1

Analysis: Leon's is adequately liquid. Its current ratio is almost exactly the same as the 2 : 1 norm in years 2007 and 2008, and over 2 : 1 in 2009.

15.2.2 Quick Ratio

Definition: (current assets – inventory) ÷ current liabilities

The quick ratio recognizes that inventory, though a current asset, is less liquid than other current assets, and its availability to pay off obligations is questionable. Hence, inventory is removed, and the more liquid current assets are compared to current liabilities.

2007	2008	2009
$\dfrac{(\$252,885 - \$75,640)}{\$126,837}$	$\dfrac{(\$266,686 - \$92,904)}{\$129,585}$	$\dfrac{(\$287,317 - \$83,957)}{\$122,558}$
= 1.40 : 1	= 1.34 : 1	= 1.66 : 1

Analysis: Leon's is adequately liquid. Its quick ratio is well above the 1 : 1 norm in all three years.

15.3 Profitability

Once it has survived extinction in the short term, a company has an objective of profitability to meet. Profitability ratios express some measure of profits against the resources used to create them. In this way the results are scaled. This means that the results of different-sized companies can be compared. You would not expect the same dollar amount of profit from IBM and a corner grocery store, but you might expect the same percentage return on their respective assets. The profitability ratios we shall calculate are return on sales (%), return on assets (%), and return on shareholders' equity (%).

15.3.1 Gross Profit on Sales (%)

Definition: (gross profit ÷ sales) × 100%

This ratio measures what is left over out of sales after the direct cost of sales is deducted. In a retail organization such as Leon's the direct cost is the replacement of the inventory that has been sold. It is a very useful control measure that monitors whether the company is controlling its merchandising activities effectively. If sales revenue or inventory are being misappropriated, this ratio will be lower than what would be expected from the official profit markups.

Canadian company law does not require disclosure of the direct costs as a separate category, but Leon's has chosen to report it anyway. It is always calculated internally, for control purposes.

2007

$$\frac{\$274,195}{\$637,456} \times 100\%$$
$$= 43.0\%$$

2008

$$\frac{\$300,016}{\$740,376} \times 100\%$$
$$= 40.5\%$$

2009

$$\frac{\$283,361}{\$703,180} \times 100\%$$
$$= 40.3\%$$

Analysis: Leon's has suffered a small reduction in its gross profit as % of sales between 2007 and 2009, falling from 43.0% to 40.3%.

In 2008 and 2009, it is just over 40%. A 40% gross profit ratio is consistent with a 66-2/3% markup on costs. For example, if an item has a cost of $600, a markup of 66-2/3% would add $400 to make the selling price $1,000. The $400 gross margin is 40% of the selling price.

15.3.2 Return on Sales (%)

Definition: (operating income ÷ sales) × 100%

This ratio measures what is left over out of each dollar of sales after all the operating expenses have been paid. It measures many things that are under the control of the management (such as the total number of employees and their remuneration) and also a number of things that are outside management's control (such as the purchase price of raw material inputs). The more carefully management controls the costs under their influence, the higher this ratio will be.

2007

$$\frac{\$91,023}{\$637,456} \times 100\%$$
$$= 14.3\%$$

2008

$$\frac{\$94,136}{\$740,376} \times 100\%$$
$$= 12.7\%$$

2009

$$\frac{\$82,534}{\$703,180} \times 100\%$$
$$= 11.7\%$$

Analysis: The operating income as % of sales fell from 14.3% in 2007 to 12.7% in 2008, and 11.7% in 2009.

In the case of Leon's, the company has given us comprehensive information about its expenses, so we can do a complete vertical analysis of the component parts of the income statement, expressing each item as a percentage of the sales revenue:

	2007		2008		2009	
Sales revenue	$637,456	100.0%	$740,736	100.0%	$703,180	100.0%
Cost of sales	363,261	57.0%	440,360	59.5%	419,819	59.7%
Gross profit	$274,195	43.0%	$300,016	40.5%	$283,361	40.3%
Operating expenses:						
Salaries, etc.	$103,661	16.3%	$116,591	15.8%	$103,977	14.8%
Advertising	32,008	5.0%	33,752	4.6%	34,732	4.9%
Rent & taxes	10,486	1.6%	11,268	1.5%	12,165	1.7%
Other expenses	22,983	3.6%	28,016	3.8%	33,391	4.7%
Amortization	14,034	2.2%	16,253	2.1%	16,562	2.4%
Total operating expenses	$183,172	28.7%	$205,880	27.8%	$200,827	28.5%
Operating income	$ 91,023	14.3%	$ 94,136	12.7%	$ 82,534	11.8%
Income tax	32,529	5.1%	30,746	4.1%	25,670	3.7%
Net income	$ 58,494	9.2%	$ 63,390	8.6%	$ 56,864	8.1%

Analysis: Leon's had an increase in sales revenue. In 2007, sales revenue was $637,456; by 2008, it had risen to $740,376, which is a 16% increase. Despite having made this increase in the sales revenue, the gross profit did not rise proportionately, and gross profit as % of sales fell from 43.0% to 40.5%. Operating expenses increased in dollar value but did not increase by the same 16% as sales revenue had, falling in total from 28.7% of sales revenue to 27.8%. As a result of all the above, the operating profit as % of sales fell from 14.3% to 12.7%. Taxes were a smaller percentage of the sales revenue (4.1% in 2008 instead of 5.1% in 2007). This resulted in net income as % of sales falling from 9.2% in 2007 to 8.6% in 2008.

In 2009, sales fell slightly to $703,180. The gross profit percentage stayed constant (just over 40%). Expenses rose slightly (from 27.8% to 28.5%) and taxes fell slightly (from 4.1% to 3.7%). Net income as % of sales fell to 8.1%.

Put in other words, for every $1 of sales in 2007, there was 9.2 cents left over after all outgoings. By 2008 this had fallen to 8.6 cents, and by 2009 it was 8.1 cents

15.3.3 *Return on Assets (%)*
Definition: (operating income ÷ total assets) × 100%

The return on assets measures how well the company has used its assets in carrying out its business mission. (Here, it is retailing.)

2007	2008	2009
$\dfrac{\$91,023}{\$475,226} \times 100\%$	$\dfrac{\$94,136}{\$513,408} \times 100\%$	$\dfrac{\$82,534}{\$529,136} \times 100\%$
= 19.2%	= 18.3%	= 15.6%

Analysis: Between 2007 and 2009, operating income rose from $91,023 to $94,136 (an increase of 3.4%), and total assets rose from $475,226 to $513,408 (an increase of 8%). The net effect is that the return on assets fell from 19.2% to 18.3%. In 2009, operating income fell to $82,534, while total assets increased to $529,156. Return and assets fell to 15.6%.

This steady decline (19.2%, 18.3%, 15.6%) is a worrying trend.

Comment: There is a connection between the return-on-sales ratio, the return-on-assets ratio (both are shown above), and the total asset turnover ratio (which is shown later in this chapter).

	Return on sales	×	Total asset turnover	=	Return on assets
2007					
	14.3%	×	1.34 times	=	19.2%
2008					
	12.7%	×	1.44 times	=	18.3%
2009					
	11.7%	×	1.33 times	=	15.6%

Analysis: Between 2007 and 2008, the drop in return on sales (from 14.3% to 12.7%) was partially offset by the increase in the asset turnover ratio (from 1.34X to 1.44X). In 2009, both return on sales and total asset turnover declined, so return on assets fell to 15.6%.

15.3.4 *Return on Equity (%)*

Definition: (net income ÷ shareholders' equity) × 100%

This is similar to the return on assets, in that it attempts to measure overall economic performance; however, it does so from the perspective of the shareholder, rather than the business unit. There are two differences between these two ratios.

First, the return on equity is measured on the basis of income after interest, which is then compared to the assets, net of liabilities (in other words, the owners' equity). This means, effectively, that the finance provided by borrowings and the interest cost of borrowings have both been excluded. Thus, a smaller definition of income is being compared with a smaller definition of investment. Return on equity compares the income to which the shareholders are entitled to the finances they have supplied. All other things being equal, this should result in the return on equity being the same as or higher than the return on assets. This is because interest costs on debt (low-risk) should be lower than the required return on equity.

Second, the return on equity is measured on an after-tax basis. This is because investors are really interested in what is left over for them after taxes have been paid. All other things being equal, this should cause the return on equity to be lower than the return on assets.

Because these two effects (leverage, taxes) work in opposite directions (leverage increases the return on equity; taxes decrease the return on equity), it is not always clear what the net effect will be.

2007	**2008**	**2009**
$\dfrac{\$58,494}{\$322,005} \times 100\%$	$\dfrac{\$63,390}{\$353,358} \times 100\%$	$\dfrac{\$56,864}{\$375,138} \times 100\%$
$= 18.2\%$	$= 17.9\%$	$= 15.2\%$

Analysis: Both the net income and the shareholders' equity rose in dollar value between 2007 and 2008. However, the percentage increases were different. Net income rose from $58,494 to $63,390, which is an increase of 8.4%, and shareholders' equity rose from $322,005 to $353,358, which is an increase of 9.7%. The net effect is a slight fall (from 18.2% to 17.9%) in the return each shareholder got per dollar of assets invested in the company.

When this return (around 18%) is compared with alternative investment opportunities, it is clear that Leon's is doing a good job for its investors in both years.

By 2009, the return on equity had fallen to 15.2%, which is lower than 2008 or 2007, but still a good return in a recessionary economy.

15.4 Debt

When a company uses debt to finance its activities, two things happen. First, because debt is less risky to the investor (i.e., the cost of debt is lower) and because debt interest is a tax-allowable expense for the borrower, the greater the debt, the greater the return on equity should be. Second, the greater the debt, the riskier the equity return becomes: both the variability of returns and the probability of default increase as a result of borrowing capital. Investors and creditors will want to measure the debt in relation to the equity (debt-to-equity ratio or debt-to-total-assets ratio), and will also want to measure the debt interest in relation to the income (interest cover ratio).

The two ratios, debt to equity and debt to total assets, are just different ways of measuring the same concept. It is redundant to consider both.

15.4.1 Debt to Assets (%)
Definition: (total debt ÷ total assets) × 100%

2007	**2008**	**2009**
$\dfrac{\$153,221}{\$475,226} \times 100\%$	$\dfrac{\$160,050}{\$513,408} \times 100\%$	$\dfrac{\$154,018}{\$529,156} \times 100\%$
$= 32.2\%$	$= 31.2\%$	$= 29.1\%$

15.4.2 Debt to Equity (%)
Definition: (total debt ÷ shareholders' equity) × 100%

2007	**2008**	**2007**
$\dfrac{\$153,221}{\$322,005} \times 100\%$	$\dfrac{\$160,050}{\$353,358} \times 100\%$	$\dfrac{\$154,018}{\$373,138} \times 100\%$
$= 47.6\%$	$= 45.3\%$	$= 41.1\%$

Analysis: Where debt is greater than 50% of total assets or is greater than 100% of share-holders' equity, the conclusion would be that the company has too much debt. An unhealthy reliance on borrowed funds is symptomatic of a risky company. Leon's debt ratios are well below these cut-off levels in all three years, so debt does not present a high level of financial risk.

15.4.3 Interest Cover Ratio

Definition: operating income (income before taxes and interest)
÷ interest paid

This ratio measures the ability of the company to pay interest expense out of current earnings. The earnings before interest and taxes are divided by the interest expense.

In the case of Leon's, the company has no debt that carries interest (its liabilities consist of mainly accounts payable and other non-interest–bearing amounts). Its long-term liabilities consist of deferred income taxes. Therefore, it is not possible to calculate the interest cover ratio.

A high interest cover ratio is associated with low risk and a low interest cover ratio is associated with high financial risk. With no interest payable, Leon's has no risk arising from borrowings and interest payments.

15.5 Efficiency

To be efficient can be thought of as getting a high level of sales out of a given set of assets, or, to put it the other way around, using a small quantity of assets to support a given level of sales. Efficiency ratios examine this feature by relating the assets on the balance sheet to the sales revenue.

This can be done for all assets (total assets turnover) or individual asset classes (e.g., receivables turnover, inventory turnover). In each case a judgment may be made on whether the asset is well managed or not.

15.5.1 Total Asset Turnover

Definition: sales ÷ total assets

2007	**2008**	**2007**
$\dfrac{\$637,456}{\$475,226} = 1.34\text{X}$	$\dfrac{\$740,376}{\$513,408} = 1.44\text{X}$	$\dfrac{\$703,180}{\$529,156} = 1.33\text{X}$

222

Analysis: The greater the sales revenue per dollar of assets, the more efficiently the company is operating. In 2007, Leon's generated $1.34 for every $1 of assets. By 2008, this had increased to $1.44. The company had therefore become more efficient in its use of assets. In 2009, it fell to 1.33X, so the company was less efficient in 2009.

The total asset turnover ratio can be broken down into its component elements by looking at similar ratios for each of the assets. The two assets that are most commonly examined are the accounts receivable and the inventory.

15.5.2 Receivables Turnover Ratio and Number of Days' Receivables

Companies that let their customers buy goods on credit terms probably expect to increase their sales by doing so. There is a cost, however, in that the accounts receivable have to be financed. An efficient company is one that allows customers credit terms, but is then rigorous about collecting the amounts owing. Comparing receivables to sales revenue shows the turnover ratio. The more frequently these are turned over, the more efficiently the company is operating.

An alternative way of presenting the same information is the number of days' worth of sales that the receivables represent. It is unnecessary to calculate both ratios.

RECEIVABLES TURNOVER RATIO
Definition: sales ÷ receivables

2007	**2008**	**2009**
$\dfrac{\$637,456}{\$34,966} = 18.2X$	$\dfrac{\$740,376}{\$34,507} = 21.5X$	$\dfrac{\$703,180}{\$32,634} = 21.5X$

RECEIVABLES COLLECTION PERIOD
Definition: receivables ÷ (sales ÷ 365)

2007	**2008**	**2009**
$\dfrac{\$34,966}{(\$637,456 \div 365)}$	$\dfrac{\$34,507}{(\$740,376 \div 365)}$	$\dfrac{\$32,634}{(\$703,150 \div 365)}$
= 20 days	= 17 days	= 16.9 days

Analysis: Between 2007 and 2008, although sales revenue increased by 16%, accounts receivable actually fell slightly (from $34,966 to $34,507). The receivables turnover ratio increased from 18.2 times per year to 21.5 times per year, indicating higher efficiency. The same story is told by the receivables collection period. In 2007, it took 20 days on average to collect accounts receivable; in 2008, that had fallen to 17 days; and in 2009, the collection period went down further, to 16.9 days.

15.5.3 Inventory Turnover and Inventory Holding Period

A retail company such as Leon's needs inventory so that its customers can see what they are buying. Holding inventory is, however, expensive. It has to be warehoused and moved around.

It may suffer deterioration. It has to be financed. All other things being equal, the less the inventory for a given level of sales revenue, the more efficiently the company is operating.

INVENTORY TURNOVER
Definition: sales ÷ inventory

2007	**2008**	**2009**
$\dfrac{\$637,456}{\$75,640} = 8.4\text{X}$	$\dfrac{\$740,376}{\$92,904} = 8.0\text{X}$	$\dfrac{\$703,180}{\$83,957} = 8.4\text{X}$

INVENTORY HOLDING PERIOD
Definition: inventory ÷ (sales ÷ 365)

2007	**2008**	**2009**
$\dfrac{\$75,640}{(\$637,456 \div 365)}$	$\dfrac{\$92,904}{(\$740,376 \div 365)}$	$\dfrac{\$83,957}{(\$703,180 \div 365)}$
= 43 days	= 46 days	= 44 days

Analysis: Sales revenue increased by 16% from 2007 to 2008, but inventory increased even faster. In 2007, inventory was $75,640; in 2008, it increased by almost 23% to $92,904. As a result, the inventory turnover ratio fell from 8.4 times per year to 8.0 times per year, and the inventory holding period increased from 43 days to 46 days. The company's use of inventory has become less efficient.

In 2009, turnover was back to 8.4X and inventory holding period was back to 44 days.

15.6 Market-Related Ratios

Ratios that shareholders will use in assessing the value of their shares include the earnings per share, the price-to-earnings ratio, and the dividend cover ratio.

15.6.1 Earnings Per Share
Definition: net income ÷ number of common shares

The higher the earnings, the better it is for the shareholders. Earnings will either be paid to shareholders now as a dividend, or they will get the benefit of capital growth through increased share prices if the earnings are plowed back into the company to finance growth. Whatever the total earnings, they have to be shared among the shareholders, so the greater the number of shares, the lower each share's proportion of earnings.

2007	**2008**	**2009**
$\dfrac{\$58,494}{70,777} = \$0.83$	$\dfrac{\$63,390}{70,729} = \$0.90$	$\dfrac{\$56,864}{70,714} = \$0.80$

Analysis: Leon's had a higher net income in 2008 ($63,390, compared to $58,494 in 2007), but the number of shares in issue had shrunk slightly (from 70,777 to 70,729). As a result, the earning per share increased from 83 cents to 90 cents. In 2009, EPS fell to 80 cents.

Leon's also has some share options in existence, which would enable some managers to purchase additional shares. If that were done, the number of shares would increase, but the net income would remain the same. This would dilute the earnings per share to a slightly lower level in all three years: EPS would be 80 cents in 2007, 87 cents in 2008, and 78 cents in 2009.

15.6.2 Price-to-Earnings Ratio
Definition: share price ÷ earnings per share

The relationship between the earnings of the company and the price of the shares is a judgment by the investing public on how well the company is regarded. A company with a high price-to-earnings ratio is looked on favourably, while a company with a low price-to-earnings ratio is viewed unfavourably.

2007	**2008**	**2009**
$\dfrac{\$14.19}{\$0.83} = 17.1\text{X}$	$\dfrac{\$8.30}{\$0.90} = 9.2\text{X}$	$\dfrac{\$11.80}{\$0.80} = 14.75\text{X}$

Analysis: In March 2009, the market price of an ordinary share of Leon's Furniture Ltd. was $8.30. The 2008 earnings per share were $0.90. This gives a price-to-earnings ratio of 9.2 times. This is about average for the retail sector in early 2009.

During 2007 the market price varied from a low of $12.18 to a high of $16.20. The average of these two gives a share price of $14.19. Based on $14.19, the price-to-earnings ratio for 2007 would be 17.1 times.

In May 2010, the share price was $11.80, EPS was $0.80, and P/E ratio was 14.75 times.

15.6.3 Dividend Cover Ratio and Dividend Payout (%)
Definition: net income ÷ dividend

The dividend cover ratio shows the extent to which the earnings are being paid back to shareholders as current dividend and, by implication, the level of profits being plowed back into capital growth. You can't have both!

2007	**2008**	**2009**
$\dfrac{\$58,494}{\$19,828} = 2.9\text{X}$	$\dfrac{\$63,390}{\$26,873} = 2.4\text{X}$	$\dfrac{\$56,864}{\$33,951} = 1.7\text{X}$

The same information can be presented in a different form as the dividend payout percentage:

Definition: (dividend ÷ net income) × 100%

2007

$$\frac{\$19,828}{\$58,494} \times 100\%$$
$$= 33.9\%$$

2008

$$\frac{\$26,873}{\$63,390} \times 100\%$$
$$= 42.4\%$$

2009

$$\frac{\$33,951}{\$56,864} \times 100\%$$
$$= 59.7\%$$

Analysis: Between 2007 and 2008, net income rose by 8.4%, but the dividend paid rose even more. Dividend payments went up from 27-1/4 cents per share to 38 cents per share (an increase of 39%). The dividend cover (at 2.4) is quite healthy and there is little risk of the dividend not being affordable, but it has fallen from 2.9X coverage to 2.4X cover. Also, the dividend payout increased from 33.9% of net income to 42.4%.

In 2009, the dividend cover ratio fell to 1.7X and the payout rose to 59.7%. This was because a higher dividend was paid out of lower net income.

15.7 Summary

Leon's Furniture Ltd. is profitable. It earns a good return on its assets and a good return for its shareholders; expenses seem to be well under control. The company is also very low risk. It has adequate liquidity and has negligible amounts of interest-bearing debt. A relatively high proportion of earnings is paid to shareholders as dividend. Its market price and price-to-earnings ratio imply that investors perceive it as a "normal" retail investment.

Week #7 / Lab #6

Class — Finance

The following reading is included in this week's section of the Lab Manual as it is required for class this week and will form the basis for part of next week's lab:

- *Accounting for Non-Financial Managers* by John Parkinson
  - o The Break-even or Cost-Volume-Profit Model

Lab #6 — Case Analysis with Numbers

In preparation for this week's lab:

- Complete the Cash Budgeting and Ratio Analysis Problems
- Review the material on case analysis from Lab #3
- Prepare *Johnston Processors Limited* case for discussion

Here are some questions to help you prepare...

  - o Using the course model, what is the main issue or primary problem in this case?
  - o Using ratios[†], analyse the historic financial statements. Does this analysis provide any insight into possible reasons for the company's problems?

    [†] The target ratios from Exhibit 6 were calculated using the following assumptions...

    - *Debt ratio* = current liabilities + $\dfrac{\text{long-term liabilities} - \text{shareholder loans}}{\text{total debt} + \text{equity}}$;

    - *Return on Shareholders' Equity* includes shareholder loans as part of shareholders' equity (assume that shareholder loans represents money that the shareholders have put into the company that is going to be converted to shares at some time in the future — so it is currently being treated as a loan until conversion, but should be included in shareholders' equity, not in liabilities, for the computation of the ratios);

    - *Times Interest Earned* is the same as the Interest Coverage Ratio; and

    - *Gross Profit Percentage* is the same as GPM

o Discuss the management style of the Johnstons and its impact on the company's performance.

o Analyse Marie's operating forecasts. Are they reasonable?

o Is the information available to the Johnstons sufficient to make an informed decision about the company's future? If not, what additional information is needed?

Based on the information given about the company and your assessment of its owners, rank the options open to the company. Provide reasons for your rankings.

The Break-Even or Cost-Volume-Profit Model

We can combine the features of the variable nature of sales and variable costs, and the fixed nature of fixed costs into a model that is called the Break-Even model (BE) or the Cost-Volume-Profit (CVP) model. This is a simple way of looking at the relationship between costs and revenues to determine the answers to question, such as the following:

- What level of sales is necessary to cover the fixed costs and avoid making a loss?
- What level of profit will be achieved by a given volume of sales?
- What would be the marginal effect of changing factors, such as the selling price, sales volume, the variable cost, or the fixed cost?

10.5.1. Contribution Margin

When goods are sold revenue is generated. The sales caused variable costs to be incurred. The difference between the selling price per unit and the variable cost per unit is called the contribution margin per unit. The contribution margin (CM) per unit measures how much better off the company is as a result of selling one additional unit. Conversely, the CM per unit measures how much worse off the company is if sales are reduced by one unit. The CM measures the marginal effect of a sale.

Tony's Drinks sells coffee, tea, and soft drinks. Each drink is priced at $0.80 and has a variable cost of $0.50. The contribution margin is $0.30 per drink. In other words, for every drink sold, Tony's Drinks will have an additional $0.30. If 1,000 drinks are sold in a day, the total contribution margin will be $300. If 1,001 drinks are sold, the total contribution margin will be $300.30.

10.5.2. Break-Even Point

Once variable costs are subtracted from sales revenue, the amount left behind is the contribution margin. The contribution is used to pay for the business's fixed costs. When that has been achieved, the business has reached its break-even point. It is useful to know how much business activity is necessary to reach break-even. If this level of activity is unlikely to be reached, there is no reason for the business to exist. If the break-even level is likely to be exceeded, the company will be profitable. Knowing the break-even point enables a sensible decision to be taken as to whether or not to go ahead with a business venture.

To calculate the break-even point, the fixed cost for a given period of time is divided by the contribution margin per unit. The answer indicates how many units need to be sold in that period to reach the break-even point.

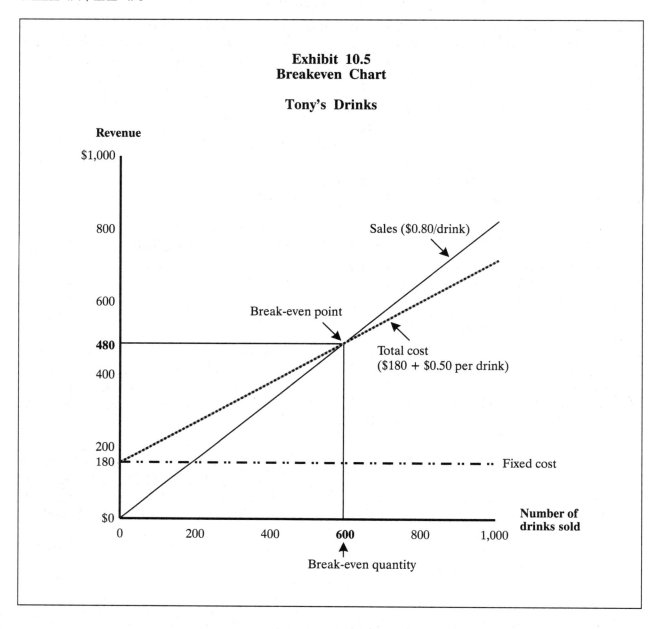

Exhibit 10.5
Breakeven Chart

Tony's Drinks

Tony's Drinks has fixed costs of $180 per day. Selling price is $0.80 per drink and variable cost is $0.50 per drink. Contribution margin is $0.30 per unit. Break-even is 600 drinks per day ($180 ÷ $0.30). If Tony's can sell 600 drinks in a day the company will break even. (See Exhibit 10.5.) If Tony's sells fewer than 600 drinks, there will be fixed costs not covered by contribution and a loss will occur.

10.5.3 Activity Above the Break-Even Point

At activity levels above the break-even point, the company will be making a profit. For every unit sold above the break-even point, the contribution margin is pure profit. The greater the number sold, the higher the profit becomes.

Earlier, we calculated that Tony's Drinks will break even if it sells 600 drinks per day ($180 ÷ $0.30). Tony, the manager, estimated that his average sales will be 850 drinks per day. His estimated average profit, therefore, will be $75. This may be calculated by totalling the $0.30 contribution margin on every drink sold in excess of the break-even point: $0.30 × (850 − 600) = $75.

Tony's Drinks
Budgeted Daily Income Statement

Sales (850 × $0.80)	$680
Variable cost (850 × $0.50)	425
Contribution margin (850 × $0.30)	$255
Fixed costs	180
Operating profit	$ 75

In addition to paying the fixed costs, an organization may have an expectation or hope about the profit level. This can only come out of the contribution margin earned from sales. Expected profit may be treated in the same way as fixed cost for calculation of the sales level required. The total of the fixed costs and the required profit is divided by the contribution margin to determine the required sales level.

Tony has decided that unless he can make a profit of $120 per day, it's just not worth getting out of bed. To make $120 profit, he has to make enough of the $0.30 contribution margins to pay the fixed costs ($180) plus $120: that is, a total of $300. To make this level of profit he will need to sell 1,000 drinks ($300 ÷ $0.30).

Based on Tony's profit expectation, if he cannot sell 1,000 drinks a day, it is not worth his while being in business. If he estimates that he can sell more than 1,000 drinks a day, then he has a potentially viable business. If his prediction is that he can sell exactly 1,000 drinks a day he has reached a point of indifference: he does not mind whether he is in business or not.

If, as above, his prediction is that he can sell 850 units per day, then his profit objectives will not be met. He will fall short by $45 ($120 − $75).

10.5.4 *Using the Break-Even Model to Analyze Changes*

The break-even model lends itself to simple (but sometimes very effective) "what if" analysis. In a "what if" analysis, the numbers, assumptions, and so on are changed to study the effect of the change. You might want to consider the effect of increasing the selling price, for example. This would increase the contribution margin but (unless the product is perfectly inelastic) would also reduce the sales volume. Or you might want to decrease the selling price, which would increase the volume but decrease the contribution margin. It is almost always the case that changing one variable will also result in change in one of the other variables. Sometimes the effects are extremely complex, with several variables changing at once.

Tony's break-even calculation informs him that he will need to sell 1,000 drinks to pay his fixed costs and get the $120 profit he is hoping for. His best estimate is that he can sell 850 drinks per day at a price of $0.80, which is not enough volume to give him his required profit. Tony is considering two alternatives: he could raise the price of drinks from $0.80 to

$1.00, in which case his volume will decrease to 600 units; alternatively, he could decrease the price of drinks from $0.80 to $0.70, in which case volume will increase to 1,600 units.

Selling price	Variable cost	Contribution margin/unit	Volume	Total contribution	Objective
$1.00	$0.50	$0.50	600	$300	Met
$0.70	$0.50	$0.20	1,600	$320	Exceeded

Both actions result in achieving his stated profit objective. Raising the price meets his requirements exactly. Reducing the price gives him his required profit, and another $20 per day. Tony would now have a good basis for making a decision. Which route he chooses would be a matter of personal preference, but both are feasible.

Another calculation to reach the same conclusion would be as follows:

Existing situation

850 units, $0.30 contribution margin per unit; $300 required; shortfall $45.

Option 1: Increase Price

Effect of decreasing volume: $(600 - 850) \times \$0.30$	=	($ 75)
Effect of increasing price: $600 \times (\$1.00 - \$0.80)$	=	120
Net increase in contribution margin		$ 45

Forty-five dollars is exactly enough to meet the $45 shortfall, so the objective has been met.

Option 2: Decrease Price

Effect of increasing volume: $(1,600 - 850) \times \$0.30$	=	$225
Effect of decreasing price: $1,600 \times (\$0.80 - \$0.70)$	=	(160)
Net increase in contribution margin		$ 65

A net increase of $45 would have been enough to meet the shortfall, so the objective has been met and superseded by $20.

The break-even model can be used to evaluate a wide range of decisions, such as using better raw materials to increase quality, using advertising to boost sales, expanding the product range, and so on.

Tony is considering the effect of advertising on his outlet. At a cost of a mere $60 per day, he can have posters put on all the transit stop benches within one kilometre of his place of business. If he does that he estimates that sales will increase by 250 units per day. His current fixed cost is $180 per day, and his contribution margin is $0.30 per drink sold.

Additional contribution margin: $250 \times \$0.30$	$75
Additional fixed cost	60
Additional net income	$15

Advertising increases his net income, so it is a sound business idea. We should also recognize that it makes his business a little riskier. His fixed cost has now increased from $180 per day to $240 per day. His break-even point has increased from 600 units a day ($180 ÷ $0.30) to

800 units a day ($240 ÷ $0.30). Although he is likely to do better, his exposure to risk is higher, as measured by the increased break-even level.

Note that in this calculation, the existing situation is irrelevant, and none of the data about the existing situation enters into the decision. The only relevant facts are those that are marginal to the decision — i.e., those that change as a result of the decision. The increased advertising spending is a marginal cost. The increased contribution from additional sales is a marginal benefit. The net effect is the marginal benefit of the decision to advertise.

Problems — Cash Budgeting

1. Using the information below, prepare a cash budget showing expected cash receipts and disbursements for the month of May, and the cash balance expected at May 31, 200X.

Planned cash balance May 1, 200X	• $60,000
Sales for May	• $800,000 half collected in month of sale, 40 percent in next month, 10 percent in third month.
Accounts Receivable balances as of May 1	• $70,000 from March sales, $450,000 from April sales.
Merchandise purchases for May	• $500,000, 40 percent paid in month of purchase, 60 percent in next month, April purchase were $400,000
Payroll due in May	• $88,000
Three-year insurance policy due in May for renewal	• $2,000 to be paid in cash.
Other expenses for May, payable in May	• $41,000
Amortization for the month of May	• $2,000
Accrued taxes for May, payable in December	• $6,000
Bank note due on May 15	• $175,000 plus $10,000 interest.

2. Prepare a cash budget for the Ace Manufacturing Company Ltd., indicating receipts and disbursements for May, June and July. The firm wishes to maintain, at all times, a minimum cash balance of $20,000. Determine whether or not borrowing will be necessary during the period and, if it is, when and for how much. As of April 30, the firm had a balance of $20,000 in cash.

Actual Sales			
January	$50,000	May	$ 70,000
February	50,000	June	80,000
March	60,000	July	100,000
April	60,000	August	100,000
Accounts Receivable	• 50 percent of total sales are for cash. The remaining 50 percent will be collected equally during the following two months.		
Cost of Goods Manufactured	• 70 percent of sales. 90 percent of this cost is paid during the first month after it occurs, the remaining 10 percent is paid the following month.		
Sales & Admin. Expenses	• $10,000 per month plus 10 percent of sales		

234

All of these expenses are paid during the month of in which they occur.

Interest Payments	• A semi-annual interest payment on $300,000 of bonds outstanding (6 percent coupon) is paid during July. An annual sinking fund payment of $50,000 is also made in July.
Dividends	• A $10,000 dividend payment will be declared and paid in July.
Capital Expenditures	• $40,000 will be invested in plant and equipment in June.
Taxes	• Income tax payments of $1,000 will be made in July.

3. Tidewater Sales Inc. expects to have a $5,800 cash balance on December 31 of the current year. The bank has required a minimum monthly cash balance for the new year of $10,000. It also expects to have a $35,200 balance of accounts receivable and $20,900 of accounts payable. Its budgeted sales, purchases, and cash expenditures for the following three months are:

	January	February	March
Sales	$24,000	$18,000	$27,000
Purchases	14,000	17,300	18,000
Payroll	2,400	2,400	2,800
Rent	1,000	1,000	1,000
Other cash expenses	1,200	1,600	1,400
Purchase of store equipment	0	0	5,000
Payment of quarterly dividend	0	0	4,000

- All sales are on account; and past experience indicates that 85% is collected in the month following the sale, 10% in the next month, and 4% in the third month. Application of the experience to the December 31 accounts receivable balance indicates that $28,000 of the $35,200 will be collected in January, $5,200 in February and $1,600 in March.
- Purchases are paid in the month following each purchase.

Prepare a cash budget for the months of January, February and March, keeping in mind that the bank requires that any excesses over the minimum required be used to pay down outstanding loans.

4. Prepare a cash budget for Parker House Ltd. for the months of April, May, and June, 2007. The firm wishes to maintain, at all times, a minimum cash balance of $60,000. Determine whether or not borrowing will be necessary during the period and how much. The bank charges 6% on any outstanding balances at month end (rounded to the nearest dollar for simplicity). Assume that all borrowing, or repaying of outstanding loans, occurs on the last day of the month, and that interest on outstanding loans is due at the end of the month. Also assume that any excess cash balances at month-end will be used to pay down any outstanding bank loans. There is no bank loan out-

standing at the beginning of April. As of March 31, the firm had a cash balance of $60,000.

Actual Sales		Budgeted Sales	
February	$80,000	April	$50,000
March	$70,000	May	$65,000
		June	$90,000
		July	$60,000

- Accounts Receivable: 50% of sales are either cash or collected in the month of sale, 40% are collected in the next month, and 10% in the month following.
- Interest Received on Bonds: $8,500 in June.
- Proceeds on Sale of Property: $25,000 cash sale received in April.
- Cost of Goods Sold: Inventory costing 40% of sales must be purchased one month in advance of sale. 50% of this cost is paid for in the month of occurrence, 30% in the next month, and 20% in the month following.
- Selling and Administrative Expenses: $35,000 per month, paid in full in the month during which expenses are incurred.
- Interest Payments: Quarterly payment on $200,000 of corporate bonds outstanding (6% coupon rate) due on April 15.
- Dividends Payable: $15,000 due on May 3.
- Taxes Payable: $20,000 due on May 15.

Problems — Ratio Analysis

1. Company X and Company Y have the following Current Assets and Current Liabilities as of December 31, 200X:

	Company X	Company Y
Cash	250,000	150,000
Marketable Securities	500,000	75,000
Accounts Receivable	1,500,000	300,000
Inventories	3,500,000	225,000
Current Liabilities	2,300,000	300,000

(a) On the basis of the current ratio, which firm appears most likely to be able to meet its current obligations?

(b) In view of your answer in part (a), are there any other ratios that you would calculate? If yes, what are they? Interpret the results of these.

2. Company A has annual credit sales of $1.5 million. On December 31, 200X the Balance Sheet of Company A showed accounts receivable of $250,000.

(a) Calculate the average collection period for Company A.

(b) If Company A's credit terms are 3/15, net 45, what does your answer in part (a) suggest about the company?

3. You are the manager of a commercial bank. Two companies have applied to you for a loan. You have been provided with the following information:

	Company A	Company B
Cost of Goods Sold	$4,550,000	$5,000,000
Inventory, Dec. 1/97	650,000	900,000
Inventory, Nov. 30/98	750,000	1,100,000

(a) Calculate the inventory turnover ratio for each firm.

(b) On the basis of your answer in part (a), which firm appears to be the least likely to default on the loan?

(c) If Company A were a manufacturer of ladies autumn dresses, and Company B were a large merchandising company (*i.e.*, Sears), would this change your answer to part (b)? If so, why?

4. Analysis of the financial statements of Company X, a manufacturing company, yielded the following:

237

	20X4	20X5	20X6	20X7	20X8
Gross Profit Margin	17.6%	16.9%	16.6%	16.1%	15.2%

(a) What types of things may have caused this pattern? (HINT: Think of the way in which gross profit is calculated on a merchandising company's Income Statement).

(b) If, when comparing your firm's GPM to that of other firms in your industry it was found that:

	GPM 20X9
Your Company	30%
Industry Average	45%

Where would you, as an astute financial analyst, recommend making some investigations?

5. On December 31, 20X4 it was found that Company Y's net profit had fallen from the previous year's level. The trend in net profit margin was:

	20X2	20X3	20X4
Net Profit Margin	7.4%	7.1%	6.6%

However, further investigation revealed that the prices on all products sold by the company had increased over the three-year period. Furthermore, unit sales had remained constant, inventory costs had actually declined, and the tax rate had remained constant. What might account for the continued decrease in the net profit margin? Assume that Company Y is a merchandising company.

6. The long term liability section of the Balance Sheet of Company W appears as follows:

Long Term Liabilities:		
7 ½% Mortgage Bonds of 2005	$2,600,000	
8% Second Mortgage Bonds of 2004	2,000,000	
10% Debentures of 2003	1,000,000	
Total Long Term Liabilities		$5,600,000

(a) If the average earnings before interest and taxes of Company W are $5,005,000; what is the interest coverage ratio of the firm?

(b) Is that an acceptable amount? What does it say about the company's ability to finance an expansion?

7. Company P is selling at a Price/Earnings ratio of 80:1. What does this indicate about the company?

8. You are a potential investor considering the possibility of purchasing shares in either Company L or Company M. You have gathered the following information:

	Company L	Company M
Net Profit 20X4	$3,000,000	$5,000,000
Preferred Stock Dividends		200,000
# Shares Common Stock Outstanding	800,000	1,200,000
Current Market Price of Common Stock	$30/share	$40/share
Dividend Payout as a % of Net Profit	60%	50%

  (a) Compute:
- i) the earnings per share;
- ii) the yield;
- iii) the price/earnings ratio; for each company.

  (b) On the basis of your analysis in part (a), which company would you invest in? Why? Assume that both companies possess the same degree of risk and that you prefer annual cash returns to capital appreciation.

9. As of the fiscal year end November 15, 2000, the Balance Sheet of Kids Inc., a large retailer of children's toys, revealed the following:

Current Assets	$3,640,000
Current Liabilities	$1,690,000
Inventory	$2,450,000

Using the appropriate ratios and guidelines developed by financial analysts, comment on the liquidity position of Kids Inc.

10. You are given the summarized financial statements (see next page) of Canadian Tire for 2001. Using financial ratio analysis, prepare a report on how well the company is doing.†

---

† Reproduced from John Parkinson, *Accounting for Non-Financial Managers*, 1st edition (Concord, ON: Captus Press, 2003), p. 248.

Canadian Tire
Consolidated Statement of Earnings
and Retained Income for 2001

			$ million
Gross operating revenue			$5,374
Less: Cost of goods sold and operating expenses			
Various		$4,874	
Depreciation		136	(5,010)
Operating income			$ 364
Less: Interest		$ 88	
Taxes		100	
			(188)
Net income			$ 176
Add: Retained earnings at start of year			860
			$1,036
Less: Cost of repurchase of shares		$ 32	
Dividends paid		31	63
Retained earnings at end of year			$ 973

Canadian Tire
Consolidated Balance Sheet
as at the end of 2001

			$ million
Current assets:			
Cash		$ 579	
Accounts receivable		959	
Inventory		441	
Prepaid expenses		14	
Total current assets			$1,993
Long-term assets (net)			2,378
Total assets			$4,371
Current liabilities			$1,110
Long-term liabilities			1,357
Total liabilities			$2,467
Shareholders' equity:			
Minority interest		$ 300	
Share capital	$622		
Retained earnings	973		
Foreign exchange adjustment	9	1,604	
Total shareholders' equity			1,904
Total liabilities and shareholders' equity			$4,371

11. Using the attached Income Statement and Balance Sheet for Donaldson Merchandising Inc., along with the industry averages given for comparison and other comparisons you feel are necessary, conduct the appropriate ratio analysis to answer the following questions.

   (a) Is the level of net working capital appropriate for this company? Why or why not?

   (b) Should an investor be concerned about the long-term viability of the company? Why or why not?

   (c) Comment on the profitability of the company and whether it is meeting its obligations to shareholders.

   Industry Averages:

EPS	$3.12
Acid Test	1.3 : 1
NPM	15%
Accts. Rec. Turnover	8x
Avg. Collection Period	45 days
P/E ratio	4x
GPM	30%
Inventory Turnover	15x
ROI	25%
Payout	20%
Interest Coverage	3.5x

Donaldson Merchandising Inc.
Income Statement
For the Year Ended December 31st, 2006

Gross Sales			$765,000
Less: Returns & Allowances			45,900
Net Sales			$719,100
Cost of Goods Sold:			
Inventory, Jan. 1/06		$ 26,700	
Gross Purchases	$535,000		
Less: Returns & Allowances	17,200		
Net Purchases	$517,800		
Add: Freight-In	10,700		
Net Cost of purchases		528,500	
Cost of Goods Available for Sale		$555,200	
Inventory, Dec. 31/06		43,000	
Cost of Goods Sold			512,200
Gross Profit			$206,900
Operating Expenses:			
Selling & Distribution:			
Building Amortization	$ 3,200		
Vehicle Amortization	2,500		
Advertising	18,000		
Wages	51,000		
Insurance	5,000		
Total Selling & Distribution		$ 79,700	
General and Administrative:			
Office Supplies	$ 500		
Rent	6,000		
Office Equipment Lease	800		
Wages	28,150		
Total General & Administrative		35,450	
Total Operating Expenses			115,150
Total Operating Income			$ 91,750
Other Income & Expenses:			
Interest Expense			4,500
Net Income before Tax			87,250
Taxes			17,450
Net Income			$ 69,800

Donaldson Merchandising Inc.
Balance Sheet
As at December 31st, 2006

ASSETS
Current Assets

Cash	$ 61,300	
Accounts Receivable	26,500	
Inventory	43,000	
Supplies	2,250	
Prepaid Expenses	4,000	
Total Current Assets		$137,050

Capital Assets

Land		$ 68,000	
Building	$150,000		
Less: Acc. Amortization	12,800	137,200	
Delivery Vehicle	25,000		
Less: Acc. Amortization	10,000	15,000	
Total Capital Assets			220,200

Other Assets

Investment	$ 50,000	
Goodwill	17,500	
Total Other Assets		67,500
Total Assets		$424,750

EQUITIES
Current Liabilities

Accounts Payable	$ 12,145	
Notes Payable	7,500	
Interest Payable	4,500	
Wages Payable	5,000	
Dividends Payable	13,960	
Total Current Liabilities		$ 43,105

Long-Term Liabilities

Notes Payable	$ 45,000	
Mortgage Payable	150,000	
Total Long-Term Liabilities		195,000

Shareholders' Equity

Common Stock	$ 75,805	
Retained Earnings	110,840	
Total Shareholders' Equity		186,645
Total Equities		$424,750

Johnston Processors Limited

Charlie Johnston, President of Johnston Processors Limited, operators of three One Hour Drycleaning franchises, sat in his office in downtown St John's and considered the information in front of him. It was March 28, 1991, and Charlie's accountant, Harry Wood, had just presented him with a draft copy of his financial statements for the year ended January 31, 1991. "This indicates that we've experienced another decrease in sales and profits," Charlie commented. "Obviously, our bankers will not like this situation at all; they may even decide to call our term loans. This would have a severe negative effect on my other companies. As you know, my wife, Marie, and my daughter, Christina, operate this company. We'll have to analyze this company's situation further to see where our problems are and what can be done to solve them." Harry, of Wood and Smythe, Chartered Accountants, nodded in agreement. "Unfortunately, we won't be able to do the analysis for you. As a small, independent firm, our personnel resources are stretched to the limit at this time of year. Why not ask someone from the University's Small Business Centre to conduct this study?"

Background Information

Charlie Johnston was the operator of several small companies in the Avalon Peninsula region of the Province of Newfoundland and Labrador. Over the years Charlie had been moderately successful, and had, in fact, accumulated considerable personal wealth, primarily as equity in various companies. Charlie's wife, Marie, was a nominal shareholder in most of Charlie's companies, but with the exception of the drycleaning franchises, did not play an active role in management. "When the kids were younger, I felt more comfortable working at home, raising our family," Marie recalled. "However, when Christina, our youngest daughter, finished high school, I found I had sufficient time to make a contribution to the businesses. Originally, I wanted to become involved in some of the existing companies, but they already had management people in place and were operating smoothly. As well, Christina was having difficulty in finding employment. Charlie and I decided that we would look for a new opportunity for Christina and me to start up."

The Johnstons' determined that a franchise arrangement would be the most suitable for Marie and Christina. They felt that franchises had several advantages, including recognition by customers, national advertising, assistance with store design and location, and advice in other areas if necessary. The disadvantages were the high initial franchise fee and the relatively expensive royalty and advertising payments required by the franchise agreement. In 1982 the family spent several months reviewing the 'Business Opportunities' sections of several business magazines and newspapers. They decided to proceed with the acquisition of a 'One Hour Drycleaning' franchise, a self-contained drycleaning store designed to operate from a shopping

---

This case was prepared by Professor Wayne King of Memorial University of Newfoundland for the Atlantic Entrepreneurial Institute as a basis for classroom discussion, and is not meant to illustrate either effective or ineffective management. Some elements of this case have been disguised. Copyright © 1992, the Atlantic Entrepreneurial Institute. Reproduced by permission.

Exhibit 1
One Hour Drycleaning
Forecast Opening Balance Sheet
(One Location Only)

Current Assets		
Inventory, parts and cleaning supplies	$ 10,000	
Fixed Assets		
Drycleaning equipment	165,000	
Other Assets		
Franchise fee	40,000	
Leasehold improvements	75,000	
		$290,000
Long-term liabilities		
Bank term loan	$232,000	
Other liabilities		
Shareholders' loans	58,000	
		$290,000

---

mall. "We felt that the concept was logical," Marie commented. "A customer could drop off cleaning, shop for a while, and then pick up the cleaned clothes on the way out." Later in 1982, the Johnstons opened their first store in St John's largest shopping center. The stores were relatively expensive to establish; the initial franchise fee was $40,000 per location, equipment cost approximately $165,000 and leasehold improvements of $75,000 were required. The opening balance sheet of a single location as required by the franchiser is presented in Exhibit 1.

Over the next four years the company prospered. Two years after the first store was opened, a second store was set up at the other large mall in St John's. A third store was started about a year after that, also in St John's. As was typical of many small business operators, the Johnstons' cash was invested in their companies. For that reason, the shareholders' advances consisted of funds borrowed personally and invested in the company, with the interest charges paid through the company account. As a result, the shareholders' advances did not provide a cushion which would assist the company in periods of slow business activity. Instead, the shareholders were dependent on the company to cover these interest charges even in poor periods.

Shortly after the opening of the third store, the company's performance began to deteriorate. Several reasons for this were advanced by Marie Johnston. "First, we can't seem to hire people who care about working any more. Consequently, our turnover is high. just as we get our employees trained to operate the machines, they leave to work at one of our competitors. Also, we have been having trouble with the machines. The manufacturer has no local repair or parts service, so even minor problems can create delays in satisfying customers' orders. We also have more competition. Presently, there are more cleaners in town than ever before. In fact, the operator of the mall where our first and biggest store is located has just allowed one of our competitors, which had a drop-off location there, to install a service somewhat similar to ours. We complained, but there doesn't seem to be much we can do about it."

About a year ago, the Johnstons had been approached by two separate groups who expressed an interest in acquiring one or more of the stores. The first inquiry was from a group of local investors who bought and sold small companies as investments. The second was from an individual who had spent more than 20 years managing a cleaning store for an owner who did not spend much time with the business. This individual had decided to investigate the possibility of acquiring his own store. At the time of the inquiries the Johnstons were not interested in selling, however, Charlie, in particular, was beginning to wonder if this option might still be open. "Interest rates have been falling for some time now. This will help make it easier for prospective buyers to meet their financial commitments. As well, the overall market for drycleaning services is increasing annually through inflation."

Organization

Although Charlie Johnston was listed on the company's records as President, he actually had little contact with it, except to review the monthly sales reports, and to negotiate lines of credit with the company's banker. Marie, as Vice-President, was in charge of the day-to-day operations, assisted by Christina, who worked full time at the stores. The accounting was done by a bookkeeper, Valarie Anthoney, who worked at Charlie's office and maintained accounting records for several of his companies.

One of the Johnstons' areas of concern was the management reporting system. The accounting for the store was done using a hand-written system, consisting of sales, cash receipt, purchase and cheque disbursement journals. Subsidiary ledgers could be prepared for accounts payable and accounts receivable. Valarie described the system as, "a really convenient way to maintain a complete set of records. We only use the Accounts Payable system here because all of our sales are for cash. Mr Johnston sometimes complains that he doesn't get enough information, but I give him a monthly list of Accounts Payable and a Monthly Sales Summary for each store. Apart from that, I really can't provide him with anything else."

Marie Johnston originally saw her role in the organization as being in the policy area. However, this had changed recently "We've had some very difficult decisions to make here in the past two to three years," she said. "Unfortunately, because of the decline in sales, we've had to insist that employees pay for their own uniforms. We've also been unable to adjust wages, except to keep pace with minimum wage movements. We laid off our store managers about a year ago, again for cost-cutting reasons. Since then, Christina and I have spent most of our time going from store to store to ensure things are running smoothly."

The Problem

After the meeting with his accountant, Charlie called a meeting with Marie and Christina and discussed the options available to them. Marie and Christina were positive about the stores and their ability to effect a turnaround. "We are the ones who know the business first hand," said Marie. "I feel that if we spent some money upgrading the stores' appearance, which we have had to allow to deteriorate somewhat, and in overhauling the equipment, we will attract our customers back. We should also increase our advertising." "I'm not so sure," replied Charlie. "We've already invested a substantial amount of our own funds in these stores. Maybe we'd be throwing good money after bad. Besides, our national advertising expenses are already pretty high. I really have no idea whether there is enough business out there for us to be successful. Perhaps I should check to see if the potential buyers from last year are still interested."

The Alternatives

After further discussion, the Johnstons summarized their options as follows:

- invest an additional $40,000 of personal funds in the stores to upgrade the appearance and equipment;
- increase bank borrowing by $40,000 for the same reason;
- sell one or more of the stores;
- close one or more of the stores.

At the Johnston's request, Valarie and Harry prepared a statement of income for each store for the most recent financial year (Exhibit 2). In addition, financial statements for the past three years were collected (Exhibits 3 and 4). Also, Marie prepared what she felt were reasonable operating forecasts to support her contention that an additional investment was justifiable. (Exhibit 5). Charlie was anxious to have the data analysed and looked forward to the report from the Small Business Centre. Exhibit 6 contains target ratios that can be used for analysis.

Exhibit 2
Johnston Processors Limited
Statement of Income
For the Year Ended January 31, 1991

	Store 1	Store 2	Store 3	Total
Sales	$396,405	$296,894	$207,989	$901,288
Cost of Sales				
Inventory, beginning	20,693	14,804	10,315	5,812
Purchases	179,988	128,842	82,449	391,279
	200,681	143,646	92,764	437,091
Inventory, ending	21,704	18,637	10,787	51,128
	178,977	125,009	81,977	385,963
Gross Margin	217,428	171,885	126,012	515,325
Expenses				
Wages and benefits	79,768	59,744	41,854	181,366
Interest charges	14,627	10,945	7,670	33,242
Travel	4,679	3,500	2,454	10,633
Royalties	38,993	29,177	20,451	88,621
Rent	55,316	38,488	26,841	120,645
Advertising	9,295	6,956	4,875	21,126
Amortization	11,500	11,500	11,500	34,500
Depreciation	19,500	19,500	19,500	58,500
Interest-long term	4,136	4,136	4,135	12,407
Other operating cost	20,984	15,701	11,005	47,690
	258,798	199,647	150,285	608,790
Net loss for year	$ 41,370	$ 27,762	$ 24,273	$ 93,405

Exhibit 3
Johnston Processors Limited
Statement of Income and Retained Earnings
For the Years Ended January 31, 1988–1991

	1991	1990	1989	1988
Sales	$901,288	$1,034,713	$1,122,879	$1,027,559
Cost of Sales				
Inventory, beginning	45,812	43,768	39,775	35,678
Purchases	391,279	403,943	441,248	401,144
	437,091	447,711	481,023	436,822
Inventory, ending	51,128	45,812	43,768	39,775
	385,963	401,899	437,255	397,047
Gross Margin	515,325	632,814	685,624	630,512
Expenses				
Wages and benefits	181,366	181,456	218,033	182,223
Interest charges	33,242	24,777	12,448	13,750
Travel	10,633	15,095	20,410	17,601
Royalties	88,621	99,288	106,297	97,483
Rent	120,645	117,624	114,487	95,175
Advertising	21,126	47,586	30,430	38,078
Amortization	34,500	34,500	34,500	34,500
Depreciation	58,500	58,500	58,500	58,500
Interest-long term	12,407	17,369	19,139	5,841
	608,730	650,156	660,768	590,096
Net income (loss) for year	(93,405)	(17,342)	24,865	40,416
Retained earning, start	198,344	215,686	190,830	150,414
Retained earnings, end	$104,939	$ 198,344	$ 215,686	$ 190,830

Exhibit 4
Johnston Processors Limited
Balance Sheet
As of January 31, 1988–1991

	1991	1990	1989	1988
Assets				
Current				
Cash & equivalents	$ 0	$ 7,332	$ 48,318	$ 19,055
Inventories	51,128	45,812	43,768	39,775
	51,128	53,144	92,086	58,830
Fixed, net book value				
Equipment	181,500	231,000	280,500	330,000
Motor vehicles	9,000	18,000	27,000	36,000
	190,500	249,000	307,500	366,000
Other, net book value				
Franchise fees	44,000	56,000	68,000	80,000
Leasehold improvements	82,500	105,000	127,500	150,000
	126,500	161,000	195,500	230,000
Investments	100,000	100,000	75,000	75,000
	$468,128	$563,144	$670,086	$729,830
Liabilities				
Current				
Current portion of debt	$ 69,900	$ 69,600	$ 69,600	$ 69,600
Bank Loans	50,000	–	–	–
Accounts payable	29,989	–	–	–
	149,589	69,600	69,600	69,600
Long-term				
Bank term loans	167,600	237,200	306,800	376,400
Shareholders' loans	45,000	57,000	77,000	92,000
	212,600	294,200	383,800	468,400
Shareholders' Equity				
Share capital	1,000	1,000	1,000	1,000
Retained earnings	104,939	198,344	215,686	190,830
	105,939	199,344	216,686	191,830
	$468,128	$563,144	$670,086	$729,830

Exhibit 5
Johnston Processors Limited
Forecast Income Statements
For the Years Ended January 31, 1992 and 1993

	1992	1993
Sales	$982,200	$1,064,860
Cost of Sales	376,476	408,160
Gross Margin	605,724	656,700
Expenses		
Wages and benefits	155,720	168,810
Interest Charges	14,600	14,600
Royalties	78,576	85,188
Rent	120,646	120,645
Advertising	34,400	37,300
Amortization	23,471	23,471
Depreciation	68,930	68,930
Interest-long term	16,400	14,400
Other operating costs	41,700	47,700
Repairs and maintenance	40,000	5,000
	600,442	586,044
Net Income	$ 5,282	$ 70,656

Exhibit 6
One Hour Drycleaning Limited
Selected Target Ratios

Current ratio	2:1
Quick ratio	1:1
Inventory Turnover	15
Debt ratio	75%
Return on assets	5%
Return on shareholders' equity	20%
Times interest earned	6
profit Gross percentage	65%

Week #8 / Lab #7

Lab #7 — Catch-up & Midterm Review

In preparation for this week's lab:

- Complete the CVP Problems

This lab will also be a chance for you to catch-up on any lab materials that you are behind on and prepare for the midterm. Come to the lab prepared with any questions you have on the midterm exam.

Problems — C-V-P

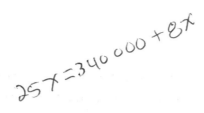

1. The productive capacity of the plant of the Wick's Corporation is 100,000 units, at which level of operations its variable expenses amount to $800,000. When the plant is completely idle, fixed expenses amount to $200,000. If the plant produced anything at all, its fixed expenses are $340,000.

   (a) Determine the company's Breakeven point, assuming a selling price per unit of $25.00.

   (b) Using only the data available, at what level of operations would it be more economical to close the factory than to operate? In other words, at what level will operating losses approximate the losses if the factory is completely closed down?

2. A firm produces a product that sells for $4.00 per unit. The variable cost associated with this product is $2.50 per unit regardless of the quantity produced, and the total fixed cost is $225,000.

   (a) How many units must be sold to breakeven? $4x = 2.5x + 22500$

   (b) What profit will result if sales are increased by 10,000 units?

   (c) Suppose it is possible to sell 170,000 units; costs shown above do not change; what unit prices must be charged to B.E.? $170000x = 2.5x + 22500$

3. The Charta Company has just been formed. The owners have a patented process that will make them the sole distributors of Product Y. Their first year, the capacity of their plant will be 9,000 units, and this is the amount they feel they will be able to sell. Their costs are: Direct Labour = $1.50 per unit; Raw materials = $.50 per unit; Other variable costs = $1.00 per unit; Fixed costs = $24,000

   (a) If the company wishes to make a profit of $30,000 the first year, what should their selling price be? What is the contribution margin?

   (b) At the end of the first year, they wish to increase their volume. An increase of $10,000 in annual fixed costs will increase their capacity to 50,000 units. They now want a profit of $76,000 and to achieve this end they also invest $50,000 in advertising. No other costs change. Under these new conditions, how many units will they have to sell to realize this profit, if their new selling price will be $7 per unit?

4. The Dore Foods Company is planning to manufacture doughnuts for its chain of coffee shops throughout the city. Two alternatives have been proposed for the production of the doughnuts — use of a semi-automatic machine, or a fully automatic machine.

   The shops now purchase their doughnuts from an outside supplier at a cost of $.05 per doughnut.

	Semi-automatic	Automatic
Annual fixed cost	$3,000	$5,000
Variable cost per doughnut	$.02	$.015

254

The president has asked for the following information:

(a) For each machine the minimum annual number of doughnuts that must be sold in order to have the total annual costs equal to outside purchase costs.·

(b) The most profitable alternative for 300,000 doughnuts annually.

(c) The most profitable alternative for 600,000 doughnuts annually.

(d) The volume level that would produce the same net income regardless of the type of machine owned.

5. Peak Performance Inc. currently sells 150 packages of training materials at a price of $750. Its variable cost is $500 per unit. Fixed costs to run the business are $25,000 per year.

(a) You are the marketing manager for Peak Performance. You are considering increasing the price to $800/unit and increasing advertising by $3,000. If this would result in sales decreasing by only 10%, would you do it?

(b) If in a slump you were only selling 80 units, would you consider taking an order for 30 units that would increase variable costs to $600/unit for this order?

(c) Would you buy a piece of machinery that would increase fixed costs by $15,000 if it would decrease variable costs to $350/unit due to lower labour requirements?

(d) Assuming you bought the machinery, would you consider dropping the price to $725, due to the cost savings on the new machinery, if it would increase sales by 10%?

6. You are the marketing manager for Sportlink Products. Your product development team has come up with an idea for a new product and together with the production department they have projected the costs to be as follows:

sales commissions VC	$42,000
advertising budget fixed	$90,000
amortization on equipment fixed	$40,000
direct labour fixed VC	$63,000
direct materials VC	$75,000
fixed manufacturing overhead fixed	$80,000

(a) You project sales next year of $600,000. How many units will you have to sell at a price of $50 to break even?

(b) If your research indicates the market to be approximately 25,000 units with 5 major competitors, what do you suggest the company do, and why?

7. You currently sell 200 units of a product at a price of $700. The variable cost to produce the product is $300. Fixed costs total $30,000. You are considering dropping the price of your product to $650, as much of your competition has done. You assume that by dropping your price and increasing your advertising budget by $9,000 you should be able to increase you market by 25%. What should you do, and why?

$$50x = 0.3x + 810000$$

Week #9 / Lab #8

Class — Operations & Sustainability

The following reading is included in this week's section of the Lab Manual as it is required for class this week:

- "The Business Case for Sustainability" by Strandberg Consulting

Lab #8 — Negotiations

To prepare for this lab, and your final topic to be covered in class later on, read:

- "Focus on 'Why' Rather Than 'What' for Successful Negotiations" by David Wachtel
- "Improving Your Negotiating Skills: Tips learned in the Trenches" by David Wachtel

No further preparation is necessary. You will be participating in a negotiation simulation/role play. Have fun... and learn something!

The Business Case for Sustainability

Strandberg Consulting

> *The following is an "evergreen" document which Strandberg Consulting continues to update to reflect the most recent benefits and statistics which demonstrate the business case for sustainability.*

Introduction to Sustainability

Although many different terms are used, such as Corporate Social Responsibility, Corporate Responsibility, Responsible Entrepreneurship, and Corporate Citizenship, CSR or corporate sustainability essentially refers to the balanced integration of social and environmental considerations in business strategy and operations. It is about maintaining economic success and achieving commercial advantage by building reputation and gaining the trust of people that work with or live around the company. In other words, it means satisfying customers' demands, whilst also managing the expectations of other people, such as employees, suppliers and the surrounding community.

Sustainability on the Rise

According to the Conference Board of Canada, sustainability is the business issue of the 21st Century. Leading corporations, not only in Canada, but also around the world, are embracing this concept and its link to economic success and competitive advantage:

- According to a 2005 KPMG survey, 68% of Fortune 250 companies now publicly report on their social and environmental initiatives as well as their financial performance

- According to McKinsey and Company, more than 90% of chief executives are doing more now than they did five years ago to incorporate environmental, social, and governance issues into their companies' strategies and operations (McKinsey and Co. 2007)

- According to PricewaterhouseCoopers' 6th annual Global CEO Survey (2003):
  - 79% of CEOs agreed that sustainability is vital to the profitability of any company, an increase from 69% the year before
  - 71% of CEOs said they would sacrifice short-term profitability in exchange for long-term shareholder value when implementing a sustainability program

Global drivers of sustainability include:
- o Legislation e.g. on pollution and environmental issues
- o Investors with the spread of CSR performance indices
- o Other stakeholders particularly NGOs
- o Commercial issues of compliance and risk management
- o The need to develop competitive advantage and brand reputation

Sustainability: A Smart Business Decision

Sustainability can bring direct benefits to a business and secure its long-term competitiveness.

Increasingly, customers want a reliable supplier with a good reputation for quality products and services. Suppliers want to sell to a customer that will return for repeat purchases and will make payments in a timely manner. The company's community wants to be confident that the business operates in a socially and environmentally responsible way. And lastly, the company's employees want to work for a company of which they are proud, and that they know values their contribution. To remain competitive, companies need to be able to adapt to these new demands from the market and the society in which they operate.

Initially viewed as a series of costs, the business case for sustainability is becoming increasingly apparent. By embracing the long-term strategic and competitive advantages of sustainability, businesses of all sizes find that they can have a significant impact, and at the same time meet — and exceed — their business objectives.

- An 11-year study of corporations by Harvard University, which emphasized stakeholder management, found socially responsible and sustainable corporations had sales growth 4 times and employment growth 8 times that of "shareholder first" companies (KPMG, The Business Case for Sustainability 2001).

- Over a 5-year period Dow Jones Groups Sustainability Index (DJGSI) performed an average of 36.1% better than did the traditional Dow Jones Group Index (World Economic Forum, 2005). "The DJSI 2008 report, affirmed a "positive strategically significant correlation between corporate sustainability and financial performance", citing that a number of its indexes have outperformed their comparative benchmarks in relation to total returns since the launch of the respective indices. The report found that sustainability strategies had a significant impact on the cost of external financing, return on invested capital, sales growth, and the fade-rate of a firm's competitive advantage." (As reported in BITC: The Value of Corporate Governance, October 2008, p. 4)

- A report by investment bank Goldman Sachs found that companies that are considered leaders in environmental, social and governance (ESG) policies also lead the pack in stock performance — by an average of 25% (Goldman Sachs, 2007).

- Innovest Strategic Value Advisors conducted a study in March 2008 and found that their Global 100 (which represents 100 leaders from the MSCI World Index that demonstrate exceptional capacity to address their sector-specific environmental, social and governance risks and opportunities) outperformed the MSCI World Index by 7.2% (annualized). It also outperformed the Dow Jones Industrial Average by 7.5% and the Dow Jones Global Titans by 8.8%. (Corporate Knights Vol. 72, p. 9).

- An A.T. Kearny analysis revealed that during the current economic slowdown, companies that show a "true" commitment to sustainability appear to outperform their industry peers in the financial markets. In 16 of 18 industries examined, companies recognized as sustainability-focused outperformed their industry peers over both a three- and six-month period, and were well protected from value erosion. Stock prices of 99 companies identified as sustainable outperformed industry averages by 15% for the six months from May to November 2008. (Sustainability companies are defined by inclusion in either the Dow Jones Sustainability Index or the Goldman Sachs SUSTAIN focus list.) This performance differential translates to an average $650 million in market capitalization per company. (2009 AT Kearney Inc. "Green" Winners).

- According to Doug Miller, chair of GlobeScan Inc., "our latest research shows that customers are not acting like they did in other economic downturns. Rather than softening their activism, consumers are more demanding than ever that companies maximize their societal and ecological contribution. It seems clear that only the best corporate citizens will thrive in tomorrow's marketplace". (Quoted in HP Global Citizenship Report 2008).

- According to Paul Herman in Sustainable Industries Sept. 2009 issue, "companies with strong management practices in sustainability, and who embed them deeply, tend to drive more quantifiable impact and results, according to HIP's research of the S&P 500", p. 51 Sept. 2009 issue.

- Business in the Community (BITC) in the UK contracted MORI to conduct statistical analysis using the financial data for a group of 33 companies who have participated in the BITC CR Index each year 2002–2007 and are listed on the London Stock Exchange. The objective of the analysis was to look for a correlation between the extent to which these companies' corporate responsibility performance (as measured by their Corporate Responsibility Index scores) and their financial performance may be linked. The performance of this group of 33 companies was compared to the FTSE All-Share and FTSE 350 groups. They found that companies consistently participating in the CR Index outperform the FTSE 350 on total shareholder return 2002–2007 by between 3.3% and 7.7% per year. They also found that higher levels of performance in the management and integration of environmental and social issues and associated governance factors, as measured in the CR Index, are associated with lower levels of stock price returns volatility. The research demonstrated the higher the company scored on the CR Index, and therefore the better the company manages its environmental and social impacts, the less volatile the stock price returns. ("The Value of Corporate Governance: The Positive Return of Responsible Business", BITC, October 2008.)

The Business Case Specifics

According to the World Business Council on Sustainable Development, business can benefit from pursuing sustainable development in two basic ways — by driving cost efficiencies and by generating top-line growth. The balance of this report is divided along these lines.

A. Driving Down Costs (i.e. return on capital including operational efficiency, workforce efficiency)

1. Cost Savings from Improved Operational Performance and Efficiencies
    - Process optimization — reduced material inputs, energy efficiency, and waste minimization
        o Sustainability Performance Ratios — potential savings equivalent to 1–3% on revenue from reduced utility, materials and waste costs (Willard)
    - Improved product quality and reduced error rates
    - Expedited permitting and improved relations with regulators:
        o Companies that satisfy and exceed regulatory compliance can develop better relations with regulatory agencies leading to less red tape and scrutiny
    - Enable bottom line costs savings through environmental operations and practices (e.g. water and energy efficiency, less raw materials needed)

2. Costs Avoided by Minimizing Business Risks and Improving Safety (i.e. risk management, including regulatory risk, license to operate, supply chain/security of supply and reputational risk)
    - Corporate responsibility provides a means by which companies can better understand and manage risk
        o Establishing a comprehensive CR policy and strategy can offset these risks, spanning legal, financial, environmental and societal risks
    - Avoids litigation, legal claims, and accident expenses
    - Mitigate risks by complying with regulatory requirements, industry standards and NGO demands
    - Social license to operate: facilitate uninterrupted operations and entry in new markets using local sustainability efforts and community dialogue to engage citizens and reduce local resistance
    - Supply chain security: secure consistent, long-term and sustainable access to safe, high quality raw materials and products by engaging in community welfare and development
    - Reputational risk: avoid negative publicity and boycotts by addressing sustainability issues

3. Cost Savings from Improved Recruitment and Retention of Talented Employees
    - Reduced recruitment and training costs
        o A survey conducted for the Conference Board of Canada (2000) found that 71% of employees want to work for companies that commit to social and community concerns
        o 70% of employed Canadians would consider changing jobs if their employers did not operate in a socially responsible manner (Scotiabank 2007)
        o 83% of employees in G7 countries say company's positive CSR reputation increases their loyalty (GlobeScan 2006)
        o Better able to attract the best and the brightest, especially amongst graduates

o Study by The Aspen Institute entitled *Where Will They Lead?* (2007), found that:

- MBA students are expressing more interest in finding work that offers the potential of making a contribution to society (26% of respondents in 2007 say this is an important factor in their job selection compared with 15% in 2002)

o Stanford University study *Corporate Social Responsibility Reputation Effects on MBA Job Choice* (2003) found that:

- MBA graduates would sacrifice an average of $13,700 in salary to work for a socially responsible company

o 40% of MBA grads rated CSR as an "extremely" or "very" important company reputation measure when job hunting (Hill & Knowlton Jan 2008)

o Recent research suggests that three-fourths of workforce entrants in the US regard social responsibility and environmental commitment as important criteria in selecting employers (p. 10 "Why Sustainability is Now the Key Driver in Innovation", Harvard Business Review, September 2009.)

- A survey by McKinsey, a global management consulting firm, shows high performers generate up to 67% more in revenues than average performers

- The career website Monster.com asked college students what they looked for in a prospective employer: a full 92 % wanted to work for a green company (p. 11 The Sustainable Enterprise Report Turning Awareness into Action). "In multiple surveys, up to two-thirds of MBAs are looking for employers who share their values." (p. 12)

4. Cost Savings and Income Produced through Improved Employee Morale and Productivity
   - Higher long-term productivity levels from:

   o More motivated, engaged and inspired workforce

   o Better trained staff from the application of higher workplace and labor standards

   o 83% of employees in G7 countries say company's positive CSR reputation increases their motivation (GLOBEScan 2006)

   o Sustainability Performance Ratio found:

   - 2% increase in employee productivity from improved company-wide teaming around common sustainability issues that transcend departmental boundaries

   - 2% increase in employee productivity from improved work environment (Willard)

   - Decreased employee turnover (Staff retention issues can cause increased workload for remaining staff, increased operating costs, loss of business to competitors, fall in customer service standards, delays developing new products and services and difficulties introducing new working practices, according to Grant Thornton IBR 2008 as cited in "Recruitment and Retention: The Quest for the Right Talent")

   - Boosted employee satisfaction and performance leads to increased customer satisfaction

   - A paper by Alex Admans of the Wharton School entitled "Does the Stock Market Fully Value Intangibles?" found a positive relationship between employee satisfaction and equity prices.
   (http://www.mercer.com/referencecontent.htm?idContent=1351955)

- Fortune magazine "Best Places to Work For" companies compiled by the Great Places to Work Institute have been studied by Wharton professor Alex Edmans who examined the shareholder value performance of these employee-friendly firms, adjusting for annual changes. He found that firms with higher employee satisfaction outperformed the benchmark — because they were under-valued by traditional profit-only investors. Mutual fund Parnassus has a Workplace Fund which draws on this approach, and has tended to outperform its benchmark significantly (Paul Herman in Sustainable Industries, September, 2009, p. 51).

B. Generating Growth (including new markets, new products, new customers/ market share, innovation, reputation/differentiation, reputation/price premium)

---

1. Increased Revenue Through Learning and Innovation

- Sustainability helps to identify new markets and price premium opportunities — enhances ability to gain access to new markets and market share through exposure from sustainability approach

- Globescan's 2003 CSR Monitor found:

  o 8 in 10 Canadians agree they would be willing to pay more for a product if produced in a socially and environmentally responsible manner

- New products through the application of new technologies and improved understanding of consumer needs — e.g. Interface; create products to meet unmet social needs and increase differentiation

- Stakeholder engagement is a catalyst for corporate innovation

- Opportunity to develop cutting edge technology and innovative products and services for unmet social or environmental needs that could translate to business uses, patents, proprietary knowledge, etc.

- Nutritionists at global beverage and food company PepsiCo cla 30% of its $43 B annual revenue comes from the sale of healthy products that are "good" for customer's health and nutrition. GE claims 80 if its "ecomagination" products generate $17 billion in revenue, or almost 10 percent of the firm's top-line. Tellab's eco-efficient equipment, which consumers 80 percent less energy for telecom customers such as Verizon, totals at least a third of its $2 billion in sales (Paul Herman, Sustainable Industries, September 2009, p. 51).

2. Enhanced Recognition and Reputation

- Sustainability is an intangible asset that has the potential to enhance corporate reputation and differentiate a brand

  o Reputation, or brand equity, is founded on values such as trust, credibility, reliability, quality and consistency

  o Reputation for integrity and respect can build customer loyalty based on distinct values differentiating the brand from the competition

  o The 2002 CSR Monitor by Globescan found 89% of Canadians have more respect for a company when the CEO speaks in favor of CSR

- o A survey by Environics International found 60% of respondents identified factors related to corporate responsibility, such as labor practices, business ethics, and environmental responsibility as helping shape their view of particular companies.

- o More than two-thirds (68%) of Canadians take a company's CSR performance into consideration when they make everyday purchases (Scotiabank 2007)

- Edelman 2007 Trust Barometer of 3,100 global respondents reveals the following: when you think of the major global companies that you trust, which are the most important activities for a socially responsible company to engage in?: 58% fair treatment of employees; 54% ensuring that products meet accepted social/environmental standards; 45% communication of both positive and negative performance; 23% CEO commitment to responsible business practices; 41% social or environmental reporting; 21% philanthropic donations or activities; 19% partnerships with NGOs or nonprofits; 15% media coverage of responsible business practices.

  - o 70–80 % of public companies' valuation in American and Western stock markets depends on expectations of the company's cash flow beyond the next three years. Companies' reputations strongly shape those expectations and corporate citizenship is the top driver of reputation, according to the Reputations Institute's 2007 global survey (p. 61 "Cultivating the Green Consumer", Stanford Social Innovation Review, Fall 2008)

3. Improved Customer Loyalty

   - Sustainability provides an opportunity to develop customers' willingness to pay increase or premium

   - Deeper understanding of customer expectations leads to more closely targeted solutions, products, and services

   - Body Shop survey conducted in 2008 finds that in Canada 77% of consumers are making more purchasing choices based on the corporate behaviour and ethics of a company than they were five years ago and 40% of those polled say that they make those decisions on a weekly basis. This, in spite of a tough economic climate.

   - Globescan's 2003 CSR Monitor survey results:

     - o Within a global context, Canada is the third most demanding market after Australia and Great Britain for corporate values to extend beyond financial gain and are the most likely to punish those companies they consider to be socially irresponsible

     - o 83% of Canadian respondents believed that the role of large companies in society should go beyond the traditional economic function

   - 67% of Canadians say would switch to "green" companies (Environics, Feb 2007)

   - 70–80% of consumers say they are switching to "green" companies; 20% actually did in 2006 (Sustainable brand study by egg, March 2007)

   - Consumerology Report, July 2008, by Bensimon Byrne, revealed:

     - o three quarters of Canadians say they consider the environmental impact when they make a purchase decision — only 20% of Canadians say they rarely or never do

     - o 40% of Canadians are very likely to make purchasing decisions to aid the environment even if it costs more

- In Canada, 34% of respondent agree to the statement "I would be more likely to purchase products or services from a company with a good reputation for environmental responsibility"; 42% in US. (Tandberg, Global retail consumers segmented by willingness to pay for products with environmental and social benefits, 2007).

- Cone Communications' 2007 Cause Evolution Survey found:

  o 79% of Americans take corporate citizenship into account when deciding whether to buy a particular company's product

  o 91% of U.S. consumers who learn about a firm's negative corporate citizenship practices would consider switching to another company, 85% would pass the information to family and friends, 83% would refuse to invest in that company, 80% would refuse to work at that company and 76% would boycott that company's products

- Cone Communications' 2009 Consumer Environmental Survey found:

  o Despite the dire state of the economy, 34% of American consumers indicate they are *more likely* to buy environmentally responsible products today, and another 44% indicate their environmental shopping habits *have not changed* as a result of the economy. Fewer than one-in-10 (8%) say they are *less likely* to buy.

  o 35% of Americans have higher expectations for companies to make and sell environmentally responsible products and services during the economic downturn and 70% of Americans indicate that they are paying attention to what companies are doing with regard to the environment today, even if they cannot buy until the future.

- Four out of five people say they are still buying green products and services today — which sometimes cost more — even in the midst of a US recession. Source: Reuters as cited in Eco-Bounty: from Eco-frugal to eco-metering, future profits will be green. www.trendwatching.com

- According to a 2008 Gallup environmental poll, 83% of respondents said they had changed their shopping and living habits over the last five years to help protect the environment (Eileen P. Gunn, "Is your Company Really Eco-Conscious?", US News and World Report, Oct. 9, 2008).

- McKinsey & Company global survey of 7,751 consumers in 8 major economies showed that 87% are concerned about the environmental and social impacts of the products they buy (p. 56 "Cultivating the Green Consumer", Stanford Social Innovation Review, Fall, 2008)

- 33% of consumers say they are willing to pay a premium for green products and another 54% care about the environment and want to help tackle climate change. (p. 61 "Cultivating the Green Consumer", Stanford Social Innovation Review, Fall, 2008)

- Edelman Trust Barometer 2007, 3100 Global Respondents: have you ever done this in relation to a company you do not trust:

  o 81% refused to buy their products or use their services

  o 74% criticized them to people you know

  o 70% refused to invest in them

- o 50% investigated more about their activities
- o 50% refused to work for them
- o 47% supported legislation controlling or limiting their activities
- o 45% ignored their attempts to communicate with you
- o 40% shared your opinion and experiences on the web
- o 36% written a letter or email complaining to the media, a politician or an official third party
- o 23% actively demonstrated or protested against them (p. 3 "Who's Listening? Who's Leading? What Matters Most?, Edelman et al)
- According to a Cone and AMP Insight Study in USA Today, the younger generation consists of the most socially conscious consumers[1]:
  - o 69% of 13–25 year olds consider a company's social and environmental commitment when deciding where to shop
  - o 83% will trust a company more if it is socially and environmentally responsible

4. Improved Access to Capital
- Improved reputation with investors, bond agencies and banks
- Enhanced credit worthiness, lower cost of capital due to greater investor confidence in company's ability to manage change
- Small but growing trend in the investment community to use environmental and social performance factors to determine risks and liabilities, and evaluate a company's suitability for investment:
  - o According to the Social Investment Organization, $609 billion of Canadian financial assets (20% of all assets under management in Canada) were invested in socially responsible investing as of 2008, up from $503 billion in 2006, a 20% increase in 2 years.
  - o According to Innovest Strategic Advisors, a company's environmental and social performance is an increasingly potent proxy and leading indicator for three drivers critical to future profitability potential: corporate agility or adaptability; durability of a firm's competitive advantage; and the quality of its strategic management.
  - o A 2003 Environics poll conducted for Environment Canada found 9 out of 10 Canadian shareholders wanted fund managers to take environmental and social performance into account when valuing companies.
  - o Socially responsible investment funds now attract about one dollar out of every nine invested, according to Infinity Wealth Management (Jerry R. Citarella, "Socially Responsible Investing", The Magazine of Santa Clarita.)

5. Improved Supply Chain Management
- Improved ability to attract and build effective and efficient supply chain relationships. A firm is vulnerable to the weakest link in its supply chain

---

[1] Cone and AMP Insight Study, *USA Today* article, 10/24/06

- Like-minded companies can form profitable long-term business relationships by improving standards, and thereby reducing risks
- See "A Guide to the Business Case and Benefits of Sustainable Purchasing" at www.corostrandberg.com for a full analysis of the benefits.

6. Enhanced ability to strategically plan for the longer term
   - Better anticipate and understand trends in society to proactively plan for the longer term as a result of new regulations, heightened societal expectations and improved scientific knowledge
   - First mover advantage by anticipating the impacts of social pressures
   - Enhanced ability to meet changing, broadening stakeholder expectations

Focus on "Why" Rather Than "What" for Successful Negotiations

David Wachtel

These two sisters focused on the "what" and compromised without asking the most important question in negotiating: "Why do you want that?" The result is that each sister only got half as much as they might, had they stopped to ask that question.

Look at it another way: The "What" is the price, contact, job, etc. upon which you have decided. The "Why" is the motivation which caused you to make that decision. Many negotiators make the mistake of thinking what they want is logical and obvious and important to everyone. A request from the other party for anything else causes the negotiation to deteriorate from solving a problem to arguing about positions.

An illustration how this works

A sales representative for a manufacturing company is calling on a customer. The customer uses a part from the manufacturer to produce their finished product. The sales representative has been charged with renewing the contract and getting an 8% price increase.

The sales representative discusses the situation with the manufacturer. The manufacturing executive tells the sales representative. "This is an item with a small profit margin, and you are one of three companies that make this product for us, nationally. If you are going to raise your prices, you are out and we are going to give your business to one or both of the other two companies. They have already indicated that they will not be increasing pricing, this year." This is "What". *Price appears to be the main issue.*

The sales representative asked the executive, "I am charged with getting the increase. What would you do if you were in my shoes?" This is "Why". *He asked the question to learn more about what is really driving the price/what issue.*

The executive answered, "This was a product where we used to have good market share and exclusivity. Other companies have begun to produce this, and are doing so at prices equal to and a bit lower than ours. Some of these products are actually better. We are losing our market share. As a result, in order to compete, we have to hold our prices flat this year. So, you can see that a price increase is not allowable if you want to still have our business."

Suddenly, it is not price, but market share and survival that are the issues. The "why" opens up a whole new arena to help negotiations.

The sales representative went back to his office and met with the engineers, sharing with them what he had been told. The customer is losing market share, other people are making a better product and their competitors are agreeing to no increase in the next year. They went to work on the "why".

The engineers were able to redesign their piece of the product, saving 15% off the cost of manufacturing. The result was they were able to come back and offer a new improved product at less cost. This enabled the sales representative to not only retain his business, but he was able to obtain an exclusive contract, eliminating his competition.

The sales representative had two choices in the conversation with the manufacturer. One was to begin to bid, defend, fight, convince, force the issue, or walk over pricing. *The second was to ask questions to learn more about the interests behind the price position.* What was learned was that it was market share, competition, and possibly design and technology, more than simply "everyone else agreed to no price increases, so if you don't, you are out." This totally changed the approach to successfully negotiating an agreement. It is important to note that there were several "whys" behind the "what" of price.

Asking for more information also requires good questioning and listening skills:

Questioning skills require three techniques

- Before you begin to ask questions, know where you are going. Randomly fired questions, without logic, makes the other party feel as if they are being interrogated and it raises tension.
- Ask for permission to ask questions.
- State why you want to ask questions.

This maintains safety and keeps tension low for the other party. They want to help you.

Other ways to find out the "why":

"**Why** are you concerned about losing market share? Is it due to simply price, or are there other reasons?"

"The product you make is very good. Costs are going up all over. **Why not** ask for a small price increase?"

Both of these techniques are valuable in helping a negotiator better understand why the other party wants something.

Listening Skills

When we are speaking with someone, we receive communication from three basic sources. These are words, voice tone, and body language.

The best negotiators are not necessarily the best speakers. They are the best listeners. They are listening for the reasons why the other party is asking for, needs, wants, or demands something. And they are listening for all the "whys", not just one. Because they are looking for the common ground from which a successful negotiation can be built. They are also looking for interests the other party may have that are not being met, that may get in the way of successfully solving the problem.

There are three listening skills:

• Selective listening: listen to everything, then select out the important information.

• Responsive: eye contact with the speaker two thirds of the time, taking notes, "I see", "Tell me more about that".

• Paraphrasing: Replay back what you think you heard and ask for confirmation and clarification. "Did I understand what you said?" As writer Stephen Covey said in his book *The 7 Habits of Highly Effective People*, "Seek first to understand, then to be understood." The other party will listen to you and work with you if they feel you understand their needs.

Why is this so important?

Typically, when two parties meet, there is an underlying desire to reach an agreement. Also, many times the "what's" are diametrically opposed. For example, in a labor negotiation the union wants to get the best deal for the members. Management wants to protect the company. However, each needs the other (no company no jobs, no employees no company), so the effort to uncover the common "whys" will show that, in reality, they both want the same thing. Simply put, employees being paid fairly working in a healthy company.

When the "whys" are examined, generally common ground is found. These also can be significant in helping creatively solve the problem. Why they other party wants something may never have occurred to the other side. In fact, it may make them appear, to the other party, as being difficult, if not irrational. *Many times, not only does this get them both working on the problem rather than each other, but it can be the solution. It uncovers the unsaid things that prevent successfully negotiated deals.*

Getting the "whys" handled for both parties is the reason we negotiate.

Improving Your Negotiating Skills: Tips learned in the Trenches

David A. Wachtel

At the beginning of training sessions, I ask students what makes them uncomfortable about negotiating. The answers generally are:

"I am afraid I will not get the best deal."

"I do not enjoy working with certain types of people."

"I am not always clear on what needs to be accomplished in a particular negotiation and how to get there."

"I can get lost in the process. While getting bogged down in details, I lose track of what I really want to accomplish."

Here are some tips to help with your negotiating efforts:

Tip #1: Negotiating is not merely a series of compromises

Most people negotiate using a zero sum process. They look at what they want, raise that 10 or 15 percent, and then engage is a series of compromises to get to a result. The effort is on the position they take, and getting as much of that position for themselves as possible. Their mission is not to get a satisfactory deal for both parties. It is to win. Many call that, "being a tough negotiator." It is extremely stressful.

The tendency is to negotiate from the standpoint of positions. Most negotiators never really stop to ask <u>why</u> they want, what they want, or even consider why the other side is negotiating.

Fisher and Ury define negotiating as "Back and forth communication where some *interests* are shared and some are opposed." The purpose of negotiating is seeing if you can get your *interests* met through an agreement. An *interest* is *why* you want something, not *what* you want. When negotiators begin working from the standpoint of interests, they can begin to work with the other party to explore alternative solutions.

What I have found interesting is the number of students who find informing the other side *why* they want something uncomfortable. They compare it to showing their cards. Negotiating does not have to be arguing over who gets the most. At its best, it is two parties working to solve a problem. The problem cannot be solved to everyone's satisfaction unless all parties understand it. <u>Why</u> the parties want something is where the process of problem solving begins.

Knowing a negotiating process is important...but...

Tip #2: It's your people skills that can make the difference

- First, you need to know how your behavior impacts others.

- Next, understand that everyone has their own preferred way of communicating and it may not be your way.

- Effective negotiators are the ones that can alter their communication style to meet the needs of the listener.

At Hautacam Consulting, we utilize Inscape Publishing's DiSC© product. It is designed to describe a person's behavior when their personality interacts with a selected environment, like negotiating on behalf of your company or organization. Using this program, students identify their natural negotiating style and begin to understand how others may view them. You begin to see why you may be more comfortable with one person and less with another. It is easier to talk to people who have similar styles. <u>We focus most of our time learning how to talk to people with less compatible</u> styles.

The first step is to build a level of understanding of the four DiSC© Dimensions of Behavior attributes, and how they interact. They are:

1. **Dominant:** Dominant people are good at making decisions. They want to control their environment, and do so by solving problems and meeting challenges. They are very direct and they are good at telling. They are self-confident but can sometimes be perceived as intimidating and arrogant. Questioning and listening does not come naturally to dominants. They tend to move toward goals without considering multiple solutions or outcomes. For that reason, others often find them impatient and uncaring. They use a bottom line approach. They are good at stating why something will not work. As a result, they may be seen as negative. To dominants, results are much more important than how people feel.

2. **Influence:** Like a person who is Dominant, influencers are good at telling but they use a less direct method. They want to convince and motivate you, rather than forcing you to do something. Rather than being task focused like a Dominant, they are focused on completing the task *with people*. Influencers see the possibilities in a plan or idea, rather than the pitfalls. At their best, they can be viewed as visionaries. The influencer may view the Dominant as "negative" and the Dominant may view the influencer as "unrealistic" or even "political". Both want to make the decision, and are leaders. Influencers like to make favorable impressions and want a relationship. They can appear to be impulsive and disorganized. Attention to detail is not an asset because they prefer to look at the bigger picture. Influencers are social, and usually know a lot of people. They want to get results, but their focus is on motivating people to get the results, together.

3. **Steadiness:** Steadiness people, like influencers when looking at new ideas will see the positive aspects. Unlike the influencer, they do not like change even if it is positive. They perceive themselves as less powerful than their environment and feel that all will be well if everyone will just work harder, together, on the status quo. They are excellent listeners, and consider things before responding. Like the influencer, they are

focused on people. They are extremely dependable, solid team players. High Dominant and influence styles that negotiate with people who are in the Steadiness style have to be careful as they like immediate responses. The Steadiness style likes to think before responding. They are very methodical, and reserved. They are opposites of dominants and influencers.

4. **Conscientious:** Like Steadiness, they are introverted and reserved. But, like the dominant, they are task and control focused. When negotiating, your statements must be factual and have a point. They are perfectionists. Their approach is indirect, reserved, business-like, and diplomatic. Unless you can give them reasons supported by facts, they do not readily accept change. They believe that if people will follow processes and procedures, many problems will be solved and change becomes unnecessary. Facts and processes are most important and people are a secondary consideration. An influencer, negotiating with a person who uses the conscientious style has to have accurate facts and support information. Detail is not a strong suit for influencers. Dominants have to have patience with the conscientious style, as dominants will want to make a decision and get on with it. A limitation of the conscientious style is that in their zeal to get all the facts, they can appear to be indecisive.

Regardless of the intensity of one or two of the attributes that an individual may have, everyone possesses some of all of them. This is identified through the Classic Profile. This profile examines the intensity of each attribute in comparison to the others. The negotiator gets a complete picture on how they tend to behave, and how to effectively communicate with different types of people. The Classic Profile includes an evaluation of how your style tends to behave in consideration of the following:

- Emotions
- Goals
- Judging others
- Influencing others
- Value to an organization
- Tendencies that can be overused
- Behavior under pressure
- Fears
- How to increase effectiveness

You may use one or more attributes less, because they feel uncomfortable. But to be most effective, learning how to use them *when needed* is important.

When people of different styles interact, it can be negative. The influencer, negotiating with a conscientious style makes a comment with a minor statistic about the quality of a product. It is questioned and cannot be supported. The steadiness style negotiating with a person in the dominant category wants to consider answers to questions. While thinking, the dominant person begins to talk again, filling the silence, pushing for an answer or decision. An influencer, negotiating with a dominant will answer questions with a story or anecdote rather than using a shorter direct approach. All of these seemingly small things can become huge in the midst of a negotiation.

To maximize your efforts, not only recognizing the style of others, but fully understanding your own tendencies and being flexible when necessary is important.

Being an effective communicator begins with being an outstanding listener...

Tip #3: The most powerful negotiating skill is listening

You learn the interests of the other party through listening. Some styles are better at this than others, but the fact is that we are typically not good listeners. Most listen to reply, not to understand.

To illustrate this, refer to the study that Dr. Albert Mehrabian, of UCLA, did on the ways we communicate:

- Words: 7%
- Tone of Voice: 38%
- Body Language: 55%

Even good listeners are asking questions and attempting to listen to the words. But words only comprise 7% of how we communicate. Communication is 93% non-verbal. It is no wonder that so much gets lost between the speaker's lips and our ears. Non-verbal communication is also important in determining the speaker's style.

Effective questioning is the first step toward learning the interests of the other party. In order to be effective at asking questions, three things must take place:

1. Know where your questions are going. Most people find randomly asked questions to be unnerving and it makes them distrust you.
2. Ask the other party if it is all right with them if you ask questions.
3. Then tell them what information you are seeking.

Use the three levels of listening to get information:

1. **Selective:** we hear things that we believe are important.
2. **Responsive:** this lets the other party know that you are, indeed, paying attention. It involves verbal and physical feedback, nodding, or asking, "Tell me more about that."
3. **Playback:** restating what you think you heard and asking for confirmation. It is also good to follow up with a confirming question. An example would be, "Have I gotten everything, or might there be something I missed?"

As you work through issues in the negotiation, playback can also be used as a "mini-close" making it more difficult for an issue to resurface later. "I missed that. When we talked earlier, we agreed on this. What did I miss? Do we need to talk about this more so I can better understand its importance to you?"

Effective questioning and listening can provide solutions to the problem. By getting the other party to talk, and listening to their responses, a positive message is sent. This greatly increases trust and keeps tension low. People will do business with you because you are perceived as:

- Trustworthy
- An adequate problem solver
- Adding value to the relationship

Effectively seeking information through questioning and listening will help develop these perceptions.

Tip #4: Develop a plan before beginning to negotiate

When I ask in training sessions, I find that few people do any in-depth planning before negotiating. I am not referring to determining how much will be spent, how long to complete a project, or what their walk-away number might be. I am talking about detailed planning, which involves trying to determine what the other side may want, and why.

Your plan should include the following:

- **Try to determine the negotiating style of the other party (DiSC© style).** This helps you think through how best to communicate and then go through the process of confirming if you were correct. If you do not know the other party at all, you will have to make educated guesses and adjust as you go.

- **What are our/my interests?** This is not what you want, but *why*. Make sure that you examine all of your interests as there may be more than one.

- **What are the interests of the other side?** A major part of the negotiation process is determining the other side's interests. This goes back to Fisher and Ury's definition of negotiations...where some interests are shared and <u>some are opposed</u>. Opposing interests are what you negotiate.

- **What do I have that I can trade that is low value to me and of high value to the other side?** In the give and take phase of the negotiation process, having considered these options ahead of time can make this less stressful. Less effective negotiators will not have considered this, and will want to go through a series of positional compromises.

- **What are three options I can use to move the negotiation from compromising to joint problem solving?** These can all begin with, "What if we tried...?", or "What if we did this...?

- **What is the very least that is acceptable?**
  You must determine:
    1. What do we aspire to?
    2. What will we be content with?
    3. What can we live with?

- **What is my <u>Best Alternative to a Negotiated Agreement</u>? (BATNA)** This is a key concept. You do not want to accept an outcome that is worse that what you may have done otherwise.

Your BATNA is what you can or will do if an agreement cannot be reached.

What you can live with in Step 6 has to be better than your BATNA. Otherwise, why negotiate?

Ask yourself what they other side's BATNA may be. Why are they talking to you? What is preventing them from doing it with someone else, or on their own?

More on planning:

In the fall of 2004, Negotiator Magazine did a reader poll. One of the questions asked had to do with planning and it was reported that as much as 40% of the time spent negotiating is internal. Sometimes, the most difficult part of planning and negotiating can be with your own team.

If thought through in advance, you can compare where you are in the negotiation to your plan. You are also less likely to agree to an unacceptable outcome. If you find yourself getting lost in comparison to your plan, you can caucus, take a time out, and rethink where you are.

Tip #5: The Top 10 Factors for Successful Negotiating

A colleague, Tony Nagle of A.G. Nagle Company, Inc., shared this list with me:

1. **Know what you want:** The clearer you are on your interests and goals, the better your chance of success.

2. **Know the other side:** Learn as much as you can about the people with whom you will be negotiating. Know their negotiating style (DiSC©), their backgrounds, hopes, fears, aspirations, and their interests. Little things do not mean a lot, they can mean everything.

3. **Consider the timing and method of negotiations:** Change the game to win–win problem solving by negotiating from interests, not positions.

4. **Prepare point by point:** Negotiators who prepare outperform those that do not.

5. **Offer benefits for accepting your offer:** You are much more likely to close if you offer the benefit...the "what's in it for them?" test.

6. **Frame your negotiation around one or two key points:** Keep it as simple as possible by framing and reframing to keep things on track and reach agreements more efficiently.

7. **Know your BATNA:** Your personal power comes from the ability to walk away if you are not able to reach an agreement. Effective negotiators not only know when to walk away, but how to walk away leaving the relationship intact.

8. **Prepare options for mutual gain:** Be creative. Find innovative ways for both sides to get their interests met. "What if we tried this?"

9. **Listening is the most powerful negotiation skill:** It will help you learn where your interests are shared with the other side, where they are opposed, and get a satisfactory outcome.

10. **Use the power of the draft:** Always put your agreements in writing.

Changing the way you think about negotiating (joint problem solving versus a series of compromises where one party may win and one may lose) is the first step toward better results. Recognizing the reasons why people act the way they do, and having the ability to communicate to a broad range of behavioral styles gives the negotiator the ability to be reach satisfactory outcomes more consistently. Following a process or strategy is fine, but understanding the styles of the people with whom you are negotiating, and altering your approach to communicate more effectively can be the key to success. Last, developing a plan in advance of the actual negotiation will give the negotiator more confidence, and lead to better and more consistent results.

Week #10 / Lab #9

Class — Human Resources & Emotional Intelligence

Readings on emotional intelligence are included in this week's section of the Lab Manual as they are required for class, and will assist in your EQi reflection that is due at the end of term.

- "The Business Case for Emotional Intelligence" by Cary Cherniss

- "Emotional Intelligence & Return on Investment" by MHS

- "Leadership Skills and Emotional Intelligence" by Ruderman et al.

- "The EQ Factor" by Steven J. Stein

Lab #9 — Effective Group Presentations & Case Practice

In preparation for this lab:

- Review the case analysis materials from Lab #3, and *Speak More Effectively* by Dale Carnegie from Lab #2

- Prepare *Linda's Bed & Breakfast* case, for discussion, using whatever case analysis tools you feel are necessary

The Business Case for Emotional Intelligence

Cary Cherniss, Ph.D.

The following 19 points build a case for how emotional intelligence contributes to the bottom line in any work organization. Based on data from a variety of sources, it can be a valuable tool for HR practitioners and managers who need to make the case in their own organizations. The Consortium also invites submissions of other research for the Business Case. All submissions will be reviewed to determine their suitability. If you have research findings that you think might help build the business case, submit them to Rob Emmerling at Emerling@rci.rutgers.edu.

1. The US Air Force used the EQ-I to select recruiters (the Air Force.'s front-line HR personnel) and found that the most successful recruiters scored significantly higher in the emotional intelligence competencies of Assertiveness, Empathy, Happiness, and Emotional Self Awareness. The Air Force also found that by using emotional intelligence to select recruiters, they increased their ability to predict successful recruiters by nearly three-fold. The immediate gain was a saving of $3 million annually. These gains resulted in the Government Accounting Office submitting a report to Congress, which led to a request that the Secretary of Defense order all branches of the armed forces to adopt this procedure in recruitment and selection. (The GAO report is titled, "Military Recruiting: The Department of Defense Could Improve Its Recruiter Selection and Incentive Systems," and it was submitted to Congress January 30, 1998. Richard Handley and Reuven Bar-On provided this information.)

2. Experienced partners in a multinational consulting firm were assessed on the EI competencies plus three others. Partners who scored above the median on 9 or more of the 20 competencies delivered $1.2 million more profit from their accounts than did other partners — a 139 percent incremental gain (Boyatzis, 1999).

3. An analysis of more than 300 top-level executives from fifteen global companies showed that six emotional competencies distinguished stars from the average: Influence, Team Leadership, Organizational Awareness, self-confidence, Achievement Drive, and Leadership (Spencer, L.M., Jr., 1997).

4. In jobs of medium complexity (sales clerks, mechanics), a top performer is 12 times more productive than those at the bottom and 85 percent more productive than an average performer. In the most complex jobs (insurance salespeople, account managers), a top performer is 127 percent more productive than an average performer (Hunter, Schmidt, & Judiesch, 1990). Competency research in over 200 companies and organizations worldwide suggests that about one-third of this difference is due to technical skill and cognitive ability while two-thirds is due to emotional competence

Paper prepared for the *Consortium for Research on Emotional Intelligence in Organizations* (www. eiconsortium.org). Reproduced with permission of the author and Multi-Health Systems Inc.

(Goleman, 1998). (In top leadership positions, over four-fifths of the difference is due to emotional competence.)

5. At L.'Oreal, sales agents selected on the basis of certain emotional competencies significantly outsold salespeople selected using the company.'s old selection procedure. On an annual basis, salespeople selected on the basis of emotional competence sold $91,370 more than other salespeople did, for a net revenue increase of $2,558,360. Salespeople selected on the basis of emotional competence also had 63% less turnover during the first year than those selected in the typical way (Spencer & Spencer, 1993; Spencer, McClelland, & Kelner, 1997).

6. In a national insurance company, insurance sales agents who were weak in emotional competencies such as self-confidence, initiative, and empathy sold policies with an average premium of $54,000. Those who were very strong in at least 5 of 8 key emotional competencies sold policies worth $114,000 (Hay/McBer Research and Innovation Group, 1997).

7. In a large beverage firm, using standard methods to hire division presidents, 50% left within two years, mostly because of poor performance. When they started selecting based on emotional competencies such as initiative, self-confidence, and leadership, only 6% left in two years. Furthermore, the executives selected based on emotional competence were far more likely to perform in the top third based on salary bonuses for performance of the divisions they led: 87% were in the top third. In addition, division leaders with these competencies outperformed their targets by 15 to 20 percent. Those who lacked them under-performed by almost 20% (McClelland, 1999).

8. Research by the Center for Creative Leadership has found that the primary causes of derailment in executives involve deficits in emotional competence. The three primary ones are difficulty in handling change, not being able to work well in a team, and poor interpersonal relations.

9. After supervisors in a manufacturing plant received training in emotional competencies such as how to listen better and help employees resolve problems on their own, lost-time accidents were reduced by 50 percent, formal grievances were reduced from an average of 15 per year to 3 per year, and the plant exceeded productivity goals by $250,000 (Pesuric & Byham, 1996). In another manufacturing plant where supervisors received similar training, production increased 17 percent. There was no such increase in production for a group of matched supervisors who were not trained (Porras & Anderson, 1981).

10. One of the foundations of emotional competence — accurate self-assessment — was associated with superior performance among several hundred managers from 12 different organizations (Boyatzis, 1982).

11. Another emotional competence, the ability to handle stress, was linked to success as a store manager in a retail chain. The most successful store managers were those best able to handle stress. Success was based on net profits, sales per square foot, sales per employee, and per dollar inventory investment (Lusch & Serpkeuci, 1990).

12. Optimism is another emotional competence that leads to increased productivity. New salesmen at Met Life who scored high on a test of "learned optimism" sold 37 percent more life insurance in their first two years than pessimists (Seligman, 1990).

13. A study of 130 executives found that how well people handled their own emotions determined how much people around them preferred to deal with them (Walter V. Clarke Associates, 1997).

14. For sales reps at a computer company, those hired based on their emotional competence were 90% more likely to finish their training than those hired on other criteria (Hay/McBer Research and Innovation Group, 1997).

15. At a national furniture retailer, sales people hired based on emotional competence had half the dropout rate during their first year (Hay/McBer Research and Innovation Group, 1997).

16. For 515 senior executives analyzed by the search firm Egon Zehnder International, those who were primarily strong in emotional intelligence were more likely to succeed than those who were strongest in either relevant previous experience or IQ. In other words, emotional intelligence was a better predictor of success than either relevant previous experience or high IQ. More specifically, the executive was high in emotional intelligence in 74 percent of the successes and only in 24 percent of the failures. The study included executives in Latin America, Germany, and Japan, and the results were almost identical in all three cultures.

17. The following description of a "star" performer reveals how several emotional competencies (noted in italics) were critical in his success: Michael Iem worked at Tandem Computers. Shortly after joining the company as a junior staff analyst, he became aware of the market trend away from mainframe computers to networks that linked workstations and personal computers (*Service Orientation*). Iem realized that unless Tandem responded to the trend, its products would become obsolete (*Initiative and Innovation*). He had to convince Tandem.'s managers that their old emphasis on mainframes was no longer appropriate (*Influence*) and then develop a system using new technology (*Leadership, Change Catalyst*). He spent four years showing off his new system to customers and company sales personnel before the new network applications were fully accepted (*Self-confidence, Self-Control, Achievement Drive*) (from Richman, L.S., "How to get ahead in America," *Fortune*, May 16, 1994, pp. 46–54).

18. Financial advisors at American Express whose managers completed the Emotional Competence training program were compared to an equal number whose managers had not. During the year following training, the advisors of trained managers grew their businesses by 18.1% compared to 16.2% for those whose managers were untrained.

19. The most successful debt collectors in a large collection agency had an average goal attainment of 163 percent over a three-month period. They were compared with a group of collectors who achieved an average of only 80 percent over the same time period. The most successful collectors scored significantly higher in the emotional intelligence competencies of self-actualization, independence, and optimism. (Self-actualization refers to a well-developed, inner knowledge of one's own goals and a sense of pride in one's work.) (Bachman et al., 2000).

References

Bachman, J., Stein, S., Campbell, K., & Sitarenios, G. (2000). Emotional intelligence in the collection of debt. *International Journal of Selection and Assessment*, 8(3), 176–182.

Boyatzis, R.E. (1999). From a presentation to the Linkage Conference on Emotional Intelligence, Chicago, IL, September 27, 1999.

Boyatzis, R. (1982). *The competent manager: A model for effective performance.* New York: John Wiley and Sons.

Goleman, D. (1998). *Working with emotional intelligence.* New York: Bantam.

Hay/McBer Research and Innovation Group (1997). This research was provided to Daniel Goleman and is reported in his book (Goleman, 1998).

Hunter, J.E., Schmidt, F.L., & Judiesch, M.K. (1990). Individual Differences in Output Variability as a Function of Job Complexity. *Journal of Applied Psychology,* 75, 28–42.

Lusch, R.F., & Serpkeuci, R. (1990). Personal differences, job tension, job outcomes, and store performance: A study of retail managers. *Journal of Marketing.*

McClelland, D.C. (1999). Identifying competencies with behavioral-event interviews. *Psychological Science,* 9(5), 331–339.

Pesuric, A., & Byham, W. (1996, July). The new look in behavior modeling. *Training and Development,* 25–33.

Porras, J.I., & Anderson, B. (1981). Improving managerial effectiveness through modeling-based training. *Organizational Dynamics,* 9, 60–77.

Richman, L.S. (1994, May 16). How to get ahead in America. *Fortune,* 46–54.

Seligman, M.E.P. (1990). *Learned optimism.* New York: Knopf.

Spencer, L.M., Jr. et al. *Competency assessment methods History and state of the art.* Boston: Hay/McBer, 1997

Spencer, L.M.J., McClelland, D.C., & Kelner, S. (1997). *Competency assessment methods: History and state of the art.* Boston: Hay/McBer.

Spencer, L.M., Jr., & Spencer, S. (1993). *Competence at work: Models for superior performance.* New York: John Wiley and Sons.

Walter V. Clarke Associates. (1996). Activity vector analysis: Some applications to the concept of emotional intelligence. Pittsburgh, PA: Walter V. Clarke Associates.

Emotional Intelligence & Return on Investment: Return on your EQ-i® investment

Multi-Health System

> *The EQ-i® is the first scientifically validated emotional intelligence tool in the world. That's impressive, we agree... but your next question is likely, "but does it work?"*

Like most business people, you need to be bottom line focused and show real results in order to get buy-in from your key decision makers and clients.

In other words, you need to prove how the EQ-i will really make a difference in:

- the TRAINING and DEVELOPMENT of your employees,
- the development of your LEADERS, and
- the SELECTION of highly qualified future leaders to your organization

We know what you're up against. It's not enough to say that it will work. You need to bring to the table evidence of a clear return on investment; that is: clear statistics and research that link the EQ-i to:

- Higher sales and profits
- Increased performance
- Improved customer satisfaction
- Decreased attrition rates
- Reduction in training costs

So we want you to hear it right from them and show you their stories of success. "They" are the reputable organizations that have used the EQ-i and gone on to see exceptional performance improvements, and real bottom line results. These success stories go beyond mere testimonials. They give evidence of what you're looking for: **specific**, **measurable**, and **scientifically validated results** that prove the EQ-i will be your most valuable and successful assessment tool for selecting and developing leaders of tomorrow.

THE PROOF IS IN THE RESULTS...
...and we have the results to prove it

American Express (Case 1)

Purpose

To predict key characteristics associated with top performance from which selection criteria can be generated

Results

This case study features information sourced from the 2007 and 2008 International Conference on Emotional Intelligence materials.

Two different metrics were used to determine success in the role of customer focused sales associates: customer satisfaction and sales. As part of a star performer study, MHS created four performance groups: 1) those who scored well on both metrics, 2) those who scored high on customer satisfaction and low in sales, 3) those who scored high on sales and low in customer satisfaction, and 4) those who scored low on both metrics. These representatives also completed the EQ-i assessment. **Those who scored well on both metrics had the highest EQ-i scores (see chart.)**

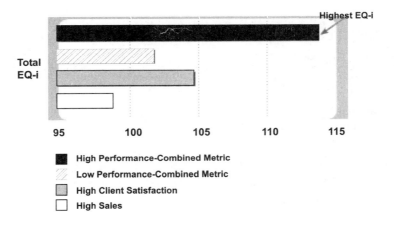

ROI Impact

The EQ-i predictive model accounted for significant differences between high and low performing sales representatives. The EQ-i accounted for:

- **48% of the variance in performance,** or in other words, almost one-half of the skill set required of a successful customer focused sales associate.

Takeaway

Using the EQ-i predictive model for Training and Recruitment leads to:

- Higher sales
- Better performance

American Express (Case 2)

Purpose

To develop a training and development program with a strong scientific basis as well as a measurable implementation and evaluation process

Results

This case study features information sourced from the 2007 and 2008 International Conference on Emotional Intelligence materials.

The EQ-i program was implemented within AMEX's Consumer Card Service Delivery Network which spanned four states and **2000 leaders**. Departmental "teams" from AMEX were assessed as a group on their EI skill sets. Each team worked on key challenge areas as identified through the EQ-i group report. The most interesting outcome from this study was the subsequent evaluation which measured the program impact in the short and long term. Using the Kirkpatrick model of evaluation (based on a 5.0 point scale), the results from the EQ-i based leadership program were outstanding.

> **900 PEOPLE SURVEYED**
>
> **Level 1 (reaction):** averaged 5 out of 5 strongly agreed that EI program was valuable, provided an awareness of EI strengths/opportunities and provided information that could be leveraged to grow and/or improve.
>
> **Level 3 (behaviour):** averaged 4.85 strongly agreed with the statement: "I have become more effective in the EQ-i areas or skills I identified as development over the past 6 months."
>
> **Level 4 (results):** averaged 4.14 out of 5 agreed with the statement: "I have seen an improvement in a business metric due to my work on EQ areas."

ROI Impact

A follow-up survey in 2004 was conducted with 50 AMEX leaders who completed the EI-based high potential program and then were promoted. This survey showed that:

- **100% of respondents** stated that knowing their EI strengths and opportunities helped them in transitioning to a higher level role.

Takeaway

Using the EQ-i for *Leadership Development* generates:

- **Smoother transitions to leadership roles = reduction in training costs**
- Better leadership performance

Fortune 100 Insurance Company

Purpose

To predict key characteristics associated with top performance and develop selection criteria for future agents

Results

First, a subjective rating was used to determine performance levels amongst General Agents (GAs) at the insurance company. Agents completed the EQ-i and were rated by two VPs as high or low performers. The sales teams of the highly rated GAs significantly outperformed the other teams in terms of sales. As you can see from the graph below, the EQ-i can be used to predict characteristics associated with high performance. High performers consistently scored higher in most emotional intelligence characteristics; most notably: assertiveness, self-actualization, empathy, problem solving, and happiness.

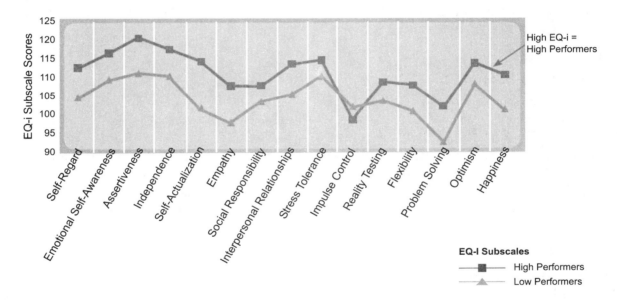

ROI Impact

The company looked at the four-year compound annual growth rate (CAGR) of their General Agent teams.! For these high performer teams,

- **Growth was 15%**, much higher than the -1% achieved by the teams of the low performing GAs.

Takeaway

Using the EQ-i for *Selection* generates:

- **Higher performing employees**
- **Decreased attrition rates**

United States Air Force (Case 1)

Purpose

To determine the differences between successful and unsuccessful United States Air Force recruiters in order to decrease attrition

Results

In 1995, USAF recruiters were suffering from high rates of first-year turnover. In their efforts to increase recruiter retention, the USAF used the EQ-i assessment to study the differences between successful and unsuccessful recruiters. Notable score differences between the two groups were evident in areas such as: assertiveness, self-actualization, stress tolerance, flexibility, problem solving, and happiness.

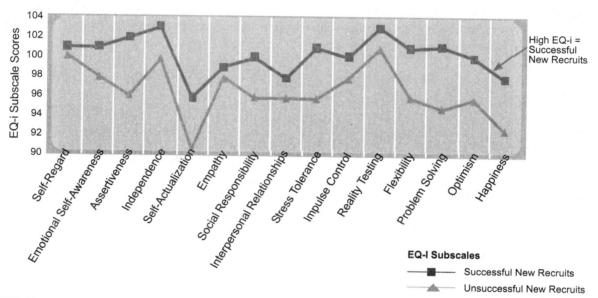

ROI Impact

Using their findings from the EQ-i, the USAF developed a pre-employment screening system. These findings led to the following:

- **92%** increase in retention,

- **$2.7-million** in training cost savings in the first year alone,

- a report to a congressional sub-committee stating that Air Force recruiters are twice as productive as recruiters in other branches of the armed forces. (Gourville, 2000; Handley, 1997).

Takeaway

Using the EQ-i predictive model for *Selection* generates:

- **Large reductions in training costs**

- **Decreased attrition rates**

- **Increased productivity**

United States Air Force (Case 2)

Purpose

To explore the impact of emotional intelligence skills on the success of USAF Pararescue Jumper (PJ) trainees

Results

In 2009, approximately 82% of those who entered the USAF PJ training were not successfully completing the program. As part of the recruiting process, trainees had been asked to demonstrate the required cognitive and physical abilities. The Air Force was further interested in exploring the impact of other factors, namely emotional intelligence skills, on trainee success. Comparing the EQ-i scores of trainees who completed the program versus those who did not, five factors were linked to successful completion of the program: flexibility, optimism, self-regard, happiness, and reality testing. In fact, trainees who scored higher in these areas were two to three times more likely to successfully complete the program.

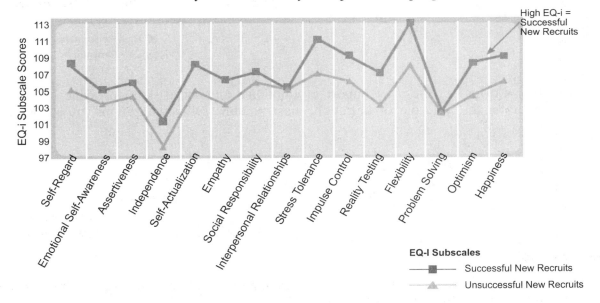

ROI Impact

This powerful information will be used by the Air Force to offer guidance to trainees regarding their potential for success in the program. The Air Force estimates the potential savings/ cost avoidance at:

• **$19 million** per year in training costs.

Takeaway

Using the EQ-i predictive model for *Selection* and *Training* generates:

• **Large reductions in training costs**
• **Reduced attrition rates**

New Zealand Telecom

Purpose

To understand the relationship between EQ-i and leadership competencies to enhance the training and coaching of leaders in their organization

Results

New Zealand Telecom categorized 70 senior leaders into high and low performance groups based on established leadership performance indicators. As shown below, high performers had significantly higher EQ-i scores than the lower performers.

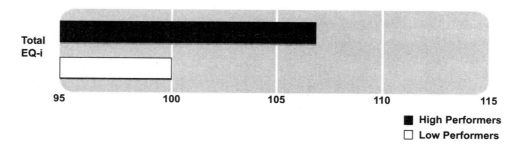

The chart below maps out the most important emotional and social skills for achieving success amongst leaders in the Telecom organization, most notably: self-actualization, stress tolerance, and happiness.

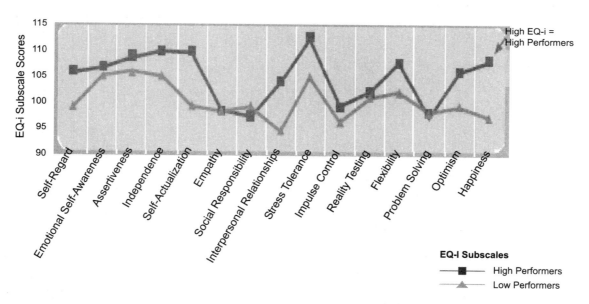

ROI Impact

The EQ-i study resulted in significant bottom line findings that New Zealand Telecom now integrates into their training and coaching initiatives.

- **48%** of what differentiated the high and low performing leaders could be attributed to EI attributes. In other words, almost **one-half** of the skill set required for successful execution of this organization's leadership competencies is comprised of emotional and social skills.

Takeaway

Using the EQ-i predictive model for ***Training and Coaching*** generates:

- **A roadmap for leadership success**
- **Better performing leaders**

Debt Collection Agency

Purpose

To assess the secrets to success in recovering client money

Results

The EQ-i assessment was completed by the company's most and least successful collections agents. The more successful collection agents had significantly elevated scores in areas that you might guess would be important for conducting collections work; areas such as: assertiveness, independence and problem solving. Other important attributes that perhaps are less obvious include: self-actualization, happiness, and the "right" mix of empathy and impulse control. We say the right "mix", because having "more" empathy or impulse control is not always the best thing.! In the case of debt collectors, the higher performers scored significantly lower than their low performing co-workers on empathy and impulse control. EQ-i analysts must look at the right mix that works for high performers from specific companies and industries.

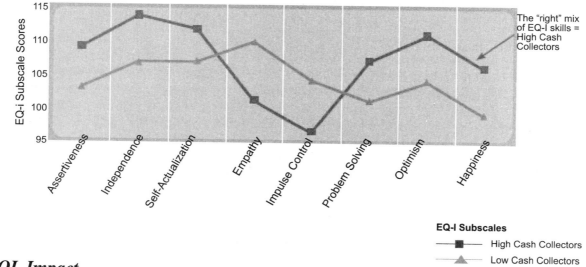

ROI Impact

The results for this study were obtained over a six-month period, with significant findings:

* Superior collectors brought in **100%** of their quotas, compared with their less successful peers, who languished at 47 percent.

* Collectors who were hired according to the new EQ-i model and were also trained against the new criteria, achieved **163% to objective** in their first year. Even low performers who had EQ-i training brought in 80% of quota within 3 months.

Takeaway

Using the EQ-i predictive model for ***Recruitment and Training*** generates:

* **Higher performing recruits**

* **Higher performance from otherwise low performers**

292

Center for Creative Leadership (CCL)

Purpose

To evaluate key emotional intelligence characteristics that define high performing leaders

Results

This study evaluated the world-famous training center (CCL), looking at 302 leaders and senior managers, some of whom were quite successful and others who were struggling. Participants were tested for emotional intelligence with the EQ-i and were also measured on leadership performance based on feedback from superiors, peers, and subordinates.

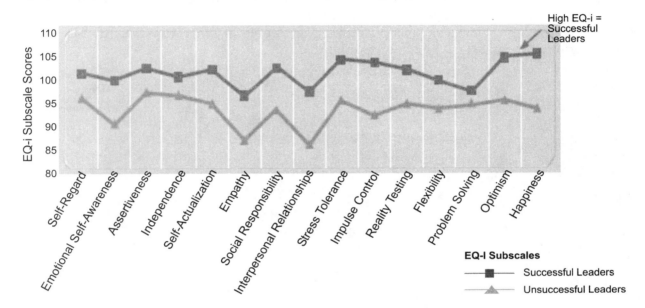

ROI Impact

The findings from this study were highly predictive, i.e:

- Eight emotional subscales predicted high performance **80% of the time**. These include: self-awareness, stress tolerance, and empathy (to name a few).

Takeaway

Using the EQ-i predictive model for **Leadership Development** generates:

- **A roadmap for leadership success**
- **Better performing leaders**

CIBC

Purpose

To determine key emotional intelligence characteristics that define successful sales representatives at CIBC

Results

The CIBC Global Private Banking and Trust team conducted a study where their high and low performing sales representatives were given the EQ-i assessment. Many EI skill-sets are clearly conducive to higher performance. As shown in the chart below, the two key EI skill-sets for success were interpersonal skills and self-actualization. Interestingly, having a lower score in impulse control in combination with higher scores in other EI areas, translated into higher performance amongst sales representatives.

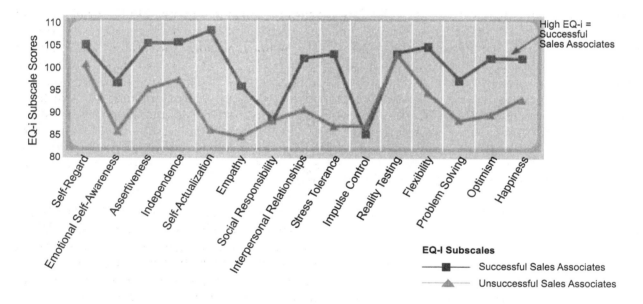

ROI Impact

CIBC now uses the EQ-i study results as a predictive model for both the selection of new personnel and in leadership development. This is because they found that:

• An individual's EQ-i test scores accounted for **32% of his or her booked sales and 71% of pipeline sales.**

Takeaway

Using the EQ-i predictive model for *Selection* and *Leadership Development* generates:

• **Better selection of sales representatives**
• **Higher performance from sales representatives**

Making the Connection:
Leadership Skills and Emotional Intelligence

Marian N. Ruderman, Kelly Hannum, Jean Brittain Leslie, and Judith L. Steed

There is growing evidence that the range of abilities that constitutes what is now commonly known as emotional intelligence plays a key role in determining success in life and in the workplace. Recent CCL research has uncovered links between specific elements of emotional intelligence and specific behaviors associated with leadership effectiveness and ineffectiveness.

Stuart is a senior manager at a well-known pharmaceutical company. He is brilliant, and everyone who knows him believes he has the potential to achieve great things. His primary strength is strategic thinking; colleagues say he has an uncanny ability to predict and plan for the future. As Stuart has advanced in the organization, however, his dark side has become increasingly apparent: he often lashes out at people, and he is unable to build relationships based on trust. Stuart knows he is intelligent and tends to use that knowledge to belittle or demean his co-workers. Realizing that Stuart has extraordinary skills and much to offer the company in terms of vision and strategy, some of his colleagues have tried to help him work past his flaws. But they're beginning to conclude that it's a hopeless cause; Stuart stubbornly refuses to change his style, and his arrogant modus operandi has offended so many people that Stuart's career may no longer be salvageable.

Every company probably has someone like Stuart — a senior manager whose IQ approaches the genius level but who seems clueless when it comes to dealing with other people. These types of managers may be prone to getting angry easily and verbally attacking co-workers, often come across as lacking compassion and empathy, and usually find it difficult to get others to cooperate with them and their agendas. The Stuarts of the world make you wonder how people so smart can be so incapable of understanding themselves and others.

What Stuart is lacking is *emotional intelligence*. There may be little hope of salvaging Stuart's career, but there is good news for managers who are similarly deficient in emotional intelligence capacities but willing to try to change their ways: emotional intelligence can be developed and enhanced.

Dealing with Emotions

In articles published in 1990, psychologists Jack Mayer of the University of New Hampshire and Peter Salovey of Yale University coined the term *emotional intelligence,* referring to the constellation of abilities through which people deal with their own emotions and those of others. Mayer and Salovey later went on to define emotional intelligence as the ability to perceive emotional information and use it to guide thought and actions; they distinguished it from cognitive intelligence, which is what determines whether people will be successful in school and is measured through IQ tests.

The concept of emotional intelligence was popularized by psychologist Daniel Goleman in his books *Emotional Intelligence* and *Working with Emotional Intelligence,* among other writings. Goleman broadened the notion of emotional intelligence to include an array of noncognitive abilities that help people adapt to all aspects of life. He focused on four basic competencies — self-awareness, social awareness, self-management, and social skills — that influence the way people handle themselves and their relationships with others. He argued that these human competencies play a bigger role than cognitive intelligence in determining success in life and in the workplace.

Mayer, Salovey, and Goleman were not the first to recognize the significance of the attributes now collectively called emotional intelligence. For years before, managers, educators, human resource professionals, and others had seen evidence that these attributes — known then by more generic, colloquial terms such as *people skills* — seemed to play an important role in separating the average from the first-rate performers. Like Goleman, many of these observers believed these skills were more important than intellect or technical skills in determining success.

Throughout CCL's more than thirty-year history, one of its primary approaches to leadership development has been to help managers and executives to understand themselves and others better, to increase their self-awareness, self-management, and interpersonal skills — in other words, to expand their emotional intelligence, although CCL has not used that term. CCL has done this through a range of programs, simulations, publications, and tools — including Benchmarks®, a 360-degree assessment instrument that measures leaders' strengths and development needs as compared with those of other leaders. Although CCL and others have long believed that people's levels of emotional competency are related to their effectiveness as leaders, little had been done to scientifically examine and document whether specific elements of emotional intelligence are linked to specific behaviors associated with leadership effectiveness and ineffectiveness — and if they are, how they are linked. With this goal, CCL designed and conducted a study that correlated Benchmarks results with scores from an assessment instrument through which people gauge their own emotional intelligence abilities (see the [Focus Box: Weighing the Evidence]). Although the findings are not sufficient to state conclusively that leaders with high levels of emotional intelligence are better leaders, they do show that there are clear and basic connections between the higher ranges of emotional intelligence and the possession of skills and abilities associated with leadership excellence. Knowing and understanding these connections can give managers and executives additional ammunition in their efforts to enhance their leadership performance.

Strongest Links

The study comparing Benchmarks results with scores from the BarOn Emotional Quotient Inventory (EQ-i™), an assessment of emotional intelligence, found that ten of the sixteen skills and perspectives assessed by Benchmarks were strongly associated with one or more

---

Weighing the Evidence

To explore whether specific behaviors associated with leadership effectiveness are connected to particular elements of emotional intelligence, CCL designed and conducted a study in which 302 managers took part. The managers, who were participants in CCL's Leadership Development Program (LDP)®, were assessed through Benchmarks®, a 360-degree feedback instrument that gives managers insights into how their bosses, peers, direct reports, and they themselves perceive their leadership strengths and development needs. The managers also completed the BarOn Emotional Quotient Inventory (EQ-i™), with which people assess themselves on fifteen components of emotional intelligence. The BarOn EQ-i was developed through nineteen years of research conducted around the world by clinical psychologist Reuven Bar-On and is published by Multi-Health Systems of North Tonawanda, New York. The results from Benchmarks and the BarOn EQ-i were correlated to reveal associations between leadership skills, perspectives, and derailment factors and aspects of emotional intelligence.

The senior-level managers in the study averaged just under forty-three years old. Seventy-three percent were male, 81 percent were white, and 90 percent had a minimum of a bachelor's degree.

---

emotional intelligence measures. In other words, higher levels of certain emotional intelligence components appear to be connected to better performance in those ten areas. Benchmarks is also designed to identify potential problem areas that can contribute to derailment, which occurs when a manager who has previously been seen as successful and full of potential for continued advancement is instead fired, demoted, or held on a career plateau. Associations were also found between two of these career-threatening flaws and certain aspects of emotional intelligence.

Let's look first at the connections between emotional intelligence and leadership skills and perspectives:

Participative management. Of all the skills and perspectives measured by Benchmarks, participative management had the highest number of meaningful correlations with measures of emotional intelligence. The essence of participative management is getting buy-in from colleagues at the beginning of an initiative by involving them, engaging them through listening and communicating, influencing them in the decision-making process, and building consensus. It is an important relationship-building skill, especially in today's management environment, in which organizations value interdependency within and between groups.

Depending on the Benchmarks rater (boss, peer, or direct report), scores in participative management were related to the emotional intelligence abilities of social responsibility (being a cooperative, contributing, and constructive member of one's social group), happiness (feeling satisfied with and deriving pleasure from life), interpersonal relationship (establishing and maintaining mutually satisfying relationships), impulse control (resisting impulsive behavior), emotional self-awareness (being in touch with one's own feelings), and empathy (understanding and appreciating the feelings of others). These correlations suggest that managers who are perceived as being skilled at listening to others and gaining their input before implementing change are likely also to see themselves as satisfied with life and good at cooperating, fostering relationships, controlling impulses, and understanding their own and others' emotions.

Putting people at ease. People who are warm and have a good sense of humor are often able to make others feel at ease, relaxed, and comfortable in their presence. The connections between this skill and emotional intelligence qualities also varied according to who did the rating. The assessments by managers' direct reports indicated that the ability to put people at ease was related to impulse control, which suggests that not overreacting in difficult situations and avoiding knee-jerk responses such as quick anger go a long way toward making people feel relaxed. The assessments by bosses indicated that managers' ability to put others at ease was tied to the managers' own sense of happiness, suggesting that a manager's disposition is a determinant of how comfortable people feel in his or her presence.

Self-awareness. Managers who were seen by their bosses, peers, and direct reports as having an accurate picture of their strengths and weaknesses and as being willing to improve gave themselves high ratings on the emotional intelligence abilities of impulse control and stress tolerance (withstanding adverse events and stressful situations without falling apart). This suggests that managers who are aware that they may easily explode into anger or become anxious in the face of difficult situations are likely to be perceived as lacking in self-awareness. The assessments by managers' direct reports indicated that self-awareness is also related to social responsibility.

Balance between personal life and work. Managers who had demonstrated to their bosses that they were adept at balancing their work priorities with their personal lives so that neither was neglected gave themselves high ratings in the emotional intelligence abilities of social responsibility, impulse control, and empathy. This suggests that if you give your boss the impression that you are a whole person with a well-rounded life, you're more likely to believe in your abilities to contribute to a group, resist impulsive actions, and understand the emotions of others. Ratings on work-life balance from direct reports were also associated with impulse control.

Straightforwardness and composure. From all rater perspectives, the leadership skills of remaining steadfast and calm during crises, relying on facts, and being able to recover from mistakes were related to impulse control. Direct reports' ratings of their managers' straightforwardness and composure were also associated with stress tolerance, social responsibility, and optimism (the ability to maintain a positive attitude even in the face of adversity), and bosses' ratings of managers' resolve and poise were related to managers' own sense of happiness.

Building and mending relationships. Bosses' assessments of managers' abilities to develop and maintain solid working relationships with people inside and outside their organizations and to negotiate work-related problems without alienating people were linked to impulse control, and direct reports' ratings were associated with stress tolerance. These connections make a lot of sense: managers who are prone to explosive outbursts and an inability to control hostility don't do much to help their relationships with their bosses, and problematic relationships with direct reports often cause stress for managers, or conversely, managers' inability to cope with stress and adversity often results in poor relationships with the people they supervise.

Doing whatever it takes. The leadership abilities of being perseverant and staying focused in the face of obstacles, of being action oriented and taking charge, and of taking a stand on one's own if required and at the same time being open to learning from others were associated by managers' bosses and direct reports with the emotional intelligence component of independence. People who rate themselves highly on independence see themselves as being self-directed and self-controlled in their thinking and actions and as being free of emotional dependency. Additionally, bosses' assessments of managers' ability to do whatever it takes were connected with assertiveness — expressing feelings, beliefs, and thoughts in a constructive way — and direct reports' ratings on this leadership skill were connected with optimism. So it appears that managers who are good at doing whatever it takes are more likely to be self-reliant, autonomous, and persistent and positive, even when they encounter adversity.

Decisiveness. Managers said by their direct reports to prefer quick, unhesitating, and approximate actions over slow and precise moves gave themselves high marks on the emotional intelligence quality of independence. This indicates that managers who characterize themselves as independent thinkers and as being self-directed and self-controlled in their actions are more likely to be seen as decisive by the people who work for them.

Confronting problem employees. Peers' assessments of the degree to which managers were able to deal with difficult workers decisively and fairly were tied to the emotional intelligence measure of assertiveness. This indicates that being able to express one's feelings, beliefs, and thoughts in a constructive way is helpful in handling employees whose performance isn't up to par.

Change management. Direct reports' ratings of their managers' effectiveness at implementing strategies to facilitate organizational change initiatives and overcome resistance to change were connected with the emotional intelligence ability of social responsibility. Peers' assessments of managers' change management skills were linked to the emotional intelligence measure of interpersonal relationship. Thus it appears that managers who are cooperative members of their social groups and who are adept at building and sustaining working relationships characterized by intimacy and affection are likely to also be good at leading change by example, involving others in change initiatives, and adjusting to changing situations.

Fast Track to Nowhere

The second section of Benchmarks is designed to identify potential problem areas that can contribute to career derailment. The study found associations between two of these career-threatening flaws and certain aspects of emotional intelligence.

Problems with interpersonal relationships. The connections between managers' difficulties in developing good working relations with others and managers' self-assessments of their emotional intelligence abilities were some of the most striking found in the study. From all three rater perspectives, managers who were seen as having problems with interpersonal relationships — a career flaw characterized by insensitivity, arrogance, impatience, authoritarianism, volatility, and other negative traits and behaviors — scored low on the emotional intelligence ability of impulse control. Interpersonal relationship ratings from direct reports and peers

299

were related to stress tolerance, ratings from direct reports were associated with social responsibility, and bosses' assessments were connected with empathy. These results suggest that no matter how strong their intellectual or technical skills, managers who care little about being cooperative and contributing members of their groups, who can't handle pressure, who easily explode and take their frustrations out on others, and who don't understand or appreciate the feelings of others may be setting themselves up for derailment.

Difficulty changing or adapting. Direct reports' ratings of their managers' resistance to change and ability to learn from mistakes were related to the emotional intelligence measures of stress tolerance and impulse control. A possible explanation for this connection is that managers who have a hard time with change often have a limited comfort zone. When they are forced outside that zone, it sets off anger and resentment, which in turn produces stress.

Points to Ponder

Four principal themes stand out from the relationships found between leadership abilities and emotional intelligence and between derailment characteristics and emotional intelligence:

- As organizations realize that the command-and-control, hierarchical model of leadership is no longer effective, they are increasingly moving toward a more participative management style. It appears that managers can more easily embrace this change and adapt to this style when they have certain emotional intelligence abilities — forming good working relationships, being cooperative and constructive members of a group, controlling anger and other impulses, and in general being pleasant to be around. Co-workers view managers with these characteristics as being effective in the participative style.

- Being centered and grounded is a valuable quality for managers. It's important for managers to give the impression that they are in control of themselves, understand themselves, and know their own strengths and weaknesses. The degree to which managers are perceived as being self-aware, straightforward, and composed and as having balance between their personal and work lives is based largely on how they react under pressure and in difficult situations. If they fall apart or flare up with anger, their leadership abilities are liable to be questioned; if they are imperturbable and resist flying off the handle, their managerial skills are likely to be confirmed.

- A willingness and ability to take action is key to effective leadership. Decisiveness and doing whatever it takes to achieve a goal are associated with independence in thought and actions. Managers who are independent do not ignore the opinions of others but are also not dependent on such input. This self-reliance helps them think strategically, make good decisions, and persevere in the face of obstacles.

- Organizations are placing increased value on interpersonal relationships, and managers who don't handle their emotions well, who lack understanding of themselves and others, and who are abrasive or abusive make others feel uncomfortable. That increases their chances of derailing.

What You Can Do

Emotional intelligence can be developed and enhanced, although doing so takes a lot of effort. Managers who are in danger of derailing because of poor interpersonal relationships are particularly good candidates for working on their emotional intelligence. In general, assessment and feedback instruments such as Benchmarks are good ways to begin improving emotional intelligence, followed by goal setting and a developmental experience that may take the form of classroom training, job assignments, simulations, coaching, or learning from a role model. Managers should identify and address any obstacles to their goals, practice new behaviors in a supportive environment, and review and reassess their behavioral changes to help lock in what they have learned.

More specifically, organizations today value managers who can put the needs of the group ahead of their personal needs — in other words, who have the emotional intelligence capacity of social responsibility. One way to develop this ability may be to involve yourself in the community through charities, nonprofit organizations, and other worthy causes. Devoting time and energy to such groups can help you see beyond your own concerns and improve your ability to be a valued member of a group. Another way to develop social responsibility is to review your individual work goals, then consider them from the perspectives of your team and organization. Ask yourself whether your individual goals facilitate and are aligned with the group and organizational goals, and what you can do to contribute positively to the larger goals.

The ability to handle stress is related to a range of leadership skills and derailment factors. Managers who are lacking in these related characteristics may want to consider stress management training. Be careful, however, to choose a program or workshop that is well designed and has a record of good results. Some of the better programs include assessment, feedback, modeling and practice of new skills, and ongoing support to keep people from lapsing back to their old ways.

Finally, the emotional intelligence ability of impulse control was related to ratings on eight Benchmarks scales. The manifestations of poor impulse control — such as aggression, hostility, irresponsibility, and frustration — are highly conspicuous to colleagues, so learning to restrain impulsive behavior can do a lot to improve a manager's interactions at work. If you have problems with impulse control, you might want to consider coaching as a way to develop composure, patience, self-awareness, adaptability, and coolness under fire. A coach can help you pinpoint your hot buttons and learn how to respond more effectively in situations of conflict or adversity.

The EQ Factor: Does Emotional Intelligence Make You a Better CEO?

Steven J. Stein, Ph.D.

What does it take to be a successful CEO? While there are hundreds of books with formulas for how to be a great leader, there are few studies of what really differentiates the great leaders from everyone else. Leadership has been described in many different ways. Traditionally it has been linked to vision, risk-taking, intelligence, technical knowledge and skill. Now, however, there is a great deal of interest in the role that emotional intelligence plays in leadership.

Some of the leading CEOs of Ontario's small and medium sized enterprises (SMEs) are found among Innovators Alliance, a CEO knowledge network of innovative, accelerated growth firms. Every member of Innovators Alliance is president or CEO of a company that has been growing at cumulative growth of at least 35% over three years and has annual revenues of at least $2 million.

These CEOs have unique characteristics that define their leadership style, characteristics that make them a successful CEO — characteristics that may described in terms of their 'emotional intelligence'.

What is emotional intelligence? There are several different views on this. The term was initially developed by psychologists John Mayer, of the University of New Hampshire, and Peter Salovey, of Yale University. Independently, Israeli psychologist Reuven Bar-On worked on a concept he called "emotional quotient" or EQ in the early 1980s. The idea was popularized in 1995 by American journalist Daniel Goleman, who wrote the first best-selling book on the subject.

According to Bar-On, emotional intelligence is a set of skills or competencies that influence one's ability to cope with life's demands and pressures. He breaks it down into five general (and 15 specific) areas: IntraPersonal, InterPersonal, Adaptability, Stress Management and General Mood. He also created the first and most widely used and validated emotional intelligence test — the BarOn Emotional Quotient Inventory (EQ-i®). The test presents 125 items that the participant rates on a 5-point scale regarding their own behaviour, thoughts and feelings. The individual data is then compared to more than 10,000 others from all walks of life that have completed the inventory. Each individual's profile provides information about emotional strengths and weaknesses, with suggestions for development.

The EQ-i has been used with corporate leaders such as the Young Presidents' Organization (YPO), Young Entrepreneurs' Organization (YEO) and at the Center for Creative Leadership (CCL) in Greensboro, North Carolina, one of the world's premier leadership training facilities. Interestingly, direct connections have been found between emotional intelligence and leadership in all of these groups.

The CEOs of Innovators Alliance recently participated in a program to test their emotional intelligence. The test was administered online and the results were discussed at the Innovators Alliance regional meetings and at the organization's annual Wisdom Exchange. Along with the test, these corporate leaders provided information — in a confidential and anonymous format — about the state of the company they were running.

Who Are These CEOs?

The final sample for the Innovators Alliance study included 76 CEOs — 61 males and 15 females. Their average age was 44 with 50% of them 45 years old or younger. Seventy percent of them have been running their companies for 15 years or less, and 45% of them have run their companies for 6 years or less. Seventy two percent of the companies were reported to have grossed less than $10 million the previous year and 47% earned less than $5 million. Thirty-eight percent of companies had less than 25 employees and 20% had more than 75 employees. Sixty percent of these CEOs founded their company.

The participants represented a number of different industries — primarily manufacturing, business services, marketing, software development and computers. The group also included professional services, organizational consulting, publishing, communications, retail, internet, property development, and financial services.

The study also looked at company performance of the Innovators Alliance members. Eighty-seven percent of these companies reported a profit in the previous year. The average previous year profit was 11%. When asked about growth, 80% of the companies reported continuous growth; 15% were flat and 5% were in decline.

So What's Their Emotional Intelligence?

The first big question the study addressed was how the participants' EQ compared to the average person. They scored significantly higher, but not by a landslide. The average score, just like the average IQ score, is 100. The Innovators Alliance CEOs averaged 104.

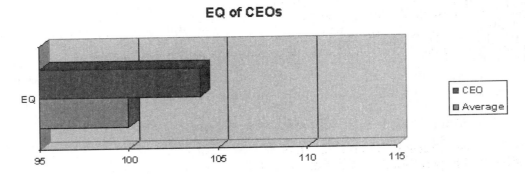

EQ of CEOs

More interesting is the profile of these entrepreneurs. Their highest score was in Independence. This is not a surprise for these high growth business leaders. After all, how could one run an organization without independence of mind, thought, and values? Independence on the EQ-i does not mean one just goes out and does her or his own thing; it implies that the CEO takes into account other points of view and then acts.

The other factor that is not surprising is their high score in Assertiveness. The Innovators Alliance CEOs are people who can express their thoughts, feelings and beliefs. The key, of course, is to do it in a non-aggressive way. Assertiveness rests somewhere between passive and aggressive.

One hallmark of assertiveness is the ability to completely disagree with someone, yet still remains friendly. Of course you wouldn't expect CEOs to be shrinking violets, but the aggressive "bullying boss" is definitely out of style. Today's leaders who rely on bullying tactics all too soon discover that there will be nobody left to be lead.

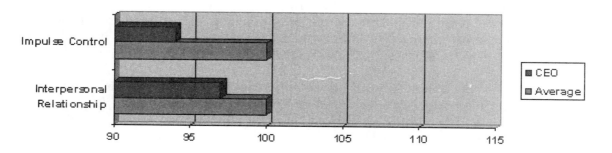

Lowest EQ Skills of CEOs

The third most important factor for success as a CEO is Optimism. This is not just "the glass is half full" kind of optimism, but optimism as a strategy, a way of dealing with difficulties. Leaders need to be resilient and having sound optimism skills to see ahead of the ball even when the next crisis is just ahead. Rather than focusing all energy on the deal just lost, the optimist thinks about what to do differently the next time around.

Earlier research looked at predictors of success in the workplace across hundreds of occupations. One factor of emotional intelligence, almost regardless of job type, consistently shows up. This factor is Self-Actualization. In presentations to business leaders throughout the world, the common response is, "let's quit the 'psych-babble,' what do you really mean here?"

Basically, there are two components to Self-Actualization as a skill. The first involves having a passion for what you do. A CEO, for example, would rather run a company than do anything else. If self-actualized, you love your work and eagerly look forward to starting each day. The second aspect of self-actualization involves being well-rounded. People high in Self-Actualization have a wide variety of interests, hobbies, and social activities. They ensure that they spend enough quantity and quality time in these pursuits.

The final emotional skill that differentiated Innovators Alliance CEOs from the general population was Self-Regard. CEOs have a high degree of Self Regard—a strong sense of self. They are aware of their strengths and weaknesses and are confident in their abilities.

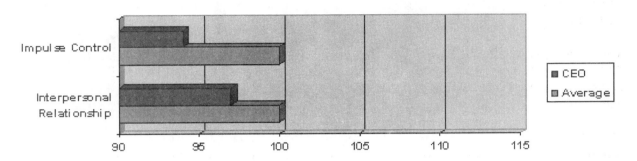

There is also what might be considered a negative side to these CEOs. They actually have significantly lower than average scores in two areas of emotional intelligence: Interpersonal Relationships and Impulse Control.

Contrary to popular belief, our CEOs are not all great at "networking," initiating, and building relationships. They are not among the most "people-oriented" groups that we've tested. This is an area ripe for development.

The ability to control impulses can help keep anyone out of trouble. Unfortunately, these CEOs, consistent with many other CEOs that we tested, were lower than average in their Impulse Control. Low impulse control can lead to poor interpersonal relationships, high anger, and numerous other difficulties. It can lead to poor judgment and decision-making.

How Do Male CEOs Differ from Female CEOs?

Perhaps one of the most asked questions when talking about executive EQ at business meetings — especially in the presence of female CEOs — has to do with the difference between male and female leaders. In the group of Innovators Alliance CEOs, like many other CEO groups we've looked at, there was no overall difference in EQ between genders. However, there were a few differences in specific factors.

The biggest gender difference was in Interpersonal Relationships. The women scored higher than the men here. Women CEOs are better at initiating, developing and maintaining relationships. Building relationships can have big payoffs both in developing your external business contacts and in working with your employees.

Two other areas differentiated the men from the women, although they did not quite reach statistical significance. Both differences favored the women. Women scored higher in Empathy and Emotional Self-Awareness. In this group, as in several other CEO groups we've looked at, the men did not outscore the women in any area. It may be that women who make it to the top have had to try harder or have additional skills.

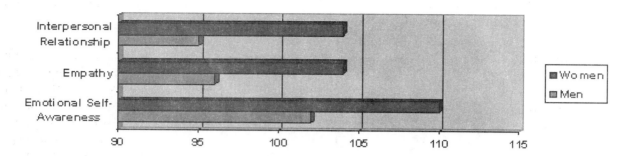

What about "superstar" CEOs?

All the Innovators Alliance CEOs are stars. They all lead successful organizations and have demonstrated their success over a significant period of time. We wanted to see if emotional intelligence could somehow differentiate the "superstar" CEOs from the rest. We set up two criteria to rank these superstars. Many groups, like Innovators Alliance and even Profit's annual Top 100 list focus on a company's gross revenues for success. We wanted to look at profitability as the criteria for selecting our CEO "superstars."

There are a number of ways to evaluate management effectiveness and successful leadership. We wanted to recognize that CEOs with sound business practices should be generating solid revenue streams as well as a healthy bottom line. To help determine these outcomes, we used two sets of criteria. In order to be considered a "superstar", a CEO had to meet both of these (either/or) conditions. First, they either had to show an average pre-tax operating profit over the past three years that was greater than 10% or have gross revenues over $25 million. Because of the difficulty CEOs of the larger companies or those in emerging industries might have in sustaining the 10% profit over three years, we allowed them to pass to the next criteria.

Second, they either had to have an average pre-tax operating profit of more than 20% over the past three years or report more than 5% in pretax profit higher than their industry three year average. Due to the diversity of industries, this rewarded those who outperformed their industry competitors and those who were able to build out a significant revenue base in emerging industries with marginal pre-tax profits.

There were only 15 CEOs that met both the first and second criteria. (There were 30 CEOs that met neither of the two criteria.) In order to do our "superstar" analysis we put all the bio history factors (age, gender, and years of experience) and EQ factor scores into a statistical formula called discriminant analysis; this analysis looks at all the information and picks out the factors that most differentiate the two groups.

There were three EQ factors that differentiated these "superstar" CEOs from the rest.

1. **Empathy**. The ability to empathize with others was the most important factor differentiating the two groups of CEOs. Empathy is often a misunderstood skill. Many people confuse empathy with sympathy. Sympathy, while a valid emotion, refers to how you

306

feel about someone else's misfortune. It often takes the form of an "I" statement — "I feel sorry about what happened to you." Empathy, on the other hand, shows that you know how the other person feels and generally starts with a "you" statement — "You must be feeling very frustrated right now."

2. **Self Regard**. As previously described, self regard involves a combination of feeling good about yourself as well as having an accurate reading of your strengths and weaknesses. High performing CEOs typically know their weaknesses and often delegate these areas to others who are more competent in those areas. Whether it's in accounting, marketing, or even interpersonal relationships, they will often have people around them who make up for the skills they lack. Or they might use a coach, especially for dealing with interpersonal prickles that get in the way of their performance.

3. **Assertiveness**. This differentiated the high performers. Being able to communicate effectively, in this case assertively, was an important element in the success of these CEOs. Interestingly, these findings parallel similar work done at the Center for Creative Leadership, looking at what makes a successful leader. Having a participatory style was one of four key leadership competencies that they found in successful leaders. One of the EI skills that were highly related to this was Empathy. A second competency they found in successful leaders was a willingness and ability to take action. Assertiveness, as measured by the EQ-i, was a key factor here as well.

What Are Their Biggest Business Challenges?

We also asked the Innovators Alliance CEOs to rank, among nine options, the biggest business challenges they were experiencing. Their selection, in order, is presented below. Their biggest challenge is hiring the right people; the least challenging issue for them is dealing with changes in technology.

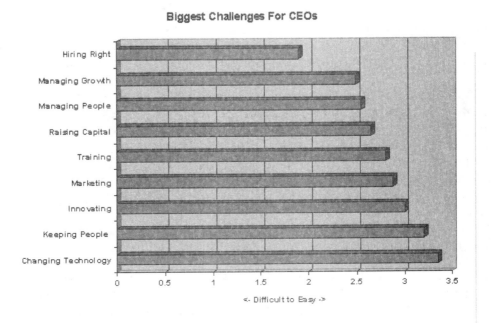

How Does EQ Relate to Real Business Challenges?

Finally, we looked at the relationship between the emotional intelligence of Innovators Alliance CEOs and their reported business challenges. There were a number of relationships between their emotional skills (or lack thereof) and their areas of greatest challenge.

Overall, CEOs with higher EQ scores overall reported being better able to keep people and to manage the growth of their company.

- Hiring the right people was easiest for CEOs who scored high on flexibility.
- Managing people was easiest for CEOs who were high in self-actualization, impulse control, reality testing, self-regard, happiness and stress tolerance.
- Keeping good people was easiest for CEOs highest in interpersonal relationship, self-regard, flexibility, optimism, happiness, stress tolerance and self-actualization.
- Training people was easiest for CEOs who were high in assertiveness, reality testing, interpersonal relationships, self-regard, flexibility, optimism, happiness, and self actualization.
- Managing Growth was easiest for CEOs who were high in flexibility, optimism, and problem solving.
- Dealing with changes in technology was easiest for CEOs who were high in flexibility, and stress tolerance.
- Other business issues were not as closely tied to the EQ factor.

Raising capital was unrelated to our measure of emotional intelligence

- Marketing challenges were unrelated to our measure of emotional intelligence.
- Managing innovation was unrelated to our measure of emotional intelligence.

Conclusion

If this research is any indication, the CEOs of a group like Innovators Alliance are high in a number of emotional intelligence skills. And that's no surprise, given the caliber of the group's membership.

Innovators Alliance (www.innovators.org) has almost 200 members meeting in 10 chapters across the province. Every member of Innovators Alliance meets several criteria — around growth rate, size and revenue levels.

As leaders of companies representing an elite 2% of the corporations in Ontario, these CEOs are helping their firms beat the economic odds. They are the firms who are hiring when large corporations are laying people off. They are growing exponentially. They are high in emotional intelligence.

Do CEOs need emotional intelligence skills to be successful? Based on EQ-i studies with Innovators Alliance, Yes.

Linda's Bed-and-Breakfast

In August of 1994, Linda Smith, owner/operator of Linda's Bed & Breakfast in Westside, 15 kilometres west of downtown Halifax, Nova Scotia, assessed the current peak season and the upcoming off season. For bed-and-breakfasts, the peak season was the middle of May to the middle of October and the off-season was the end of October through until May. The tourism and travel business had been good and had improved over the last two years, however, the off-season continued to be slow. Linda was concerned about increasing revenues during both seasons and wondered how she might do so.

Company Background and Surrounding Area

Linda, who spent 25 years in personnel administration with the federal government, originally aspired to own and operate a handicraft shop but, at the suggestion of a friend, decided upon a bed-and-breakfast. For Linda, there were four distinct advantages to this type of business. First, she could operate the business from her home. Second, there was little risk because start-up costs were low. Third, the business was easy to start because there were some basic regulations which provided an outline but were not restrictive. Fourth, the type of business provided a high degree of personal satisfaction. Linda felt that to operate successfully one had to be an early riser, a morning person and "... you gotta like people." She also attended two week-end workshops sponsored by Tourism Nova Scotia on operating a bed-and-breakfast. Early in the summer of 1992, Linda opened for business.

Westside was a rapidly growing suburban area, with a population of approximately 35,000 people, about 15 kilometres from the city of Halifax.

There was little manufacturing industry in Westside, although a small business-park was being developed. Most of the approximately 350 businesses, many of which were located on the main highway through Westside, were service oriented. There were many shops, services, and fast-food outlets, some were free standing and others were located in strip malls or major shopping centers.

The Bed & Breakfast Industry in Nova Scotia

Typically, a bed-and-breakfast was owned and operated by a home owner who provided accommodation in his/her private home. Breakfast was served in the owner/ operator's private dining area only to those accommodated. In Nova Scotia, bed-and-breakfast operations with three or more rooms were licensed and inspected yearly through Tourism Nova Scotia. An application for a Hotel License and a $5 license fee had to be submitted to the Training &

This case was prepared by Professor Jeff Young of Mount Saint Vincent University for the Acadia Institute of Case Studies as a basis for classroom discussion, and is not meant to illustrate either effective or ineffective management. Copyright © 1995, the School of Business Administration, Acadia University. Reproduced with permission.

Inspection Services Section of Tourism Nova Scotia prior to the opening of the business. This application provided for an arranged inspection. Licenses were only issued after inspection and had to be renewed on April 1st of each year.

Tourism Nova Scotia readily supplied copies of *The Hotel Regulations Act & Regulations Thereunder*, an 18-page booklet which provided important information concerning the relationship between the operation and the guests. Tourism Nova Scotia also supplied prospective bed-and-breakfast operators with a 60-page booklet which provided necessary details on hotel licensing, the Office of the Fire Marshal, the Department of Health, the Department of Transportation and Communications, Health Services Tax, and Occupancy Permits. The booklet also provided information on the Nova Scotia Travel Guide, partnerships and business names registration and construction requirements. In addition, the booklet contained useful comments and tips on a wide variety of issues, such as furniture selection and placement.

Canada Select, a national accommodation rating program, inspected, assessed, and rated bed-and-breakfasts. Owners' participation in the program was voluntary and there was an annual fee. Canada Select rated bed-and-breakfasts according to a star rating system:

1 star — clean, comfortable accommodations

2 star — clean, comfortable accommodations with some amenities

3 star — very comfortable accommodations with a greater range of facilities, guest amenities and services

4 star — the highest standard of accommodations with an extensive range of facilities, guest amenities and services

5 star — exceptional properties which are among the best in the country in terms of their outstanding facilities, guest services and quality provided.

Ratings appeared in some advertising of bed-and-breakfasts and helped travelers find appropriate accommodations. Generally speaking, the number of bed-and-breakfasts in operation in the province had increased yearly, although the total number of rooms occupied had declined since 1989. Exhibit 1 provides the number of licensed bed-and-breakfast operations within the province of Nova Scotia by year.

Since 1980, the number of licensed bed-and-breakfasts had more than tripled. The last five years had seen about 15 operations closing each year with 30–40 new operations opening each year for a net growth of 12–40 operations per year (with the exception of 1993). It should be noted that in 1995, all bed-and-breakfast operations, including one and two bedroom operations, were to be licensed. This would bring the total number of bed-and-breakfasts in the province to about 450, as there were approximately 150 one and two-bedroom bed-and-breakfasts currently in operation.

Data from Tourism Nova Scotia, with respect to numbers of rooms sold and occupancy rates in Nova Scotia for the years 1989 through 1993, are presented in Exhibits 2 and 3 respectively.

The total number of continually occupied rooms declined in 1990, 1991, and 1992. The total number of rooms occupied in 1993 almost reached 1990 levels but was still less than the number of rooms occupied in 1989.

Exhibit 1
Number of licensed bed-and-breakfast operations within the province of Nova Scotia by year

Year	Number of bed and breakfasts
1980	87
1985	155
1989	223
1990	235
1991	251
1992	268
1993	260
1993	300

Exhibit 2
Numbers of rooms sold by month and year for the Province of Nova Scotia for 1989 through 1993

Month	YEAR				
	1989	**1990**	**1991**	**1992**	**1993**
	Number rooms sold				
January	1,138	959	581	943	586
February	1,111	1,000	724	916	847
March	1,412	1,555	819	936	856
April	1,636	1,351	986	1,040	1,082
May	3,294	2,683	2,613	2,662	2,355
June	6,686	6,176	6,437	5,669	5,523
July	13,534	12,298	12,289	11,680	13,385
August	15,045	13,667	14,154	13,135	15,405
September	9,920	9,377	8,260	8,257	9,344
October	4,240	4,320	3,756	3,715	4,014
November	1,511	1,234	1,040	1,147	1,265
December	1,269	853	679	698	708
TOTAL	60,796	55,473	52,338	50,798	55,370

The summer season started with the long week-end in May and ended with the long week-end in October. In terms of occupancy rates, August, July, September, and June, tended to be the busiest months, respectively, followed by October and May.

These growth patterns may continue for the next few years but some regions of the province, the Valley and South Shore in particular, appeared to have reached close to a saturation point with the numbers of bed-and-breakfasts in operation. There appeared to be some room for continued growth in other regions, such as northern Nova Scotia. In the bed-and-breakfast industry, the emphasis was on providing increased and improved services. Better services might include improved quality of food and rooms and an increase in the availability of private bathrooms.

Exhibit 3
Occupancy rates by month and year for the Province of Nova Scotia
for 4989 through 1993

Month	YEAR				
	1989	1990	1991	1992	1993
	Occupancy rate (%)				
January	12	10	6	10	6
February	13	11	9	10	10
March	14	15	8	10	9
April	16	12	9	10	10
May	21	15	15	14	13
June	30	27	28	23	22
July	55	46	48	45	49
August	59	54	53	50	55
September	44	42	35	20	36
October	22	24	20	20	20
November	13	12	10	11	12
December	12	9	7	7	7
TOTAL	32	29	27	26	27

Current Operation

On May 2nd, 1992 Linda opened for business in her four-bedroom, modern, split-entry home. The house was situated on a large, trim and tidy lot, one and one-half blocks from the main business thoroughfare in Westside. Linda had 3 rooms, 2 with double beds and I with a set of twin bed for rent and the rooms could accommodate a maximum of 6 people. There were two four-piece, shared bathrooms, one upstairs and one downstairs. Rates for the summer season were $40 per night, double occupancy and $35 per night single occupancy. Rates for the winter season were $35 per night, double occupancy and $30 per night single occupancy. Linda's bed-and-breakfast was a three-star operation, licensed with Tourism Nova Scotia, and was open year round.

Located within 15 minutes of the Halifax International Airport, with easy access to major highways 101, 102, and 103, Linda's bed-and-breakfast was easy to find and was within convenient walking distance of major shopping malls and a flea market. Museums, playlands and other attractions were within a five minute drive.

A "quiet retreat for the tired traveler" was the operating rule at Linda's. Breakfast was served from 8:00 a.m. to 9:00 a.m. and included cereal (choice of three), fruit or juice, toast, muffins, homemade jam, tea, coffee, or milk. Special dietary needs could be accommodated with prior notice, arrangements could be made for breakfast to be served in the guest's room and light refreshments were available in the evening. Linda tended to keep her breakfast menu fairly simple and nutritious, avoiding fried foods, because she believed "fried foods don't sit well with people". Her menu was easy to serve, was fast and, more importantly, allowed Linda to spend more time talking with her guests than in the kitchen.

Exhibit 4
Numbers of rooms sold by month and year for Linda's Bed and Breakfast for 1992 through 1994

Month	YEAR		
	1992	1993	1994
	Numbers of rooms sold		
January	—	0	1
February	—	3	3
March	—	0	10
April	—	0	2
May		5	4
June	0	13	17
July	4	31	55
August	9	40	58
September	17	24	37
October	3	6	—
November	2	6	
December	0	-	
TOTAL	35	122	187

Laundry service, stamps, and bridge tokens were available upon request and there was a portable phone and directories in the living room and a phone and directories in the TV room downstairs. Other amenities included an upstairs sitting room with two daily newspapers, a spacious and quiet back deck with tables and chairs, and a TV room with VCR, board games, playing cards, and books. There was plenty of free parking and arrangements could be made for transportation to and from the airport and the downtown areas. Check-out time was 10:00 a.m. and no smoking was permitted indoors and no pets were allowed. Linda's business had been growing steadily as shown by Exhibit 4 which presents the number of rooms sold by month and year for 1992–1994.

Linda had no full-time or part-time employees but had occasionally hired a student to help on busy weekends. There had been no problems with guests, and should there be, the RCMP office was just five minutes away. The business operated largely on a cash basis, American money was given fair exchange, no credit cards were accepted for payment, but Linda Would take personal cheques, none of which had been returned by the bank.

Linda's Current Marketing Strategy

Linda's catered mainly to tourists and to business professionals. The business focused on the needs of the individual guest and on providing outstanding service. At the moment, a student at the local academy had taken a room for several weeks. This was good for cash flow but Linda did not want to turn her business into a rooming house and she was a bit resistant to this type of business. Linda saw her clientele in terms of four groups 1) tourists, those who lived elsewhere and were literally touring the area; 2) visitors, those who lived elsewhere but were originally from Westside or nearby or had ties to the area and were visiting friends or family; 3) business travelers, those visiting businesses in the greater metro area; 4) other, a catch-all group of those not fitting any of the first three groups, for example, the student. Linda believed that at least 85% of her business came from the first group.

Linda's strategy for promoting her business could be seen in terms of a series of informal and formal activities. Generally, Linda's aim was to have people know "... who you are and where you are" and she felt it was important to be seen as part of the broader community.

Informally, Linda promoted her business through networking during the course of every-day social and business activities. She was active in Girl Guides, Professional Secretaries International, and a local business association. Linda also relied, to some extent, on word-of-mouth advertising done by business associates, friends and more importantly, satisfied guests.

On a more formal basis, Linda had engaged in a number of marketing activities over the last three years. In 1992, Linda placed a sign on her front lawn to advertise her business and to identify it to guests (cost $147). She ran one small ad once in each of the two daily newspapers (total cost — $182) and placed one ad in Atlantic Adventure (cost — $25). She purchased space in a local newsletter (cost — $45) and in a local, community-oriented sports schedule (cost — $72). In 1992, Linda's Bed & Breakfast was included in a Metro guide to bed-and-breakfasts (cost $135) as well as a provincial guide book (cost — $5) and an Atlantic bed-and-breakfast book (cost — $25). Linda developed a 3-inch x 6-inch cardboard brochure which described her business, identified its location and listed its amenities (cost in 1992 — $312). These brochures remained a key source of advertising and were distributed mainly at tourist bureaus at entry points to the province and in the Metro area. In 1992, Linda also paid $223 to have her brochures available at two stores in a major food chain located on the south shore of the province. She also paid $62 to have her business card printed in a flyer promoting local businesses.

In 1993, Linda ran an ad in one local daily paper (cost $170) as well as one ad in The Clansman (cost — $76), one ad in the Masthead (cost — $54), the latter were tourist-oriented publications, and one ad in a south-shore newspaper ($117). Linda also placed a business-card ad in brochures for a musical which played in Halifax and which were distributed to those attending (cost — $81). She also continued to buy space in the local, community-oriented sports schedule (cost — $156) and had space in the local newsletter at no charge. In 1993, Linda's Bed & Breakfast was again included in the Metro guide to bed-and-breakfasts (cost — $120) as well as the provincial guide book (cost — $5). Additional brochures for the year cost $120.

In 1994, Linda stepped up her advertising, most ads had tended to be business-card size, and again she had purchased a one-time-only space in each of the two local daily papers (total cost — $164) and in the brochure for those attending the musical (cost — $43). Additional ads were placed in Vic Clansman (cost — $140), Family Tree (cost — $35), and a fiddling competition paper (cost — $40). Linda also continued to buy space in the local, community-oriented sports schedule (cost — $156) and this year, had placed an ad in a flyer supporting seniors' games (cost — $50). Linda's operation was again listed in the metro area tourist brochure (no charge) and the Nova Scotia guidebook to bed-and-breakfasts (cost — $5). In 1994, Linda's Bed & Breakfast was also listed in the Quebec (cost — $30) and the Canadian (cost — $41)

314

bed and breakfast guidebooks. Inclusion in the Atlantic bed-and-breakfast book was estimated at $25 and additional brochures would likely cost $120. Since 1993, Linda had had an ad (at no charge) in a commercial travelers' brochure.

While there was currently no bed-and-breakfast association, Linda was registered with CheckInns and its 1-800 number (cost in 1992,$20; in 1993, $144; and in 1994, $305). Charges for CheckInns were based on 10%) of the room cost plus GST, for example, a room which rented for $40 resulted in a fee of $4.28 to CheckInns. Approximately 40–45%, of Linda's business was booked through CheckInns.

In terms of 1993 promotions, Linda gave away ball-point pens inscribed with her business name and address at Halloween to neighborhood children (total cost $170) and had planned to do so again in 1994 (total cost — $178). In 1994, Linda also provided a prize (two nights free accommodation, for two) for a local school fair (total cost — $89).

Linda estimated that 40%–45%, of her business was a result of Check-Inns and 85% of her guests were tourists, but there had been no formal, longrun evaluation of her markets or marketing activities. Occasional informal surveys of guests had shown that the brochures available at tourist bureaus in the Metro area and at entry points into the province had been successful. One person had a copy of the ad from *The Clansman* in her hand when she checked in. With respect to paying for brochures to be distributed through a grocery chain, Linda said, "It was mistake number 1. It didn't do a thing for me."

Linda planned to continue her ad in the local sports schedule, "... to be community minded.", but for 1995, planned to "hold back" on many of the other forms of ads, other than the guidebooks, "to see how things worked Out."

The 1994 Nova Scotia Travel Guide showed a total of 192 bed-and-breakfast operations in the province, 13 of which were in the Halifax–Dartmouth and Metro area. The Metropolitan Area Tourist Association listed 14 bed-and-breakfasts in its guide, 5 of which were not listed in the Provincial Guide. Most of these 18 bed-and-breakfasts were located in the cities or in the coastal areas at least 30 minutes drive from Linda's. Linda's closest competitors were in Waverley (20 minutes drive), Enfield (20 minutes drive), and Windsor (25 minutes drive) and, from her point of view, represented no real competition.

There were no bed-and-breakfasts in the immediate vicinity and Linda saw a local motel, which was located just around the corner, as her main competition. However, there appeared to be a good working relationship between the two business owners, as each sent clients to the other when no vacancies were available. Linda believed her competitive advantage was her attention to guests' special needs, the one-to-one service, and the creation of a sense of being at home.

In terms of pricing, Linda had been told by several business colleagues that her prices were a little high. She opened her business later than many bed-and-breakfasts and based her prices on those of other operators. She also based her prices on a comparison between what they offered and what she offered. She felt her slightly higher price was justified because of the better service and accommodation she provided. The Guide *to Bed and Breakfast and Country Inns of Metropolitan Halifax–Dartmouth, and Surrounding Areas*, prepared by the Metropolitan Area Tourist Association, profiled at least 18 bed-and-breakfasts. There was some obvious variability in terms of location, distance to downtown Halifax or Dartmouth, and amenities. However, with amenities roughly comparable to those offered by Linda's, in Halifax city some single rooms rented for $30 or $35 per night, double rooms rented for $40 or $45 per night. In Dartmouth single rooms were available for $32 or $40 per night with doubles being available for $40 and $45. In the areas surrounding the cities, single rooms were available for $25, $30, $35, and $40 and double rooms were available for $35, $40, $45, $50, and $60. Rooms in areas surrounding the cities were comparable to Linda's, although they may not be close to Linda's and may not be considered as direct competition by Linda.

Linda's business plan, which more of a mental outline than a detailed plot, included the goal of having an average of 1 room booked per night every night for the entire year. She had thought about "putting things down on paper" but at present the business was "fun" and she didn't want it to become "work." At this point in time, Linda wanted to know how she could increase business, particularly during the off-season.

Exhibit 5

Nova Scotia visitor traffic flows 1992 — Westside area

Party pass throughs — represents the number of no resident party trips passing a specific community without stopping.

Party stops — represents the number of no resident party trips involving a stop of less than one half hour in a specific community.

Part visits — represents the number of no resident party trips involving a stop of more than one half hour, but not overnight, in a specific community.

Overnight party trips — represents the number of no resident party trips involving a stop of one or more nights in a specific community.

Of the 32,100 tourist parties who stopped in Westside, 20,400 stayed overnight, which translated to approximately 44,250 visitors who booked into some kind of accommodation, campsite or fixed roof.

REASONS FOR TRIPS

Reasons	Pass throughs	Stops	Visits	Overnight	Total
Business	103,400	100	4,000	1,500	109,000
Pleasure	96,800	500	2,100	5,900	105,300
Friends/ relatives	146,200	600	4,100	12,200	163,100
Other	28,200		500	800	29,500

ORIGIN OF VISITORS

Origin	Pass throughs	Stops	Visits	Overnight	Total
Atlantic Canada	148,700	500	5,200	9,200	163,700
Other Canada	166,700	500	4,500	8,900	180,600
International	62,100	100	900	2,300	65,500
TOTAL	377,500	1,100	10,600	20,400	409,800

Weeks #11 & 12 Labs #10 & 11

Labs #10 & #11 — Group Presentations

The final two weeks in labs will be spent presenting your final projects. Your Teaching Assistant will assign what week each group will present.

Presentation practice rooms will be available. Instructions on booking a room will be given in labs. Do not underestimate the value of practice, practice, practice, both individually and with your team, particularly in a room similar to the one you will be presenting in. The most successful teams work together to smooth out their presentations' rough spots ahead of time.

It is expected that when your group is not presenting you will be listening attentively, asking good questions, and learning about effective presentation skills by watching the other groups' presentations. Remember, participation marks are still being determined.

Solutions

Solutions — Cash Budgeting

1.

Cash Budget
Month Ending May 31, 200X

Cash Balance, Beginning		$ 60,000
Add Receipts:		
March Receipts	$ 70,000	
April Receipts	360,000	
May Receipts	400,000	
Total Receipts		830,000
Total Cash Available		$890,000
Less Disbursements:		
Merchandise Purchases: May	$200,000	
April	240,000	
Payroll	88,000	
Insurance	2,000	
Other Expenses	41,000	
Bank Note	175,000	
Interest	10,000	
Total Disbursements		756,000
Ending Cash Balance		$134,000

2.

Ace Manufacturing Company Ltd.
Cash Budget Worksheet
Months of May, June, July

	March	April	May	June	July
Net Sales	$60,000	$60,000	$70,000	$80,000	$100,000
Collections:					
month of sale 50%	$30,000	$30,000	$35,000	$40,000	$ 50,000
month after 25%		15,000	15,000	17,500	20,000
2nd month 25%			15,000	15,000	17,500
Total Receipts			$65,000	$72,500	$ 87,500
Net Purchases	$42,000	$42,000	$49,000	$56,000	$ 70,000
Payments:					
month after 90%		$37,800	$37,800	$44,100	$ 50,400
2nd month 10%			4,200	4,200	4,900
Total Payments for Purchase			$42,000	$48,300	$ 55,300

Ace Manufacturing Company Ltd.
Cash Budget
Months of May, June, July

	May	June	July
Cash Balance Beginning	$20,000	$ 26,000	$ 20,000
Add Receipts	65,000	72,500	87,500
Total Cash Available	$85,000	$ 98,500	$107,500
Less Disbursements:			
Cost of Good Manufactured	42,000	48,300	55,300
Selling and Administrative	17,000	18,000	20,000
Interest	0	0	9,000
Sinking Fund	0	0	50,000
Dividends	0	0	10,000
Capital Expenditure	0	40,000	0
Taxes	0	0	1,000
Total Disbursements	$59,000	$106,300	$145,300
Cash Excess/Deficiency	26,000	(7,800)	(37,800)
Minimum Cash Balance Required	20,000	20,000	20,000
Borrowing Required	0	27,800	57,800
Surplus Cash	6,000	0	0
Cash Balance, Ending	$26,000	$ 20,000	$ 20,000

3.

Tidewater Sales Inc.
Cash Budget Worksheet
Months of January, February, March

	January	February	March
Net Sales	$24,000	$18,000	$27,000
Collections:			
December A/R	$28,000	$ 5,200	$ 1,600
month after 85%		20,400	15,300
2nd month 10%			2,400
Total Receipts	$28,000	$25,600	$19,300
Net Purchases	$14,000	$17,300	$18,000
Payments:			
December A/P	$20,900		
month following 100%		$14,000	$17,300
Total Payments for Purchase	$20,900	$14,000	$17,300

Tidewater Sales Inc.
Cash Budget
Months of January, February, March

	January	February	March
Cash Balance Beginning	$ 5,800	$10,000	$14,900
Add Receipts	28,000	25,600	19,300
Total Cash Available	$33,800	$35,600	$34,200
Less Disbursements:			
Purchases	20,900	14,000	17,300
Payroll	2,400	2,400	2,800
Rent	1,000	1,000	1,000
Other Cash Expenses	1,200	1,600	1,400
Purchases of Store Equipment	0	0	5,000
Dividends	0	0	4,000
Total Disbursements	$25,500	$19,000	$31,500
Cash Excess/Deficiency	8,300	16,600	2,700
Minimum Cash Balance Required	10,000	10,000	10,000
Borrowing Required	1,700	0	7,300
Surplus Cash	0	6,600	0
Loan Repayment	0	1,700	0
Cash Balance, Ending	$10,000	$14,900	$10,000

SOLUTIONS

4.

Receivables:

	February	March	April	May	June	July
Sales	$80,000	$70,000	$50,000	$65,000	$90,000	$60,000
50%	$40,000	$35,000	$25,000	$32,500	$45,000	$30,000
40%		$32,000	$28,000	$20,000	$26,000	$36,000
10%			$ 8,000	$ 7,000	$ 5,000	$ 6,500
			$61,000	**$59,500**	**$76,000**	

Disbursements: 32 000

Purchases	$28,000	$20,000	$26,000	$36,000	$24,000	
50%	$14,000	$10,000	$13,000	$18,000	$12,000	
30%		$ 8,400	$ 6,000	$ 7,800	$10,800	
20%			$ 5,600	$ 4,000	$ 5,200	
			$24,600	**$29,800**	**$28,000**	

Parker House Ltd. Cash Budget
for the months of April, May, and June, 2006

	April	May	June
Beginning Cash Balance	$ 60,000	$ 83,400	$ 60,000
Add: Receipts			
from Sales	$ 61,000	$ 59,500	$ 76,000
Interest			$ 8,500
Proceeds on Sale of Property	$ 25,000		
Total Cash Available	$146,000	$142,900	$144,500
Less: Disbursements			
Purchases	$ 24,600	$ 29,800	$ 28,000
Selling & Administrative	$ 35,000	$ 35,000	$ 35,000
Interest	$ 3,000		$ 85
Dividends		$ 15,000	
Taxes		$ 20,000	
Total Disbursements	$ 62,600	$ 99,800	$ 63,085
Cash Excess/Deficiency	$ 83,400	$ 43,100	$ 81,416
Minimum Cash Balance	$ 60,000	$ 60,000	$ 60,000
Cash Surplus	$ 23,400		$ 21,416
Borrowing Required		$ 16,900	
Ending Cash Balance	$ 83,400	$ 60,000	$ 64,516

4.   (a) *Key*: How is Gross Profit calculated in a merchandising company?

Net Sales – Cost of Goods Sold = Gross Profit

To achieve the stated pattern:

i)   Cost of Goods Sold must be increasing at a faster rate than sales (*i.e.*, cost of purchases increasing at a faster rate than selling prices).

ii) Sales are declining while cost of goods sold remains constant or increases.

(b) The problem must lie in one of the two components of GPM (*i.e.*, Sales or Cost of Goods Sold). As such,

i)   **Check your selling prices.** Are they consistent with those charged by other firms in the industry? If your prices are lower, all other things being equal, this will be reflected in a lower gross profit margin than that of the industry as a whole.

ii) If your selling prices *are* consistent with those of the industry as a whole, then the problem must lie within your **Cost of Goods Sold**. As such, you should check the following:

- Raw Materials (Mfg. Company) Costs vs. those of industry.

- perhaps your purchasing department is doing a poor job, (*i.e.*, not taking advantage of quantity and sales discounts);

- poor speculative buying;

- not looking for substitutes that are cheaper, etc.

- Direct Labour Costs vs. those of industry.

- Problems with Manufacturing Overhead Costs being out of line with those of the industry. For example, you may have outdated and inefficient machinery resulting in frequent breakdowns, costly downtime, and resultant dis-economies of scale.

5.   *Key*: Analyze effects of components of Net Profit.

		Given Information
	Net Sales	increasing
–	Cost of Goods Sold	declining
	Gross Profit	increasing
–	Operating Expenses	?
	Net Profit Before Tax	?
–	Taxes	constant
	Net Profit	declining

(a) Operating Expenses (*i.e.*, wages, salaries, rent, etc.) are increasing at a faster rate than gross profit.

(b) Rapid increase in other expenses (*i.e.*, Interest on outstanding debt or interest on new debt issues).

SOLUTIONS

6. (a) Key Ratio: Interest Coverage = $\dfrac{\text{Earnings Before Interest and Taxes}}{\text{Annual Interest Payments}}$

Interest Due Yearly:

$$
\begin{array}{rcl}
7.5\% \times \$2,600,000 & = & 195,000 \\
8\% \times \$2,000,000 & = & 160,000 \\
10\% \times \$1,000,000 & = & \underline{100,000} \\
\text{Total Yearly Interest} & = & \$455,000
\end{array}
$$

$$
\text{Coverage} = \frac{\$5,005,000}{455,000}
$$

$$
= 11 \text{ times}
$$

(b) The rule of thumb is generally that the interest coverage ratio should be > 3:1, so this ratio appears quite healthy. The firm appears to have plenty of room in its capital structure to use debt financing.

7. When a company is selling at a very high P/E ratio, it normally indicates that the firm is a "growth industry"

i.e.
- it pays out very little to its stockholders in the form of dividends;
- instead, it retains most of its earnings and re-invests it in the company;
- shareholders are normally compensated for the lack of dividends by a rapidly increasing share price (*i.e.*, capital appreciation);
- IBM was a notable example of a company that for years paid out virtually no dividends but whose market price rose rapidly.

It may also indicate that the firm is overvalued and as such potential investors should be wary of an impending "correction."

8. Key Ratios:

(a) Earnings/Share = $\dfrac{\text{Net Profit (Less Preferred Dividends)}}{\text{\# Shares of C/S Outstanding}}$

Dividends/Share = $\dfrac{\text{Net Profit} - (\text{Preferred Dividends} + \text{Retained Earnings})}{\text{\# Shares of C/S}}$

Yield = $\dfrac{\text{Dividends / Share of C/S}}{\text{Price / Share of C/S}}$

Price/Earnings = $\dfrac{\text{Price / Share of C/S}}{\text{EPS of C/S}}$

		Company L	**Company M**
i)	EPS	$= \dfrac{3,000,000}{800,000}$	$= \dfrac{(5,000,000 - 200,000)}{1,200,000}$
		$= \$3.75/\text{sh.}$	$= \$4.00/\text{sh.}$

ii) Yield $= \dfrac{\$2.25/\text{sh.}^*}{\$30.00}$ $\qquad = \dfrac{\$1.92/\text{sh.}^*}{\$40.00}$

$\qquad = 7.5\%$ $\qquad\qquad = 4.8\%$

* dividends per share $\qquad$ * dividends per share

$= \dfrac{(3,000,000 \times .6)}{800,000}$ $\qquad = \dfrac{(3,000,000 \times .5) - 200,000}{1,200,000}$

iii) P/E $= \dfrac{\$30/\text{sh.}}{\$3.75}$ $\qquad = \dfrac{\$40/\text{sh.}}{\$4.00}$

$\qquad = 8 \text{ times}$ $\qquad\qquad = 10 \text{ times}$

(b) On the basis of the analysis you should invest in Company L because it has a higher yield and lower price/earnings ratio. Even though it has a slightly lower EPS, because its market price is lower, you can make the money that you have to invest go further.

9. Current Ratio $= \dfrac{\text{Current Assets}}{\text{Current Liabilities}} = \dfrac{\$3.64M}{\$1.69M} = 2.15{:}1$

Acid Test $= \dfrac{\text{Current Assets} - \text{Inventory}}{\text{Current Liabilities}} = \dfrac{\$3.64M - 2.45M}{1.69M} = .7{:}1$

Using the rules of thumb developed by financial analysts (current ratio should not be less than 2:1, and acid test should not be less than 1:1), it would appear that Kids Inc. is experiencing a liquidity problem due to what appears to be excessive levels of inventory. The acid test looks poor once inventory is removed, but the current ratio is OK, so it must be the high inventory that has inflated the current ratio.

However, Kids Inc. is closing its books on November 15, 2000. As a retailer of children's toys, Kids Inc. will be entering its peak selling season (the six weeks leading up to Christmas), and one would expect inventory levels to be at their highest in anticipation of this peak period. As such, the low acid test figure does not represent any cause for alarm regarding the liquidity position of Kids Inc. If however the acid test ratio revealed a similar figure in January 2001, after the Christmas rush had passed, then there would be considerable cause for concern regarding the ability of Kids Inc. to meet its current obligations to suppliers, creditors, employees, etc.

SOLUTIONS

10. **Liquidity analysis**

Current ratio: Definition: $\dfrac{\text{current assets}}{\text{current liabilities}}$

$$\frac{\$1,993}{\$1,110} = 1.8:1$$

Reasonable liquidity, close to the norm of 2:1

Quick ratio: Definition: $\dfrac{\text{current assets} - \text{inventories}}{\text{current liabilities}}$

$$\frac{\$1,993 - \$441}{\$1,110} = 1.4:1$$

Relatively high liquidity, well above the norm of 1:1

Profitability analysis

Return on sales %:   Definition: $\dfrac{\text{operating income}}{\text{sales}} \times 100\%$

$$\frac{\$364}{\$5,374} \times 100\% = 6.8\%$$

This is a relatively low margin business, and Canadian Tire is probably operating at the low end of the range.

Return on assets %:   Definition: $\dfrac{\text{operating income}}{\text{total assets}} \times 100\%$

$$\frac{\$364}{\$4,371} \times 100\% = 8.3\%$$

A very modest return on assets

Return on equity %:   Definition: $\dfrac{\text{net income}}{\text{shareholders' equity}} \times 100\%$

$$\frac{\$176}{\$1,604} \times 100\% = 11.0\%$$

This is a modest return for a business investment. Would shareholders have been better off if they had invested in shares of other companies?

Debt Analysis:

Debt to Assets %:   Definition: $\dfrac{\text{total debt}}{\text{total assets}} \times 100\%$

$$\frac{\$2,467}{\$4,371} \times 100\% = 56\%$$

Debt to equity %: Definition: $\dfrac{\text{total debt}}{\text{total equity}} \times 100\%$

$$\frac{\$2,467}{\$1,904} \times 100\% = 130\%$$

The debt is a little on the high side being over the norm of 50% (debt to assets) or its equivalent 100% (debt to equity).

The "minority interest" is problematical in this analysis. It refers to shares in subsidiary companies held by outside investors. It has been treated as equity here to calculate the debt to equity ratio, but it has been ignored above in the calculation of the return on equity.

Interest cover ratio: Definition: $\dfrac{\text{net income (before interest and taxes)}}{\text{interest paid}}$

$$\frac{\$364}{\$88} = 4.1$$

This is safe: earnings would have to fall to one quarter of their present level before interest payments were under threat.

Efficiency Analysis

Total asset turnover: Definition: $\dfrac{\text{sales}}{\text{total assets}}$

$$\frac{\$5,374}{\$4,371} = 1.2$$

Assets are turned over 1.2 times per year. This is not a capital-intensive business, so this ratio is relatively low.

Receivables turnover ratio: Definition: $\dfrac{\text{sales}}{\text{receivables}}$

$$\frac{\$5,374}{\$959} = 5.6$$

Receivables collection period: Definition: $\dfrac{\text{receivables}}{\text{sales} \div 365}$

$$\frac{\$959}{\$5,374 \div 365} = 65 \text{ days}$$

Receivables are turned over 5.6 times every year, in other words the average age of receivables is 65 days. In most retailing businesses this would be excessive, but Canadian Tire credit accounts are much like credit cards, and charge a high interest rate, so it is not a wasted investment.

Inventory turnover: Definition: $\dfrac{\text{sales}}{\text{inventory}}$

$$\frac{\$5,374}{\$441} = 12,2$$

Inventory holding period: Definition: $\dfrac{\text{inventory}}{\text{sales} \div 365}$

$$\dfrac{\$441}{\$5,374 \div 365} = 30 \text{ days}$$

Inventory is turned over 12.2 times per year, in other words it is held for only 30 days on average. For a retailer of non-perishable goods this is a highly efficient.

Market Based Analysis:

Earnings per share: Definition: $\dfrac{\text{net income}}{\text{number of common shares}}$

There were approximately 75 million common shares in issue

$$\dfrac{\$176}{75} = \$2.35$$

Dividend cover ratio: Definition: $\dfrac{\text{net income}}{\text{dividend}}$

$$\dfrac{\$176}{\$31} = 5.7$$

This is very safe: there are $5.70 of earnings for every $1 of dividend

Summary: Canadian Tire is a solid, but perhaps unexciting, company from a financial perspective. Its liquidity is OK. Its profitability is low. Its debt is on the high side. Its efficiency is good. Interest and dividends are well covered.

11.   (a) Net Working Capital = $137,050 − 43,105 = $93,945

Current Ratio = $137,050 ÷ 43,105 = 3.2:1

Compared with the rule of thumb of > 2:1 but < 4:1 this appears adequate.

Acid Test = ($61,300 + 26,500) ÷ 43,105 = 2 : 1

Compared with the rule of thumb of just > 1 : 1 this appears high — perhaps there is too much cash on hand (not too much in A/R according to the receivables ratios) that could be invested to earn a greater return.

Accounts Receivable Turnover = $719,100 ÷ 26,500 = 27x

OR Average Collection Period = ($26,500 × 365) ÷ 719,100 = 13.5 days

Compared with the industry averages of 8x and 45 days it would appear that A/R might be collected too quickly thereby lowering the risk but also the potential return.

Inventory Turnover = $512,200 ÷ [(26,700 + 43,000)/2] = 14.7x

Compared with the industry average of 15x this appears just right